The People of the Bat

The People of the Bat
Mayan Tales and Dreams
from Zinacantán

Collected and translated by
ROBERT M. LAUGHLIN

Edited by
CAROL KARASIK

SMITHSONIAN INSTITUTION PRESS
Washington and London

Edited by Karen Siatras
Designed by Alan Carter

Cover: Village elders of Zinacantán.
Photograph by Mark L. Rosenberg, 1967

LIBRARY OF CONGRESS CATALOGING-IN-PUBLICATION DATA

The People of the Bat.

Bibliography: p.
1. Tzotzil Indians—Legends.
2. Tzotzil literature—Translations into English.
3. Mexican literature—Translations from Tzotzil.
4. Indians of Mexico—Legends.
5. Tzotzil Indians—Social life and customs.
6. Indians of Mexico—Social life and customs.
I. Laughlin, Robert M.   II. Karasik, Carol.
F1221.T9P46 1988   398.2'08997   87-20754
ISBN 0-87474-590-X

British Library Cataloging-in-Publication data available

The paper used in this publication meets the
minimum requirements of the American National
Standard for Performance of Paper for Printed
Library Materials Z39.48—1984

Manufactured in the United States of America

Contents

The Burden of Days
TALES

Introduction

Zinacantán is a small Mayan community in the highlands of Chiapas, the southernmost state in Mexico. Isolated by rugged mountains, the twelve thousand inhabitants of Zinacantán maintain a traditional way of life. They continue to work their fields by hand, celebrate the old gods, and affirm the truth of myths and dreams while defending themselves against modern social pressures and ancient demonic forces. The bat god, from whom they take their name, still haunts the landscape.

There is not a single monument today to testify to the glory that was Zinacantán. Throughout the Classic Maya period (200–900 A.D.) the Chiapas highlands remained outside the political and cultural dominion of the major Mayan centers. When the cities fell, Zinacantán became a thriving market, gaining impressive local control over the trade of precious feathers, salt, and amber. Despite perpetual warfare with the lowland Chiapanecs, Zinacantec merchants maintained a network of trade relations that stretched from Guatemala to Tabasco and north to the Aztec Empire. At the time of the Conquest the fame of the merchants of Zinacantán was so great that simply to be a native of that town was deemed an honor.

In 1524 Zinacantán capitulated without a hint of resistance to a handful of Spaniards, doubtless believing that the town would profit by the defeat of their enemies, the Chiapanecs, and the Chamulans. Four years later the Spaniards established the town of San Cristóbal de las Casas as the political and commercial center of Ladino supremacy in the highlands. Yet Zinacantán continued to be the Indian "capital" of the region. Zinacantecs served the Spanish forces as porters and warriors in expeditions in the highlands and in the Lacandon jungle. Then, as now, the Zinacantecs astonished the Ladinos by their haughty mien.

When the first Dominicans arrived in Zinacantán in 1544, the friars discovered

> an infinite number of idols; they worshipped the sun and made
> sacrifices to it, and to the full rivers, to the springs, to the trees of
> heavy foliage, and to the high hills they gave incense and gifts. . . .
> [The Zinacantecs] called themselves Zotcil Vinic which is the same
> as saying batman. . . . Their ancestors discovered a stone bat and
> considered it God and worshipped it (Ximénez, 1929:360).

Despite the friars' attempts to make good Christians of the Zinacantecs, they eventually collected enough idols to supply a huge
bonfire in the plaza. The bat that was the symbol of Zinacantán at the
time of the Conquest became, under Catholic instruction, the devil.

For three centuries Zinacantecs endured a fate as bitter as that of
any Indian segment of Mexico. So exorbitant were the tributes of
cacao exacted from the Indian communities that Bishop Bartolomé
de las Casas and the chiefs of Zinacantán sent pleas directly to King
Philip II, who responded to their eloquence by lowering these tributes throughout Mexico and Central America. But from the Conquest
to the Revolution and even decades beyond, "history" was for the
Zinacantecs what they defined in a sixteenth-century dictionary as
"the book of suffering, the book of hardship"—famines and epi-
demics, tributes and taxes, servitude and destitution (*Diccionario en
lengua sotzil*, p.190).

Until the early nineteenth century Zinacantecs engaged in extensive trade, carrying cacao and coffee from Guatemala to Tabasco, and
tobacco to the Pacific slopes. But tropical diseases and dispossession
of their goods by the Ladinos severely curtailed their traditional occu-
pation. Economic exploitation by landowners, political officials, even
priests, was the order of the day.

When the misery of the Indian communities became insupport-
able, the gods descended from the skies to aid the oppressed. In the
first years of the eighteenth century, when an insatiable bishop was
demanding even higher tithes, a hermit appeared in a hollow tree in
Zinacantán and built a chapel for the Virgin. Another Virgin was
discovered in a corn field in Santa Marta, a cross fell from "heaven"
in Cancuc. Native leaders donned priestly robes, held Mass, and ex-
horted the worshippers to murder the oppressors. By the year 1712
the "Tzeltal Rebellion" had spread to thirty-two towns. An army of
four thousand rebels was ready to march on San Cristóbal. Reinforcements arrived from Guatemala and Tabasco. The rebellion was bru-

tally crushed, its leaders were hung, their heads displayed on stakes before the church doors, their bodies quartered and exhibited at the entrances to the towns.

For over one hundred and fifty years the memory of this ruinous defeat kept the Indians subdued, but once again, in 1867, there were new stirrings. "Talking stones" dropped from heaven and were picked up by a Chamulan girl. A cult of Saint Rose, including saints, priests, and native Masses soon flourished. Growing religious and economic independence led to violent reprisals. In December 1868, military forces sacked the church. Devotees assassinated a meddling Spanish priest the following May. A month later the Tzotzil Indians of Chamula began their "War of the Castes," which took the lives of more than a hundred Ladino ranchers. Rebels camped on the outskirts of San Cristóbal until June 21, when government troops attacked. Three hundred Chamulans were dead by nightfall. Savage raids on Tzotzil villages snuffed out the revolt.

As late as 1910 the plight of the Chiapas Indians was "probably the worst of all in the nation" (Cosio Villegas, 1956, 4:227). From the fall of Porfirio Diaz to the defeat of the reactionary forces of General Pineda in 1924, Zinacantán was invaded by waves of contending armies. The land reform policy promised by the Revolution did not reach Zinacantán until the early 1940's.

Conditions have changed rather dramatically in the past twenty-five years. Since 1950 the National Indian Institute has built roads, schools, clinics, and stores in the Chiapas highlands. Other government programs provide legal, administrative, and economic recourses for the Indian population. Despite continued exploitation, explosive population growth, and scarcity of land, the Indian communities are beginning to experience a degree of economic prosperity.

In 1958, when Zinacantecs first told me their tales and dreams, the hamlets of Zinacantán were separated by gleaming forests of oak and pine. Wisps of smoke rose from the tall black pyramids of thatch nestled in the green corn fields. Men ran down muddy trails, urging on their convoy of mules, or strode jauntily along the highway, weaving a coil of palm fiber for a new hat. Their Mayan profiles slanted obliquely under straw platters spilling yards of pink and purple ribbons. Brief white shorts set off their brown muscular thighs as they paraded at the head of their flock of womenfolk. The women, bowed under bristling bundles of firewood, drew shawls across their faces as the cars raced past.

Now the forests ringing the hamlets are mostly knee-high stumps. Low tile roofs cover the adobe or brick rectangles. Trucks, few mules, carry corn. Store-bought sombreros and long pants far outnumber beribboned platters and white shorts. Most boys are bareheaded. Those who can, wear watches on their wrists and carry radios in their plastic shoulderbags. Girls stare boldly and may even smile.

But the electricity is still dim, meals are still cooked on wood fires, dogs still bark and roosters still crow through the night, men still lead the way, mist swirls past the ragged limestone cliffs, and the thunderbolt crashes, shaking the mountains to their foundations. The profile is still Mayan.

Of Wonders Wild and New

Shortly before the arrival of Cortés, the capital of the Aztec Empire, Tenochtitlan, was shaken by a series of ill omens.

> Anyone dreaming anything about the end of the Empire was ordered to the palace to tell of it. Night and day emissaries combed the city, and Tenochtitlan paid tribute in dreams. . . . But finding no good in the thousands offered, Moctezuma killed all the offenders. It was the massacre of the dreamers, the most pathetic of all.
>
> From that day there were no more forecasts, no more dreams, terror weighed upon the spirit world . . . (Séjourné, 1957:42).

Once the conquistadors had subdued the native people, the friars set about converting the multitudes to Christianity, asking, "Have you practised witchcraft? Do you believe in the devil? Do you believe in dreams?"

Dogs dream, and cats dream. Horses dream, and even pigs, say the Zinacantecs. No one knows why; but there is no question in the mind of a Zinacantec why men dream. They dream to live a full life. They dream to save their lives.

While we take extraordinary pains to distinguish between

dreams and "reality," the Zinacantecs would call our wisdom sheer blindness. We seem to concern ourselves only with what transpires "on the earth's surface," as the Zinacantecs describe the material world. In Zinacantán, however, it is the inner reality that motivates, explains, and clarifies the irrational, hazardous events of our lives. There must be a reason for poverty, sickness, and death, for all the disagreeable happenings that bring sadness to our hearts. The reasons are not to be found "on the earth's surface" but in the "soul." Dreams are the means to "see in one's soul" or to "see with one's soul."

When still a fetus, every Zinacantec is bestowed with a soul by the ancestral gods, who reside in the surrounding mountains and who jealously guard and sustain the souls of their descendants, so long as they live in humility and righteousness. The soul, say some, is lodged in the back of the head, others locate it in the heart. Under cover of darkness the soul sits on the tip of its owner's nose and surveys the world, or it wanders abroad.

The soul is believed to be composed of thirteen parts. It is immortal, but it, or parts of it, may be dislodged from the body by fright, by the excitement of sexual intercourse, by a divine beating, or by witchcraft. When a person is ill, a shaman can determine the state of his patient's soul by "pulsing," since the soul resides also in the blood, permitting the shaman to listen "as if to a telephone."

There are men and women whose souls are inherently "clever" or "strong," and there are others whose souls are "ignorant." To qualify as a shaman, an individual's soul must be clever. There are, however, degrees of cleverness and strength, both among shamans and among ordinary citizens.

Should the "crimson hour" strike, when the ancestral gods, the saints, and the sun withdraw their grace, and the soul is permanently lost or consumed, it departs from the body in the shape of a fly. For nine days it retraces its steps on earth. Then it undertakes its journey to the otherworld, ferried across the chthonian river on the back of a black dog. The "ghost" soon reaches a fork in the road. To the left is a broad path, to the right, a crooked trail, the first leading straight down to hell, the place of "burning bones," the second winding up to "heaven." For as long as the soul was alive on earth, that many years it will suffer in hell or delight in heaven, wandering steadily until it is reborn in a baby of the opposite sex, belonging, some say, to the same patrilineage. If, however, the soul was "sold to the earth" by a witch, it must first labor in the fields of the Earth Lord until the contract has been fulfilled, at which time the soul may begin the slow process of reincarnation.

In addition to the soul, everyone has a "companion animal spirit" whose identity is consonant with his personality, with the strength of his soul. Some would say that the individual person and the individual animal have the same soul. These animal spirits reside in corrals inside Great Mountain overlooking Zinacantán Center. They range from jaguars to coyotes, deer, anteaters, foxes, raccoons, weasels, opossum, squirrels, hawks, and owls. Every day the ancestral gods transform these wild animals into sheep and cows so they may graze peacefully. At night they are changed back into their pristine forms and are fed by the assistants of the ancestral gods, the "embracers" and "bearers." If the individual earns the disfavor of the ancestral gods by breaking moral codes or by failing in his duties, his companion animal spirit will be heaved out of the corral into the woods, where it soon will become the target of a hunter's bullets or the prey of a witch's soul. Its death and the death of its owner are usually simultaneous.

The identity of a person's companion animal spirit is revealed in dreams. While shamans, because of their superior vision, are aware of their animal spirits, many Zinacantecs remain ignorant of them throughout their lives. If a shaman determines by pulsing that an illness is caused by the ejection of his patient's animal spirit from the protective corral, he will reveal the animal spirit's identity to its owner and speedily perform the necessary ceremonies to restore it to divine custody. Shamans alone are credited with the power to change their animal spirits if they perceive that their animal spirits have died. To keep body and soul together, and the animal spirit safely corralled, requires more than diligent and responsible activity on the earth's surface; it requires vigilance and boldness when awake or asleep.

Whoever sees, dreams well. Whoever aspires to shamanhood must appear three times before the ancestral gods at the mountain shrine of Calvary. There the initiate acquires his knowledge of prayers and rituals, diagnosis and treatment, and receives the gourds and flowers that he will use in curing ceremonies. Not all shamans have these dreams, but then not all shamans are powerful; some are dismissed as being mere "chicken-eaters," quick to take advantage of the ritual food offered by the patient's family.

Although shamans never enter into trances, they are credited with supernatural vision. When an individual falls ill, he seeks the aid of a shaman who can see best whether he is the target of divine punishment or the victim of a "crimson heart," an "eater of souls." The shaman, who is viewed not as a priest but as a lawyer for the defense in a celestial court, may assemble as evidence his patient's dreams. If the patient loses his soul, he may learn from his dreams where on the earth's surface the shaman should pray for his soul's recovery. Often a shaman can follow in his dreams the fate of his patient, discovering whether the sickness is susceptible to treatment. Although healing may involve the use of herbal remedies, steambaths, or bloodletting, its basis is advocacy through prayer. If necessary, a shaman will descend into the underworld to rescue his patient's soul from the forces of evil beneath the earth's surface.

It is a Zinacantec truth that people are resentful and envious of the good fortunes of others. If their anger and hatred of a particular person becomes sufficiently strong, they may seek the aid of a shaman who is known to wield his power with malevolent effects. One of the principal practices employed by a shaman who indulges in witchcraft is to "sell the soul" of his enemy to the Earth Lord, secretly offering up prayers and lighting candles in remote caves that are acknowledged to be the Earth Lord's domain. Everyone must be on guard lest his soul be devoured by the soul of one of these witches, for every night these evil souls emerge to hunt their victims. Build yourself a new house and you won't have to wait long for nightmares, for a witch is trying to weaken you so that your soul will "shrink" and your body "slacken." To further confuse and frighten his enemies, a witch's soul rolls three times, it is said, before a cross and transforms itself into an animal—a black dog, a cat, a long-haired, rank-smelling goat, a cow, or a horse. In any of these shapes he will visit his victims.

Dreams, then, are not mere portents, they are fields of battle. Zinacantecs must defend themselves or seek a shaman's defense against the wily witches who can see both the souls and the companion animal spirits of their enemies. A shaman, if he is strong, may share the burden of his patient's sins as he struggles in his defense. The combats between shamans are not only verbal assaults but physical wrestling matches or armed encounters in the dream world.

As well as being tests of endurance, dreams are a principal means of communication between mortals and the divine. Zinacantec religion is a blend of pre-Columbian native theology with medieval and modern Catholicism. In their pantheon reside Christ and Mary (who are also sun and moon), the saints, and the Indian ancestral gods. They all may be addressed individually or collectively as "Our Lord." In divine opposition stand the Earth Lords, or Thunderbolts, guardians of the wilderness and the forces of nature. Like the Faustian devil, they can bestow both treasure and death. It is believed that without the aid of both Our Lord and the Earth Lords a Zinacantec's life comes to a speedy close.

The ancestral gods are in steady contact with shamans, advising and aiding them, punishing them if they should be remiss in their duties. These same deities invest with power the bonesetters, midwives, musicians, and office holders. When a religious official wishes to request a loan, an ancestral god suggests to him in his dream whom should be visited; but before the offical pays his call, his coming has already been announced. Perhaps simultaneously Our Lord has appeared before the second man to request a loan, and so the religious official can expect to be welcomed and rewarded with the desired sum. To refuse such a divinely inspired request is believed to invite a supernatural beating and possible death.

An ordinary person may save his own soul in the midst of an oneiric combat if he "remembers Our Lord." Failing that, he may, upon waking, light candles and offer prayers at the cross before his door. Ordinary people, it is said, see the ancestral gods only after praying for their aid.

The major saints also appear to the ignorant mortal in dreams, Saint Sebastian as a soldier, Saint Lawrence, the patron saint of Zinacantán, as a priest. The saints request services, intervene on behalf of their servants, express reproval, or offer consolation.

Dreams provide a vantage on the present action of the soul, but they also cast a view of the future. There are three rules which guide a Zinacantec in interpreting his dreams: (1) dream imagery casts a reverse image of what will happen in the waking state (e.g., "We won't marry the girl we dream about and we won't dream about the girl we marry."); (2) dream imagery presents a metaphoric statement of future events (e.g., to see a house afire is to get a fever); (3) dream imagery reflects future events exactly (e.g., to be involved in a fight is to be involved in a fight). These three kinds of interpretation, however, seem to be quite randomly applied.

Two Zinacantec concepts provide further guidance. It is believed that an individual's possessions are representative of himself, have acquired his soul. Corn, too, shares its soul with the farmer, his family, and his farm tools. Thus, the loss in one's dream of a horse, money, or clothing imperils one's own health. To sell corn is to lose one's child. To lose one's hoe is to lose one's crop. Furthermore, there is a matrix of ominous associations with the earth. Since the Earth Lords are thought to be Ladinos, to meet with a Ladino in one's dream is to confront death. To enter a cave, a car, a Ladino's house, a church is to enter the Earth Lord's lair, to be "sold to the earth." Snakes are the Earth Lord's daughters, so encounters with serpents and women alike may have horrifying connotations. To dream of touching a woman's privates "is like touching a horrible, cold snake" one man remarked. Earth Lords, like Ladinos, are fabulously wealthy; to discover treasure, to receive money is to receive an infernal gift. Water, too, being within the Earth Lord's domain, is icy to the touch. Food and drink that are happily consumed in one's dreams are products of the nether world, transferring their subterranean chill to the dreamer's body.

Sickness and death are prophesied with overwhelming regularity. The calamitous tone of Zinacantec dreams would seem to render each new dawn unbearable were it not for a series of qualifications, equivocations, and uncertainties that clothe the dreamer in protective armor. Dream interpretation finally depends on the individual circumstances of the dreamer and his state of mind.

The dream is a measure of the man. Presented with a disaster, or a formidable opponent, how does the dreamer respond? Does he meet the challenge, elude or vanquish his tormentor? The dire consequences are avoided if he recovers his clothes, extinguishes the fire, flies to protection, scares off the buzzards, or throws the bull.

Whatever may be interpreted as divine advice and consent lightens the dreamer's burden. Not only does he communicate intimately with the gods in his dreams, but he can turn to them for aid afterwards in prayers. While many nightmares may seem to the dreamer to be a severe trial, they can constitute a powerful ego-building force, reinforcing a man's or a woman's relationship with the gods, and with self.

"Dreams are all lies!" "Dreams always come true!" Both sentiments are heard. It is not uncommon for a sleeper to awaken in the pitch black of night and arouse his family to describe in minute detail the visions of his soul. He may be told roughly to quiet down and let the others sleep, but if his dream is particularly frightening or uncanny it will stir up a lively discussion. A dream that cannot be explained is thought to be merely the soul's madness. Just as in our consciousness we have idle thoughts, so in our sleep we have idle dreams, it is argued. The standard, and eminently secure response is: "Sometimes they come true, and sometimes they don't!"

The prophetic value of dreams is reinforced by the elasticity of Zinacantec dream logic and the generous time span that is allowed for a dream's prophesy to unfold. If it is not clear whether the figure that is seen in a dream is actually a devil, a god, or a saint in disguise, his identity is usually revealed by later events upon the earth's surface. Dream motifs, too, are often made intelligible only by later events. The effects of many dreams are felt immediately upon waking; but the Zinacantecs in their practical way have given their dream prophesies considerable temporal leeway. A man dreamt that he lost his mule's tether, and to be sure, one year later the poor mule died, just as had been forewarned!

The consequences of a dream vary from the purely private to the public. Although dreams are not considered valid evidence in a court case involving disputes between individuals, they are brought to court in matters that affect the entire community. If a drought or an epidemic is threatening the town and there is a question whether the town should finance a major series of ceremonies in the mountain shrines, the shamans may air their dreams in court. Shamans will also advise the magistrate if they have seen that a saint desires new vestments, or if an ancestral god has requested a new cross. Perhaps the most dramatic public response to a dream occurred in the hamlet of Thunderbolt Lake in 1969, when a boy dreamt that a bell was buried in the hill overlooking the lake, and that he should dig it up. An ancestral god led him to the very site. The boy enlisted the support of a political leader who consulted a "talking saint" and learned that the boy's dream was true. A ceremonial circuit was made of Zinacantán Center with offerings to the Earth Lord, the saints, and the ancestral gods. The tools were blessed in the chapel of Thunderbolt Lake. For two weeks in the height of the corn farming season the digging continued, bolstered by ritual meals, sacred music, trips to "talking saints" and spiritualists. It was divined that the bell was held in the unyielding grasp of two saints. Finally the search was abandoned, but not before some seventy-five men had wielded picks and shovels to dig a thirty-foot deep hole in solid limestone (Rush, 1974).

The content of dreams, myths, and business on the earth's surface is molded to form a cohesive structure of belief. The treasure hunt in Thunderbolt Lake was consciously and unconsciously modeled after the legend of a similar hunt in Zinacantán Center, also inspired by dreams ("The Priest and the Bell—The Epidemic and Me"). The symbolic sources of myths and dreams undoubtedly flow from a common reservoir.

The spiritual power and spiritual sanctions that are invoked in the soul's wanderings reflect explicitly the cultural values of Zinacantán. The saints and the ancestral gods teach men to beware of surface reality. The gods reveal themselves to mortals in intimate communication, rescuing them and chastising them. Men in positions of authority are reminded to carry out their responsibilities conscientiously. A musician is urged not to neglect his instrument. A shaman is instructed by the gods whether his patient will recover.

The dreams of Zinacantán reveal an uncompromising world of fear and affirmation, where coincidence and clairvoyance are commonplace and the demonic and divine are immanent. Though the soul wanders on perilous paths, Zinacantecs bear their fate with astonishing grace and humor.

I imagine that there will be some who will cower on the earth's surface, shuddering as they peer into this "separate reality," not daring to discover the wonders wild and new. But those whose souls are clever should find plenty to attract them, remembering that dreams are a universal commodity, and that one curious dream is the root of our reality.

Timeless Tales, Sacred Scraps

In the beginning who really knows how it was? No Zinacantec can flash a photographic memory of the origins or the outlines of the cosmos. Scraps of knowledge are passed on to the younger generation, but Zinacantecs are unconcerned about the gaps, the conflicts, the inconsistencies. They know that the world and mankind have both survived multiple creations and destructions, but they do not agree on the number or sequence of events.

Long ago there were three suns in the heavens. Long ago Christ created the earth, sea, and sky. Once the world was inhabited by jointless men and women unable to bend their knees in humility. There were others so keensighted they could discover the gods' treasures hidden in the mountains. And there were people who ate their babies, calling down upon themselves a rain of boiling water. Some were drowned, some became dwarfs banished to the underworld, some, for their rude replies, grew tails and turned into monkeys. Evidently there is little need to stratify these earliest inhabitants of the world chronologically except perhaps to note whether they lived before or after the flood.

At a later stage in the history of the world animals still talked and men traveled as thunderbolts. Spooks and jaguars were rampant. Saints appeared to request new homes.

While the immoral behavior or miraculous events of distant times are believed to continue today, the past is not always at the horizon. The familiar mountains and valleys were the sites of the early creations and destructions. As the waters flooded the valley of Zinacantán Center, Noah floated his boat "like a railroad car." Christ planted his corn there. The Spaniards rescued Saint Sebastian from jaguars' jaws and Lacandón arrows in the forest nearby. No one knows when the next flood will engulf the town in punishment for disobedience. But every Zinacantec knows that in the valley of Zinacantán Center protrudes the Belly Button of the World. Just as familiar surroundings have an ancient past, so, too, mysterious characters of the past intrude into the present. Under cover of darkness Spooks and saints still roam the earth.

Despite the Zinacantecs' lack of compulsion to recall an origin for every aspect of the present world, to an extraordinary degree their tales reveal the Zinacantec musing over his cosmic journey. Man has not developed from monkey, but the monkey, like the dwarf, is a fallen man, atoning for his primeval disrespect for authority ("The Flood"). Beasts of burden are the helpless victims of man, the animal who walks upright. Woman is also man's victim ("What's Man Like?"). Occasionally, through her clever audacity and courage, she shows herself a fitting match for both men and Spooks.

The early inhabitants of the world were few, but they were stronger, cleverer, healthier, and wealthier than the people of today. Yet they were disobedient, evil—and so brought punishment on themselves. Now "some have lice, and some are well off." The gods made a bargain; now soul-loss takes one of every two.

In tale after tale the Zinacantec wrestles with the problem of his fall from grace. "Where does the responsibility lie?" he asks. His answer is contradictory, as many-angled as the historical facts warrant. "It is the Ladino, the wenching priest, who brought divine punishment upon our town. But, too, the negligence of the elders— or was it the shamans, or even the entire town which shares the guilt?" His conclusion: "Only Our Lord knows. As for us, we only know that we eat."

Zinacantec tales about the beginnings of the world and subsequent misfortunes may bear a moral weight, but they are remarkably free from our concerns for historical accuracy. Zinacantecs possess a philosophy of time where, "There is no firm line drawn between traditional narrative and today's reality. That which occurs today is proof of what happened in the past, and what happened in the past can be repeated at any moment" (Guiteras-Holmes, 1961:310). As a result, their memory remembers forwards; a later event is described in terms of a former one. The legendary acts and actors often do not pass by one after the other, but rather they appear motionless on a revolving stage. Time and place lose their relevance.

"When the Soldiers Were Coming" recounts the origin of a number of place names that later proved to be archeological sites testifying to the extent of trade between Zinacantán and neighboring towns in the post-Classic era. We are reminded constantly of the former wealth of the town, and the employment of its citizens in foreign wars. We see the Zinacantecs not so much as simple corn farmers, but rather as the proud merchants admired by Fray Antonio de Remesal in the sixteenth century. Legends of Indian kings, invading armies, military alliances with the Aztecs or Mexicans, conflicts with the Chiapanecs and the Lacandóns—these may refer to any number of characters and events over the past millenium.

Often the course of history is shaped by the intervention of spirits drawn from Zinacantán's pantheon. The spiritual world of Zinacantán is largely revealed through tales of dramatic encounters with saints or Spooks, demons or deities. While the personification of natural forces and the human characterization of supernatural beings give an immediacy to sacred belief, these narratives provide only isolated views of the religious system.

Ritual activity is almost constant in Zinacantán, but the cord between myth and ritual is exceedingly slack. "When the Church Rose and Saint Sebastian Was Saved" partially explains Zinacantán's chief dramatic ritual, the Fiesta of Saint Sebastian. "Our Lady of the Salt" relates the supernatural origin of Zinacantán's economic resource. The rites and sacrifices associated with waterholes are described in "The Donkey and the Spring" and "Saved from the Horned Serpent." Explanations for the "whys" of every ritual are difficult to elicit. Apparently the simple explanation, "This is the way our fathers and mothers have done from the beginning" has been sufficiently satisfying.

To say that the tales reveal the Zinacantec musing over his legendary journey, reminding himself of the supernatural dangers that persist even today, does not mean that he is staggering under the burden of the past, cowering from fear of the present. In fact, the past is borne very lightly, almost cavalierly. During most of his waking hours the ordinary man, caught up in the innumerable petty affairs of daily life, gives little thought to the supernatural world.

Zinacantecs possess an iconoclastic spirit. In religious ceremonies they juxtapose ribald comedy and solemn devotion, and their myths and legends repeat this reckless balance. Cosmic motifs are mixed with sexual perversity in the bizarre pre-Columbian myth, "A Bellyful." Gods and saints display surprising human failings. Christ is a mischievous prankster, much like the wily rabbit that rises from the dead ("How Rabbit Won His Hat and Sandals").

The very flatness of history permits an old man like Xun Vaskis to reminisce about his life in the same manner that he would tell stories about the gods. The listener may be regaled with a myth, a legend, a historical, explanatory or fanciful account, a fable, or a fairy tale. Even gossip about the deviations of one's neighbors may become, in time, part of the community's traditional narrative.

Zinacantecs make a distinction between "ancient words" or "words of the past" and "recent words" or "hearsay." But there is no sharp division between the "truth" and simple entertainment. In Zinacantán, myths, legends, and folktales are one, sources of both moral instruction and delight.

I had thought originally that, "Behind the story which a man tells lies the original whole, a sort of Platonic ideal of the story, from which he draws according to the emphasis of his immediate interest, his memory, his learning and his gifts" (La Farge, 1947:48). In his initial contribution to the study of myth Lévi-Strauss recognized the futility of searching for the "true" or the "earlier" version: "There is no single 'true' version of which all the others are but copies or distortions. Every version belongs to the myth" (Lévi-Strauss, 1963:218). After poring through texts collected in Zinacantán by other students in recent years, I am more impressed than ever by the depth of the reservoir of mythical and legendary material. "Pure" tales are as rare as "pure" cultures.

Despite enormous variations in style and content, Zinacantec narrators emphasize that they are merely repeating the ancient words handed down by their parents, grandparents, and, rarely, great-grandparents. Innovations are frequent, but they are never acknowledged. A tale speaks time-honored truths; conscious alterations are deemed lies.

After years of studying the Zinacantecs in their homes, in their fields, in bars, at court, and at market, listening to hour upon hour of conversation, gossip, joking banter, talk of prices and fiestas, sickness and success, the outsider, who feels that at least he has become a knowledgable quasi-member of the community, is confronted with a mystery: only rarely has he been present at the spontaneous telling of a tale from the past. Furthermore, the ability to tell a tale well is not the basis for great admiration. There are, it is true, individuals whose narrative talents are recognized and appreciated, but the real source of their prestige lies elsewhere. Yet under almost no other circumstances did I see such an open display of enjoyment as that which enlivened the facial and gestural expression of a storyteller in action.

A factor contributing to the scarcity of public narration is the staggering consumption of alcohol in every public situation. But perhaps an even more restrictive force is the avoidance of verbal display unless supported by ritual or political position. Storytellers have no such support.

Certainly there are few Zinacantecs who, when asked, are unable to oblige with a personal version of one of the many well-known narratives of the past. On several occasions the raconteur would explicitly state that he had been told a certain tale "so he would not

grow up to be lazy like the buzzard man," and so forth. Narrators
introducing a tale were just as likely to attribute it to their mother as
their father. The contribution of Lol Sarate, in his early teens, to this
collection demonstrates that verbal skill in telling tales is learned at
an early age.

Tales are not usually told on public occasions for entertainment,
but they are told at wakes. They are told to children around the
hearth of an evening. They serve to while away the time after a hard
day's work in the tropical lowlands or on the roads. They may be
traded between a host and his guest for entertainment and the exchange of information. Since few Zinacantecs read or write in their
own language, tales are the sole means for relating the deeds of the
past. If storytelling is not appreciated as an art in itself, nevertheless
folktales are valued as part of the town's treasure.

Zinacantecs would never suspect that they share the town's treasure
of tales with the peoples of Europe, Africa, India, and Asia. Some
Zinacantec folktales derive from the myths of the Classic Maya and
others from the myths of Classic Greece. The search for outside influ-
ences on Zinacantec oral literature has led to distant events and cultures, confirming the incredible power of folk motifs across space and
time.

What is unique or foreign in Zinacantec oral literature and
where does that literature fit into Middle American oral traditions?

Laying aside the problems of universal motifs, and before indulg-
ing in comfortable generalizations, two discoveries in the course of
my research should serve as warning flags. "What's Man Like?"—a
tale with undoubted European influence—had one scene that was
absent from any of the collections I had reviewed. Moreover, woman's "pestiferous wound" seemed so typical of Zinacantec imagina-
tion that I concluded it must be a local innovation. But this product of
Zinacantec genius, I learned entirely by chance, had been forecast
almost literally by none other than François Rabelais in his *Second
Book of Pantagruel*. Later in the course of study, a legend that told how
Christ punished a farmer's disrespect by turning his crop to stone
("When Our Lord Was Chased") was found to be widely distributed
in Middle America, yet absent in large collections of texts from Spain,
Cuba, and Puerto Rico. The logical conclusion would be that this was
a special "Indian" adaptation of Biblical lore to fit Middle American

ideas. Alas, Oskar Dähnhardt uncovered a thirteenth-century Latin manuscript of this very tale. He discovered that the legend was brought to Europe from the Near East by the Crusaders!

If one were to be overly scrupulous, European elements could be found in nearly every tale. Magical adventures, picaresque heroes, Christian homilies, and animal tales are the stuff of Spanish oral literature that the Zinacantecs have had four and a half centuries to transform. Nobody presented with two collections of tales, one from Zinacantán, the other from Spain, could confuse the two. The ravishing princess, the true bride lost in enchanted sleep in the depths of the magic mountain, rescued by a lovesick and repentant suitor who, with the aid of a golden bird, vanquishes the giants guarding her door—this is not a Zinacantec tale. Only a vague echo reverberates through the oral literature of Zinacantán; an orphan rewarded with a magic token that is lost and retrieved by faithful animals ("The King and the Ring"), a hero who vanquishes the ogre and wins the princess ("How Toenails Won a Bride"), a magic flight ("John, Head of Gold"), the Bear's Son, Cinderella, and the Castle of Going and No Returning ("Journey to Irdivolveres").

Several versions of the Spanish picaresque have been adopted nearly intact. But significantly the picaroon—Peter, John Skin, Johnny Fourteen—is an Indian, his hapless victim a Ladino.

Some Zinacantec folk interpretations of biblical events or of the lives of the saints vary little from their European equivalents; others show a profound assimilation with pre-Columbian beliefs. Traditional Spanish Catholic hostility to the Jews was adopted by the Zinacantecs who conceive of them only as the persecutors and, indeed, murderers of Christ. Zinacantecs' fear of Blacks derives in part from Spanish political rather than religious motives. What could better suit the conquistadors' desires to ensure that no alliance be made between fugitive Black slaves and the native Indian population than horrendous tales of Black cannibalism and supersexuality?

Most puzzling of all are the tales of necrophagous witches. If these tales originated in the Old World, they have undergone a change in Middle America with a new emphasis either upon the efforts of a husband to be rid of his wife, or the husband's concern with his sexual identity. "The Man Who Lived a Dog's Life" bears a remarkable similarity to a tale from the Arabian Nights (Hoopes, 1968:100–105). The husband in the Middle Eastern tale eventually forgives his wicked wife and they live happily ever after; the hero of the Zinacantec version lets his evil bride starve to death.

Spanish folklore, while not deficient in fantasy, is stamped with realism. The "Never-Never Land" of the Grimm's tales is not so prominent as the humorous, pessimistic anecdotes of everyday life. The hand of justice strikes Everyman in the dusty street. This realism is evident in Zinacantec tales where even the most fanciful events are described in down-to-earth terms, where the deities and demons speak the same familiar phrases of anyone's next-door neighbor. Pessimistic humor is a commonly shared trait, but while the Spanish stories delight in the absurd scrapes and misperceptions of fools of a thousand varieties (particularly priests), the Zinacantec does not bear fools or priests lightly. Usually the foolish victim is an outsider: a Chamulan, a Spook, or a Ladino. Here the vagaries of priests, their amorous adventures, are the subject not of humor, but outrage.

The depth of moral concern of Spanish oral literature is equalled in Zinacantec tales, but in Zinacantán it is expressed with somberness, righteousness vindictively triumphant, or injustice unhappily endured.

It is doubtful whether realism, pessimistic humor, or moral concern can be transported intact from one shore of the ocean to the other. While particular elements, even phrases, may flourish unchanged with almost magical powers of survival, the tone of an oral literature as a whole is dependent upon cultural conditions. Though there is no way to ascertain if the oral traditions of Zinacantán were as somber before the Spanish Conquest, there are surely good historical grounds for Spanish-introduced pessimism in Zinacantán!

Tales brought by the Spanish were adopted by many other peoples of Latin America, the Caribbean, and the American Southwest. After perusing the substantial collections of folktales recorded in central Mexico, where Spanish influence is very evident, the Zinacantec oral tradition seems peculiarly autochthonous. An intuitive judgment of the number of tales with *pronounced* European qualities would not raise the estimate above twenty percent of the total collection. Clearly, though European influence is strong, it is far from predominant.

Motifs that at first were assumed by me to be uniquely Mayan (some with an ascertainable time depth of over four centuries) can be found far to the north of Chiapas. Not only motifs, but even dialogues, despite their translation from a variety of unrelated languages, exhibit astonishing similarity. Suggested here is the early existence and current perpetuation of an extensive culture area that embraces not only Guatemala, Chiapas, and Yucatan, but also the southern half of Veracruz and the entire state of Oaxaca.

Prominent traits in the traditional narratives of this vast culture area are tales of the buzzard man, horned serpent, long-haired devils, thunderbolt spirits who singly, or accompanied by whirlwind, hawk, or other aerial *naguals*, defend the town from enemy attack. Descriptions of the underworld, tales of the flood and of multiple creations and destructions agree in many particulars. An interesting parallel occurs in native descriptions of the supernatural creation of the Church of Saint Sebastian in Zinacantán, of a Mixe pre-Columbian plaza, and of Chichen Itzá.

Common motifs demonstrably adapted to post-Conquest life are the arrival of a mysterious person (a saint) who begs the people to build him or her a home and the loss of the church bell either by robbery or through carelessness of the town elders.

Zinacantec familiarity with motifs present far to the north and to the south are added evidence for extensive commercial activity in both directions in the past.

In the Mayan area, a reading of the Guatemalan epics reveals several correspondences with Zinacantec myths: the theme of a god either transformed into an animal or slain while perched in a tree, gorging on fruit or honey; the use of bathing girls to tempt an enemy army to destruction; stiff-legged forebears; wasps and bees as tools of war; thunderbolt defenders; and Thunderbolt Girl. Contemporary Mayan folktales manifest a slightly closer relationship to Zinacantán than do non-Mayan tales. There is but one motif whose distribution appears to be limited to Guatemala and Chiapas; the origin of corn—brought to man by a raven that steals it from a cave.

Clues to the antiquity of folktale elements found uniquely in Chiapas are practically non-existent. There are suggestive remarks by early chroniclers regarding the "Black Lord," or Spook, and the pre-Columbian god Votan, who may survive behind the mask of Saint Sebastian. There are accounts of the War of Saint Rose, or "War of the Castes," of 1868–71. But there seem to be no other historical happenings prior to the twentieth century that can be identified with any security.

With the advance of scholarship the number of motifs peculiar to the Chiapas highlands has dwindled dramatically. The Charcoal Cruncher, a witch whose head comes off and rolls about searching for burning embers to eat, has appeared, under various disguises, in British Honduras and El Salvador. Spreading terror through all the Indian towns, the Spook seems to be native to the highlands. Perhaps the one tale unique to Zinacantán is "The King and the Ring," the saga of a boy who went from rags to riches, became the king of Zinacantán, and was escorted to Mexico City amidst great fanfare, never to return—a hapless betrayer, preserved by the betrayed.

It is not surprising to find that in the oral literature of Zinacantán personal relations, whether between man and god, between stranger and Zinacantec, among fellow townsmen, or between family members, are shaded with distrust. Threats to the social order exist everywhere, in the earth, in the community, in the dark of night, and within the human soul. Chaos is averted, but there is no lasting security and no true salvation. Few mythic antagonists are ever reformed; they are generally rejected and destroyed. A frequently unpredictable universe, whose evil manifestations are easier to batter down than to set right, may have been the creation not of Zinacantecs alone, but of Zinacantecs laboring under the domination of Ladinos. Zinacantecs recall a wealth of timeless tales suffused with a profound sense of loss. And yet they have no memory of the greatness of their Mayan ancestry.

The hesitant teasing out of tales began in my front yard in Zinacantán. The storytellers' toils were accompanied by idle chitchat, bowls of beans, and, when appropriate, bottles of cane liquor or beer, so that their stories would reflect, as they should, hours of leisurely companionship. The choice of narrator was limited by the trials of establishing close relations. The most insignificant and unpremeditated actions—the one-time sharing of a drink, the giving of a ride—proved to be the determinants of the final list of contributors. Titles are my own invention.

"Talk of many things. . . . of cabbages and kings"—no scholar's array of evidence to prove a favorite theory, no logical design, just a few samples of the talk of the town to whet the appetite of those who dare to wonder "why the ocean boils and whether pigs have wings."

Imagine an archeologist attempting to reveal a buried civilization with only the potsherds he finds littering the surface of the ground—so has been my frustration in trying to gain an understanding of life in Zinacantán from this random collection of tales and dreams.

The comparative material displayed in the commentaries is no less random. Scattered far and wide in fieldnotes, mimeographs of federal Indian development programs, in missionary publications, in journals of linguistics, ethnopoetry, and folklore, tucked into anthropology monographs, this material defies easy discovery. Even after examining every scrap that reached my attention, it became clear that there is only the spottiest knowledge of the role of dreams and folk literature in the daily lives of the Indians of Middle America.

The People of the Bat is an endeavor to present a common tradition through the personal styles and interpretations of a variety of townspeople who made no claim to special knowledge but who told with relish what came to their minds during a few mornings and afternoons of their lives.

One thing is certain—they don't need my observations nor my renderings. I would have been content, quite selfishly, to have let their words resound in my ears and their burden be stored in my heart, amen. They never would dream of the care that has been lavished on their ordinary words—the hours, the years spent by countless persons laboring with reels and typewriters and word-processors, computers and Linotrons to reproduce their voices, then to reduce their words to writing for the amusement and edification of mere strangers.

For those of us who assume without question the value of literacy, may this volume intimate the exuberance of living speech!

The stories and dreams of Zinacantán are paraded here in black stripes. But in Zinacantán the real words rush heedlessly into tomorrow, recreating and repeating, forever and forever.

—Robert M. Laughlin

A Note on Pronunciation

For those game to pronounce the Tzotzil words the vowels are *a* as in father, *e* as in gem or the *a* in fame, *i* as in safari, *o* as in cold or the *au* of caught, *u* as in the *oo* of woo. The glottal stop ' is a constriction of the throat that is used by Brooklyners pronouncing "bottle," and by Hawaiians referring to their native state. *j* is h, *tz* is ts, *x* is sh. Apostrophes following the consonants *ch*, *k*, *p*, *t*, and *tz* indicate glottalization that gives the consonant an explosive quality. Stress is on the final syllable unless marked with an acute accent.

In the Land of the Night Sun

DREAMS

May there not arise,
   May there not pass,
The seeming good,
   The evil,
He of the fiery heart,
   He of the crimson heart,
In unison circle,
   In unison shine.
Watch over me,
   Regard me,
At dusk,
   At dawn,
Wherever I travel,
   Wherever I journey,
Where I climb down,
   Where I climb up,
At dusk,
   At dawn.
I, who am Thy orphan,
   I, who am Thy beggar,
I, Thy ashes,
   I, Thy dust,
My beauteous Father,
   My beauteous Lord.
Awaken my soul,
   Awaken my heart,
Uncover my face,
   Open my eyes,
Grant me my path,
   Grant me my course,
Where I shall find a little,
   Where I shall earn a bit,
Whether a splinter of Thy cross,
   Or a sliver of Thy passion,
Whether a handful of Thy sunbeams,
   Or a handful of Thy shade.

Romin Teratol

Day unto day uttereth speech,
And night unto night uttereth knowledge.

—*Psalms*, 19

He was an enigma. Dignified, meticulously dressed in traditional Zinacantec clothing, he seemed the epitome of the exotic. Almost sphinxlike he listened as I tried to learn the folklore of Zinacantán. After twenty years of friendship Romin is still an enigma.

Drawing from bits of gossip, personal observation, and Romin's reminiscences, I will outline his path through life, not ignoring the "trivial" childhood events that loomed large in his memories.

Romin was conceived in 1933, reputedly in the woods, the son of a Zinacantec salt merchant and an ex-Chamulan woman. He was raised by his grandmother, mother, and maiden aunt.

His six years in the school system were initiated by the lopping off of his shoulder-length hair. As an only child it was a struggle learning to play with his peers, but he won one hundred and sixty marbles. Many school days were spent in the woods with a slingshot. During fiestas he served as an assistant to the ensign-bearers' musicians. In the afternoons when school let out, he received crackers from a strange man. He learned it was his father.

Aged twelve, Romin watched his corn crop fail. He volunteered for the coffee plantations down on the coast, but the recruiter did not let him go until his head was shaved. For two months he worked with seven fellow townsmen on thirteen plantations. He saw his first movie. He shook with malaria, grew homesick, had his savings stolen on the train.

Returning home, Romin was appointed sacristan, a post he held for four years while he earned money doing roadwork on the side. Then he became a puppeteer and agent of the National Indian Institute.

At the age of twenty-six, after one rejection and a lengthy courtship, Romin was married to a girl of high social standing within the community. Their first child, a daughter, died in infancy. The three sons and two daughters who followed have been more fortunate.

Shortly after his marriage Romin became the self-styled "interpreter of anthropology for Harvard University." For many years he was the principal informant of the Harvard Chiapas Project, serving as typist, transcriber, and translator of hundreds of native texts. Together with Anselmo Peres he collaborated in the compilation of *The Great Tzotzil Dictionary of San Lorenzo Zinacantán*. This task took Romin to Santa Fe, New Mexico, in 1963, and to Washington, D.C., in 1967. His eyes were assailed with new sights: the Pacific and Atlantic oceans, snow, blacks, subways, television, the assassination of a president, a football game, the march on the Pentagon.

Between these two journeys abroad Romin spent a year in office as Senior Steward of the Holy Sacrament. Later he served as Ensign-bearer of Saint Anthony.

Romin is a worried man. Romin worries about his debts, but he pays them. Romin worries about the cost of major enterprises, but he carries them out. He calculates and recalculates the expenditures; he always falls short. When he built his house he found to his chagrin that he needed more beams. He remembered how painful it was dragging logs from the mountaintops. One dark night he and his friend, Rey Komis, crept out behind the old courthouse where the lumber for a new courthouse was piled. They hoisted the heavy beams onto their shoulders and transported them to an empty house for safekeeping. A week later Romin admitted sheepishly that his heart could not be at rest with those beams in his roof. He would just have to chop them up for firewood.

Romin's "friends" and "enemies" change roles with lightning speed. Yet in a pinch Romin is a loyal friend. He worries about his enemies, sure that everyone resents his new wealth and his American associations. He is fearful of being seen in public with anthropologists. Yet he asked to be the godfather of my daughter. He always invites his American friends to the important rituals in his public and family life. With a sad smile sliding across his face, he drunkenly accuses them of abandoning him "as if he were an aging whore." He is exuberantly boyish, running around his yard carrying his dog and exclaiming, "My son! My son!" Romin is deeply religious and conservative. He carried out his stewardship with such an attention to the fine details of ritual that his colleagues met to ask him to relax his high standards. During his stewardship he had an affair with an American artist, and according to his wife and his enemies, he was so befuddled that he could not respond effectively to the most minor demands of his office. He prays with the deepest conviction every night at bedtime. He prays with mock seriousness under the most absurd circumstances, collapsing in laughter. He walks past the hundreds of mounds in the jungle at Palenque and asks with wonder, "Where have all the souls gone?" When questioned about the date of the annual rain ceremony in Zinacantán he replies, "If it rains early, the ceremony is early, otherwise it is held late for then the rain is sure to come soon!"

He is an affectionate father, scrupulously filling his shoulder bag with fruit for his children whenever he goes to market. And yet when he hears his son crying in the house, he knocks on the door and shouts, "I will sell you to the Ladinos in San Cristóbal, I am the baby-eater." He feeds his drunken compadre's children for days on end without complaint. He taunts his compadre mercilessly for his irresponsibility.

Romin may now have cirrhosis; his month-long binges have turned him a brilliant yellow. One night Romin looked at his hand, "Isn't it strange we must all be food for worms someday!"

He loves his wife, shares the latest gossip, his dreams, and many jokes with her, often at his own expense. He is not violent, he says. Because he was an only child he never had brothers teach him how to fight. His wife complained to him that she was richer when she was single. She could buy sandals with the money from her flowers. That's why, he says, he hit her with a sandal.

He never can make up his mind. He ponders every possible course of action, frets over everyone's reaction to his pettiest affairs. Yet in less than a minute he decided to travel with me to far off New Mexico, and later pioneered the first artesian well in Zinacantán. He is so diplomatic, so eloquent, so reasonable, so aware of cultural relativity, he would be a worthy representative to the United Nations—when sober. He is sullen, remorseful, melancholy, body and soul racked with aches and pains. He frowns with concentration seeking to penetrate and explain the religious concepts of Zinacantán. With a wink and a secret smile he gulls his friends. He tells the most obscene jokes and laughs contagiously. Cheerfully, with the greatest dedication, sensitivity, and care he transcribes, translates, and interprets. No one is his equal—when sober. He is no longer an informant, he is an anthropologist, drunk or sober. But who is he really? "I am the son of god and the son of a devil!"

In his dreams Romin is constantly defending himself against the attacks of wild beasts, murderous men, and lecherous women. His wife is the victim of his near-mortal assaults. At best she is a fellow sufferer in his dreams.

Although the ancestral gods offer him divine aid, there is never a lessening of his anxiety. With a frequency unique to Romin in this company of dreamers, he must lift his wings and flee heavenward.

I Say Goodbye to a Corpse

On Tuesday, January 29, 1963, I, Domingo de la Torre Perez (Romin Teratol), had a dream at dawn.

They summoned me at my home to go talk to a friend of mine who was wounded and who was shut up in the office in the courthouse of Zinacantán.

I came to see which of my friends was wounded. And the wounded person spoke to me. He said, "I'm José Cabrito."

I didn't want to answer José because he was about to die, and because he had been put in a plain white coffin in anticipation of his death. I saw him wounded in my dream because he must actually be wounded. And so I didn't want to talk to a corpse and I withdrew.

When I withdrew, his stepfather, Mariano Hernandez Nuj of the town of Zinacantán, started to shout at me. "Look, Domingo, maybe you don't want to talk to poor José because you were there when they cut him up with a machete and he's an enemy of yours."

"No, Uncle Mariano. He is a friend of mine, but right now I don't have the time to chat. I have to do an errand and I can come back in a little while if he is still alive. Or if he dies, too bad. He's not the only one who can die. I can come back later on to chat with him when there's more time for chatting, but I can't now. I'll tell you frankly, Uncle Mariano, if he were a good friend of mine I'd go in and see how he was and what happened to him. But he'll have to look after himself because I don't know how to cure and I don't know how to defend his life, and because he was going to kill me once with a machete. That's why I don't have to talk to a corpse," I said to Mariano Nuj.

"Don't be like that, Domingo," he told me. "Go in and chat with José!"

So I went in and chatted with José who was stuck in the plain coffin. "What happened to you, José?" I asked him. "Why are you going to die?"

"Well, I don't know, Domingo. They say I'm going to die. My back is badly cut up and I can't stand the pain anymore. That's why I'm just waiting for my death here in the coffin, so they can simply go and bury me. I summoned you, Domingo, to say goodbye forever because we were friends." And I shook hands with the wounded man, or the corpse as we say.

When I finished saying goodbye, the wounded man told his mother to buy some meat and to invite me to a farewell meal. And I, Domingo, understood that a corpse was inviting me to supper. I withdrew from there, I went home, and I woke up.

It is believed that to chat or shake hands with a corpse leaves bad "wind" in our bodies, because corpses are cold. But to say goodbye to a corpse is good because they won't take our souls, although they still will leave us a little sick. The coffin in which the corpse was stuck looked white because it wasn't varnished, and some people here in Zinacantán always buy them like that when they are poor and can't pay for a good coffin. Varnished coffins cost more, that's why people buy them plain and that's why they are seen in dreams.

Pooh on Him and Pooh on Me

I, Romin Teratol, dreamt at dawn, Tuesday, the twelfth of February. God, My Lord, I had a terrible dream.

I don't know why, I was going to San Cristóbal with my compadre, Lol Brinko (Robert Laughlin).

On the other side of Window Pass a table was standing in the middle of the road, and a Ladino was sitting there, writing.

There was a privy at the side of the road and my compadre, Lol, went to take a shit. But when he finished shitting, he didn't know how to put his pants on. He put the front part in back.

Now a Ladina girl was there and she told my compadre that his pants were on wrong. So he turned his pants around, but his fly was covered with shit. The Ladino who was sitting at the table, writing, saw it and scolded him.

I was standing nearby. Afterwards I went to shit, but when I finished shitting I was covered with shit too. My shit jumped up and landed smack on my chest.

Maryan Chiku' and Maryan Martinis were standing there now. Maryan Chiku' removed the shit from my chest. He threw it at my mouth and it landed with a smack on my cheek. I removed it and was going to throw it at his face, but he told me to throw the shit away for good or else he would throw more at me. I got rid of it.

Then I went to wash myself in a little gully. The spring was beautiful. It wasn't a bit muddy. All the shit came off my hand and then I woke up.

When I awoke I was terrified, because that is a very bad dream. It means accusations of carnal sin, false accusations. Maybe it has to come true, because once I saw that dream come true. But who knows when it will be. Only Our Lord knows if the gods will still watch over me, will still stand up for me, because the resentful people beside me and behind me want to become more powerful. God, there are so many resentful people. Maybe later they will lie that I am guilty.

An Owl Screeches, I Kill a Black Cat

On Thursday, February twenty-eighth, I dreamt I was sleeping at my mother's. It was dark. And then a screech owl arrived and called by the side of the house.

I was very scared because it is said that if a screech owl comes and calls next to the house we will die, because that bird is a messenger of death. I went out to look. I was going to kill it.

A man was standing in back of the house. With his pine torch flaming, he was looking for a way to break in.

Now I was terrified. My head felt as if it had grown. I was struck dumb. I took out my machete. I was going to chase him, but I could no longer find him. I shouted, but because of my fear I couldn't shout loudly. When he disappeared, my fear passed a bit.

Later, a black cat came in and found me in my bed. Before I realized it, it was curled up on top of me, asleep. I caught it and threw it outside, but it kept coming back in.

Then I caught it and stretched it. I pulled it by the legs. I cut off its head. All its guts came out. The black cat lost the battle. It was dead.

I went to get rid of it outside. It bit my fingers. It still fought back.

When I woke up I was terribly scared. I couldn't get back to sleep until I lit my lamp to guard me. I was terribly scared from being so terrified in my dream. I was terrified in my dream because of all the resentful people, behind me, beside me. They want me to get sick. They want to leave behind a little sickness.

My Hoe Is Stolen, I Am Chased and Fly Away

God, My Lord, I, Romin Teratol, had a terrible dream last night.

I was on the other side of Sweet Water, the stream that runs by my mother's house.

A boy arrived and spoke to me. "What are you doing, Romin?" he asked.

"I'm looking for my hoe. I had it at work yesterday, today it's gone. I don't know who came and stole it. My laborer was Markux Teratol. Maybe he took it home with him, because I went to my mother's house for a minute and when I came back I couldn't find Markux."

"Markux didn't take it. I saw who took your hoe. It was the son of Antun Masan, the third prefect. And your hoe wasn't the only thing he took. He abducted a girl. So who knows if he will come back. He probably fled. Try saying a word or so at the courthouse to see if the magistrate will send one of his constables after him," the boy told me.

But I returned to my mother's house.

Night fell suddenly. I was walking on the hill above the house. Before I knew it, a bunch of men were swarming in with flashlights. I was terribly scared because I thought they were coming to kill me. I hurried to the other gate, but there I met a mob of women and they were trying to catch me too.

I flew into the sky, in the dark. And when I came down to earth, all the men and all the women came chasing after me in a rush.

I flew again. I did a turn around the church roof and returned home. I ran into my house and picked up my machete, but when I opened my door, they stormed in. They shot me three times. The bullets hit me in the ribs.

I attacked them with my machete, but they grabbed my machete away. I made myself a pistol to fight back. I shot them but they didn't die.

And then they caught me. They tickled me. I simply shouted. I screamed.

My wife shook me. "Wake up! What's happening to you? What do you see?"

God, My Lord, I awoke.

I prayed to Our Lord, I prayed to Saint Lawrence. I couldn't get back to sleep. God, there are so many resentful people, behind me, beside me.

I dream too much when I don't pray at bedtime. When I pray at bedtime, when I cross myself at bedtime, I don't dream very often. When I don't pray, I dream so much.

I Am Nearly Stoned, I Drink Chicha, I Pull a Pebble from My Leg

I went to a fiesta in San Andrés. Many of my countrymen were already gathered there. I met Maryan Chiku' from Zinacantán Center, my compadre, Maryan K'obyox, and his brother-in-law, Mikel Sarate. Lots of children were playing with them.

Then a cow arrived. The children started throwing stones at it. The owner of the cow came and gave the children a good bawling out, but the children threw stones at him too, and scared him away. Even I was scared because they almost hit me with the stones.

I circled around and went to find Maryan Chiku'. But when I reached the place where the older people had assembled, it had already grown dark. When it was good and dark, Ladinos started to play their guitars. The fiesta was in full swing now. But it wasn't by the church, it was in the meadow.

There were many young Ladina girls squatting in the hollow. They showed me their asses, their pussies.

Little by little I climbed to the top of a hill. And there were two barrels of chicha. I went into the store to buy some, because I longed to drink a little. But the chicha was terrible. It was undrinkable.

I went to look for more. There was a store at a crossroads and I found better chicha there. I was with my compadre, Maryan K'obyox, and his brother-in-law, Mikel Sarate. We drank one large gourdful apiece. It tasted very good.

When we finished drinking, we went to look for more. A man from San Andrés was selling some. "Buy some chicha, friend! My chicha is excellent," he said. We bought some. We went inside his store.

Now my compadre, K'obyox, started to quarrel with his brother-in-law. "See here, Mikel, you bastard, let's fight!"

"Take off your shirt!" Mikel shouted.

He got scared and was about to leave, but my compadre, K'obyox, began to laugh. "Let's drink some chicha in good spirits. The chicha tastes wonderful!"

Afterwards—I didn't see how it happened—all my clothes fell into a river. My tunics, my shirt, my neckerchief, my hat were sinking. They were caught on a strand of wire.

Quickly I jumped in to get all my things. I even stole an old neckerchief from the river.

I put on my clothes. I was laughing and joking contentedly with my friends. We reached a small stream. There were boards stretched across the water. We sat down on the bridge.

Now I had a cut in my leg. I began to lift up the scab little by little. I saw a green pebble embedded in my leg. I picked it out.

And then there was another one. They kept spilling out. Now I saw that it was my legbone. My legbones were rotten. They hurt. I told my friends, "I can't make it home now."

"Your leg is useless," they told me.

I tried to walk, but my leg wouldn't get any stronger. It was breaking, because the whole support to my leg had come out.

God, My Lord, I sat down on the edge of the gully and cried. I sobbed to myself that I was just a leftover, now that I had had an accident when I was still young.

When I woke up I was still crying.

"What happened to you?" asked my wife.

"I had a terrible dream," I told her, but I couldn't talk clearly because I was crying.

"Why don't you have a curing ceremony for yourself? Offer a few candles, because there are so many envious people behind us, beside us," said my wife.

I prayed to Our Lord. I prayed to Saint Lawrence because I was so sad. God, the next holy morning my heart was in two.

I Stab My Wife

God, My Lord, I, Romin Teratol, dreamt at dawn today, the ninth of March.

It seemed I lost my temper. I caught my wife by the door of don Chavel's house. I grabbed her. I threw her to the ground. I was about to hit her with a machete. But I couldn't get her because the machete was heavy and I wasn't able to whack her.

Then I grabbed a knife. I stuck it in her stomach. It was hard to get the knife in. I was watching to see if she was dying. But when I tried to stick the knife in deeper, I shouted.

While I was in the midst of my dream, my wife was already up, grinding corn. She heard me shouting in my bed and came to wake me. "What's happening to you? What do you see?" she asked.

And I woke up. I awoke when I was holding the knife. I told her, "It seemed as if it was you I was killing and I shouted when I stuck the knife in."

"Oh, how horrible! I shouldn't have wakened you. I should have let your soul get a good scare. If only I had known it was me you were killing! It's probably just because you'll kill me one of these days," she said.

I Am Chased by Women

God, My Lord, I don't know why I dream so often.

Last night, around two in the morning, many women came to the house where I was sleeping. First they knocked on the main door, but no one answered.

Then they broke in. They reached the door to the very place where I sleep, and they knocked on it. I didn't open it because I knew they were evil people. And I knew it was night. They broke in again by themselves.

I jumped out of bed. I pushed against the door, but they forced it open. But they didn't come in because the light was on.

I shouted to the landlord, but I couldn't yell. I was struck dumb with fear.

Then I screwed up my courage. I went out and wrestled with the women. There were a great many. I didn't see if they were Ladinas or my own people. I couldn't see well because it was dark.

Just as they were about to kill me, I remembered what could be done to unnerve them. I took off my pants, turned them inside out, and threw them in their faces. All the women fled into the street.

I wasn't afraid anymore. I found a stick lying by the door. I picked it up and whacked a woman's leg with it. Her leg broke immediately.

But now I wasn't able to close the big door. And they came in to find me again. This time I hurried inside the landlord's house, where they sleep in separate rooms.

The women headed straight for the place where I had been sleeping, but again they didn't go in, because the light was on. They didn't see me because I was hiding inside the other house. And then I woke up, terribly scared, and that's how it ended.

Maybe there are witches who are tormenting my soul. Or maybe the earth where the house is standing is dangerous, I don't know.

I See a Bull Slaughtered

On Saturday, the thirteenth of April, I dreamt that a man came to my house.

"Romin," he said. "I've come to talk to you. Are you well?"

"I've been well for a few days, sir," I answered.

"Oh, even those few days are a help, son."

"They're a help, sir," I said.

"Would you like to take a little bit of meat, son? There is still some left over. We haven't finished paying for it all ourselves."

"Where are you bringing it?" I asked.

"Oh, nearby," he said.

I went to the place where the bull was to be slaughtered, but who knows where, in the woods.

The bull was caught. It took a lot of people to catch it, because the bull was terribly big. And they divided it up equally among the young and the old.

I didn't see if I received some of that beef. I woke up.

It was then that Telex K'o got sick, the one who lived on the ridge. It was his soul I saw, indeed, since that was when he died. That's how we see those who have been caught by witches.

I Carry Rocks, Find Honey and Pine Needles, Fly from Ladinos

God, My Lord, I, Romin Teratol, dreamt at dawn, Sunday, the twenty-first of April.

I saw that I was a sacristan. I went with the stewards to the town of Five Pieces to celebrate the Fiesta of Our Lady of the Rosary. My mother wasn't there and neither was my wife. I simply went alone to celebrate the fiesta.

I was bringing back my little presents in a basket. I simply was coming home all by myself with my little piece of meat and my tortillas.

On the way I met the civil authorities, the justices of the peace, the syndic, the magistrate.

"Romin," said the magistrate. "You will take a burden!"

"What is my burden, sir?" I asked.

"It's nothing much, son. You will carry away these rocks."

"Ah, all right, sir. I wonder if you have a wheelbarrow? I'll carry them over to the edge of the path."

"Take that one!" they told me.

I got the wheelbarrow. I carried off the limestone piled where the civil authorities were standing.

Then I hurled the wheelbarrow down at them.

"Damn, that friend of ours doesn't realize that he nearly killed us!" I overheard them say. I didn't answer.

"Why am I carrying rocks?" I said to myself. "Am I a criminal? Am I guilty? Hell! It would be better if I left. I'll go meet up with the stewards."

I picked up my little basket and went to meet the stewards on the path. Before I knew it, I was at Ak'ol Ravol Ranch, looking for work. Many of my countrymen were there. We couldn't even find a place to sleep at the foot of the cliff, and when I looked next, it was already light.

I went to the woods and found two honeycombs to eat. My

other countrymen discovered two bagsful of yellow-jacket comb, so I snitched some of theirs. Now I couldn't possibly finish eating all the honey.

I didn't see how I and several of my countrymen came to this side of the ranch. I was with compadre K'obyox and Karmen, Old Serafina's son. We were taking a stroll. My land was being hoed, so we passed by to look at it.

Then we saw a ball of pine needles on a branch. The tree was on the top of a cliff, leaning way out. We wrecked the ball of pine needles and dropped it over the ledge. A black robe was rolled up and stuck in the middle of the pine needles, but we threw it over the cliff because we thought that a highwayman or a robber had slept there. So we got rid of it all.

"But let's leave our gourds here!" compadre K'obyox told me. "They'll come in handy for drinking water tomorrow."

"But won't they get lost?" I said. "I think it's better if we hang them from the top of the tree so they won't be seen."

I climbed up and hung compadre Maryan's gourd on a high limb. I left it there, because it was bigger, but I kept mine.

As soon as I reached the ground, a bunch of young Ladinos appeared. We were terribly scared because we had wrecked the pine needles and the robe. We thought that it might be their sleeping place.

They came up to Karmen, Old Serafina's son. "What's your name?" they asked.

"My name is Karmen," he said.

"Karmen what?"

I told Karmen he'd better not tell his last name because they might catch him later if it was their sleeping place we had destroyed. And Karmen didn't tell them his last name.

We left. Now we were on the road to Zinacantán Center. There next to the white house at the edge of the ranch was another group of Ladinos. But we couldn't understand their language. Their Spanish sounded awful. Their pants were different too. They wore the same white baggy pants as the people from Big Lake. And mixed with them were people from Paste'. They were stealing corn.

Then they saw us and came toward us.

I told compadre K'obyox, "See here, compadre, be patient, take my gourd! I'll see what I can do."

I gave him my little gourd. I carried my basket of tortillas and meat that I got in Five Pieces and I went looking for the top of a cliff. I flew with my basket of tortillas, but I didn't fly far off. I just landed in a river.

More robbers caught me there. "Romin! Romin!" they called one after the other, but I couldn't shake all their hands. I tried to throw them in the river when they grabbed my hand, but they didn't fall.

A man from Paste' came up to me. "Do you know where we got our permit?" he said.

"Where?" I asked.

"From Our Holy Father Saint Ignacius."

"But that's Our Holy Father Esquipulas, of course," I said.

"No, he is the younger brother. There is an older brother."

"Is it the one who lives in Burrero, then?" I asked.

"Oh yes, do you know him?"

"I know him if that's who it is."

"Well, it's his letter that I've brought here giving me permission to travel. I can even enter houses," said the man from Paste'.

Now I thought to myself, "It would be better if I went to Our Holy Father Saint Lawrence to see what the situation is, if he has given the robbers a permit to walk abroad or not." I told that man what I was going to do, so that the crowd of people gathered there would make room for me to fly.

"I'll go talk to Our Holy Father Saint Lawrence to see what kind of permit he will give me. Once I have spoken to him, I will come back here and circle over their heads. First I'll fly off and talk to Saint Lawrence."

I carried my little basket with my little portion from Five Pieces. And I flew to the west to pray to Our Lord.

Then, in the middle of my dream, my wife woke me. "Get up, the sun is already high!" I woke up. The sun had risen. And my dream was cut short.

"What could my dream mean? It said thus and so," I told my wife.

"Who knows what that dream could mean. Maybe you'll die. Why did you fly?" she said.

Well, that dream of mine means something. Who knows if I'll

die or not. Or if it's a lesson for me from Our Lord. It has two meanings, good and evil.

I Am Late for Work and Am Chased by Ladinas

God, My Lord, I, Romin Teratol, dreamt in the evening of the day before yesterday, Sunday, the fifth of May.

I was on my way to work in San Cristóbal. Then I met Xun Vaskis, the current second sacristan, and Anselmo Peres, the shaman.

"Where are you going, Romin?" they asked.

"I'm going to work," I said.

"If you are going to work, then wait a minute, we'll go by bus, because this bus is going. You'll arrive quicker in it."

I got in the bus next to the Church of Saint Anthony in San Cristóbal. But the bus just stood there.

So I got off the bus. "It's better if I go on foot. I'll arrive quicker, because it's getting late. It's my job!" I said to myself.

Xun and Anselmo got out too. "Romin!" they said. "Do you like the Ladina girl over there? She is really pretty. She wants to get married."

"Ah, but I can't because I have to hurry off to work. It's a good idea if only I weren't busy. Maybe you should talk to her yourselves because I don't have the time at all."

I went to work. But then I couldn't remember where to go. I tried to look for the place where I worked, but I simply forgot where it was. I went to the center of San Cristóbal to ask. "No, it isn't here. I don't know where it is," said the Ladinas.

I found an auto repair shop. I asked the workers there. They were Tenejapans and Chamulans and Ladinos. One of the Tenejapans had a wife who worked as a maid. I knew her. The woman was from Deer House hamlet.

"Can I spend the night here? I have a bed. I've come to look for my blanket," I said to the Tenejapan.

"I don't know if you left your blanket here. I haven't seen it," he said.

"Never mind," I said. "I was just asking."

I left, and then I met Telex Kirivin with his wife, his mother-in-law, Tonik Nibak, and his sister-in-law, Petu' Nibak.

I bought a quarter pint of cane liquor and gave them each a drink. We finished the quarter pint. I don't know how we got inside a Ladino's house.

Telex went way inside the house. I remained standing by the door. The Ladinos and Ladina girls were planning to kill us.

"Telex, come on out! If you bring out my sack I'll take it," I said. He handed it out to me. The Ladina girls were about to shut the door. Night was beginning to fall.

I picked up two rocks. They were good and big. When one of the Ladinas tried to grab me, I quickly threw the rocks at her. I beat her with my fists too, and she landed way off on her back. She was thrashing about in the street.

Then I fled. Poor Telex and his wife, his mother-in-law, and Petu' probably were killed. I didn't see them again.

That dream is just envious people tormenting me. They are angry since I built my little house.

I Am Jailed for Nothing, Chickens Talk to Me

Last night, too, I left my house. I went to speak to the clerk and Chep Ok'il, but who knows what I was going to tell them.

As I was crossing the square, the magistrate called me. "Come over here, Romin! You're going to rest in jail awhile."

"What is my crime, sir?" I asked.

"I don't know, son. You'll hear soon. Go take a rest first!"

I was put in jail. Suddenly it grew dark. I didn't see the two other prisoners who were spending the night there until one of them spoke to me.

"God, is it you, Romin, who has been put in jail too?" said the gentleman.

"It's me, sir!" I said.

"What were you accused of?"

"I don't know, sir. They jailed me for nothing. 'You'll hear soon!' they told me."

"But you can't be very guilty then, son. They'll probably let you leave in a little while."

Then Maryan Burito was standing at the jail door.

"Father Maryan," I said. "Won't you please go tell my wife that I won't be coming back tonight because I was put in jail. She probably thinks that I got drunk. I was supposed to come here for just a minute on business. How would she know that I've been jailed? Please go tell her for me. Have her ask someone to bring me my blanket because it's too cold for me to sleep here. I'll pay you a little for making the trip."

"All right, I'll let her know," said Maryan Burito. He went off to tell my wife.

I didn't see how I got out of jail. The next time I looked, I was already at home.

There was a very bright moon. I looked up, and on the hill above my house were flocks of chickens and lots of chicks too. I went to drive the chickens off my land because they were digging up the ground so badly.

"Could those be good chickens?" I asked my wife. "Or could they be evil?"

"I'm a good chicken. Don't be afraid!" The chickens answered me!

"So you're dumb devils, then! That's why you travel at night." I hit them with my hat.

"So you think you're a man! Let's fight and see! Don't you believe that I'm a chicken—I'm a human being," they all told me. I was terribly scared. I was screaming.

Since I probably was screaming loudly, my wife said to me, "Why are you screaming? Wake up!"

I told my whole dream to my wife, and then I prayed to Our Lord. God, but the envious people certainly torment me all the time. It's too much!

I Find Beautiful Stones, See a Snake, We Fly Away

God, My Lord, I, Romin Teratol, dreamt a little bit just before dawn this morning, Wednesday, the eighth of May.

I was in the shade of Women's Rock, digging under the trees for little stones. They were very beautiful round stones.

Now I hadn't seen it until my wife shouted, "Watch out! Look at the snake next to your foot!"

Damn, I looked. Then I saw it. It almost bit my foot. It was a horrible thick coral snake, lying on top of the leaves.

I picked up my machete. I cut the snake in half. Now the front end rose to bite me. I swished the machete at it again and chopped off its head.

Then we fled because the snake had a master who might come to kill us.

My wife didn't know how to fly. I knew how to fly, of course. I carried my wife and I flew with her. We flew, and when I woke up I was still flying.

That dream means a devil is tormenting us. It's our souls being tormented by the Earth Lord when he is walking abroad.

I Am Offered Three Stones

God, My Lord, I, Romin Teratol, dreamt last night, the ninth of May.

I was standing next to the house of Old Maryan Sarate, the land commissioner.

Several stewards were gathered in Petul Buro's yard. I thought very highly of the one who spoke to me. He is the present Senior Steward of Our Lady of the Rosary, Maryan Peres from Paste', the former magistrate.

"Romin," he said.

"What is your command, sir?" I asked.

"See here, son, I want to ask you if you're still working at jobs."

"It still seems so, sir, because I am very poor. I can't find anything on the holy earth. There ought to be a little contribution here at the feet of Our Lord," I said.

"Have you stored up a little of your money?" Two people asked me that, Maryan Peres and Chep Vob from Paste', the former Steward of the Holy Sacrament.

"God, you wouldn't believe it, sir. I haven't any at all. It doesn't accumulate, because I have to buy my little bit of corn. It's just completely used up."

"Well, son, we want to say a few words to you, a few words of advice, if you will accept them."

"Please then, My Father, please then, My Lord, because I don't know how to make my plans."

"See here, son, since you find that your money doesn't accumulate, it would be better if you sat here beneath the feet of Our Lord. Give up the search for jobs. Because, son, your little share is set aside. I'm telling you openly, pray to Our Holy Father the Martyr, and he will show you right away, even tonight, if you pray to him. He has set aside your little share. It's true. It isn't idle talk. We have seen it. What he has set aside for you is very beautiful.

"You see, son, that's the way it was when I was a boy. I used to look for roadwork all the time, but the money didn't accumulate.

"Then I entrusted myself to Our Lord. I prayed to Our Lord. I prayed a lot to Our Lord. God, now I can say it openly, I have my own little bit. Our Lord presented it to me. I settled down. I didn't go looking for jobs. If you want your favor, son, try praying to Our Holy Father the Martyr, because he has kept your little present. I'm showing you now, son. This is yours," said the Senior Steward of Our Lady of the Rosary.

He showed me three little rectangular stones. The stones were bright blue. They sparkled like glass.

Then I woke up. I didn't see how the matter turned out.

I started to wake myself up thoroughly. "What could that dream of mine mean, My Lord?" I said in my heart. "But that was a good one," I said to myself. I have a little present. The trouble is, who knows what kind of present Our Lord wants. And besides, who knows which of Our Lords it was. That dream was a proper one, of course. It wasn't a persecution. It was advice, because Our Lord is going to favor me. So forget the poverty. I suffer so much.

I Scold a Shaman

Just before dawn this morning, the tenth of May, I dreamt. Three shamans were celebrating Cross Day at Sweet Water Well. It is my mother's and Old Antun Konte's well. The shamans were assembled at Markux Teratol's house. Old Antun Konte was there, Markux Teratol was there, and his older brother, Maryan Teratol, the one whom I had asked to offer the candles for my new house.

"See here, Romin!" said Maryan Teratol. "Today we are friends, you bastard! That was a beautiful thing you did to me! Do you remember that you beat me out of your house when I was about to offer the candles?"

"If that's what you say, father, but I know that I was sober. I wasn't completely sober, the way I am now. I had drunk a bit, but I remember."

"But why did you trick me, then? Where was my present? Where was the food that should have been given to me when I was escorted home?"

"Ah, if that's what you're talking about, father, why should I give you your present? Did you finish offering the candles for my house? Now you ask for your present! You just went to sleep! All you did was dig the hole for the chicken in the middle of the floor—the gift for my house. And then you fell to the ground. And your ass just missed going into the grave. I asked you the favor, but to pray, to pray to the Holy Fathers, the Holy Mothers. I asked you to offer my candles before Our Holy Lord. Then see what you did to me! You just kept asking for cane liquor every few minutes. And you never prayed. Do I want a shaman like that? Is your shamanhood yours alone? Wasn't it given to you by Our Father and Our Mother?"

"Is that right, son?" he said.

"Yes, indeed, father! It isn't as if I got so drunk. All the helpers that I brought there saw it. Even two justices of the peace saw it. My brother-in-law, Maryan Tanchak, was there. My compadre, Palas Muchik, was there. Both of them are justices of the peace. It isn't as if I'm accusing you falsely of your crime, father. The justices of the peace told you to pray, but you only asked for more cane liquor. You never even prayed at the four corners. My musicians planted the candles. 'We'll just plant the candles ourselves if the shaman won't pray!' they said. 'God, My Lord, am I going to light my candles myself?' I said to myself. We simply decided to light my candles before Our Lord. As for you, you were left behind asleep."

"I knew it! That's your kind of stupidity!" his wife told him. "I thought your crimes were great!"

"Ah, forget it, Romin. Let's not squabble. Forgive me, because I got drunk."

He calmed down. He probably thought I would run him out, beat him off, that's why he had planned to give me a scolding. And he was going to ask for his present, but he learned the truth about it.

He didn't say another word. His wife had looked at me angrily, but she learned the truth about it too. They became friendly. And that's how the matter ended.

Maryan Teratol tried to torment me in my dream, but my soul is a bit powerful too. Even though I'm not a shaman, my soul is strong. If my soul were stupid, then I'd probably be dead this morning—but no, not yet! Our Lord won't discard me as long as I remember him.

I Ride a Flying Cow

I was at Ak'ol Ravol Ranch. I was with some Chamulans at the church.

"Go, Romin," a Chamulan said to me. "Go, bring this!" But it wasn't clear what I was to bring. "Go and bring it, because it is needed very badly right now."

He gave me a black cow. Quickly I mounted it. The black cow jumped over the fences, the tall trees. It flew high above the meadow.

On the return trip, the cow gored me. My leg was pierced and the blood flowed.

But the cow spoke to me. "I will cure your wound," she said. "It won't take long to cure." And she licked my leg. It healed immediately.

And then I woke up. I told my wife my dream.

"Who knows what it means," she said. Just in joking she told me, "Probably it's because you are a witch. Why else would you dream of black cows?"

I think it's a bit of a torment. That's what I tell myself.

And that's the way it all is.

I Work in the Belltower, Give Advice, Distribute Corn

God, My Lord, I, Romin Teratol, dreamt at three o'clock this morning, Monday, the first of July.

My compadre, Lol Brinko, was going back to his country, it seemed. "See here, compadre, I'm leaving. We'll talk together again when I return. You stay and work with this boy, but only work here.

Don't work on the ground!" he told me. "And write only in Tzotzil!"

The place where we were to work was where the bells are rung in the tower of the church in Zinacantán Center. The seat was too narrow for two people to sit on. I tried it twice, but I had a hard time getting out because I was afraid I would fall.

"As for me, compadre, I don't know if after a day of this I'll still be alive in the evening. Can't you find a good place for us to work?"

But the bells were really beautiful. Around their rims was a great deal of writing. The bells were engraved in Tzotzil.

I never saw how we got down from the tower. The next time I looked, I was standing on the road to Paste', near the school house.

There I met the gringo priest. "Where did you go?" I asked him.

"I haven't gone yet. I'm going to see George. He's come to speak to the magistrate in Paste'. The magistrate settles cases in Paste' now, not in Zinacantán Center anymore. I don't know whom George asked for permission to come here, because he certainly never asked *my* permission," said the priest.

"Why has he come to speak to the magistrate?" I asked.

"Because he has had bad chest pains. He is in great pain, so he's come to buy a little land from the magistrate."

I began to wonder what use the land was to him. "Probably it's for him to be buried in," I said in my heart.

"Why do you look so unhappy?" asked the priest. "Can't such a thing be said?"

"Isn't he buying a little land so he can be buried on it? Isn't he dying?"

"No, he is simply buying some land."

"Ah, then you can't say he is buying a little bit of land because he is sick. What you mean to say is that he is buying land so that he can work on it," I told him.

"Yes, of course, that's right!" he said.

As for me, I went on to Paste'. And when I arrived, all the men were assembled. Old Maryan Sarate was there. All the shamans were there. They were meeting because they wanted to offer candles so that the price of corn would come down. The people of Zinacantán Center didn't want to give money for the ceremony. Only the hamlets wanted to give money.

"I just don't know what to do," said Old Sarate. "Hell! We don't agree."

Then a shaman from Paste' arrived and Old Sarate gave him a

good dressing down. "As for you, don't interfere! Do you remember that you scolded me once very sharply at the courthouse?"

"It wasn't me, sir. I never scolded you, sir. I certainly don't remember it!" said the gentleman.

"Well, forget it, then," said Old Sarate. "I really don't know if we should give up or not. Hell! The people of Zinacantán Center don't want to get involved."

I was just standing there like a fool, listening to the talk. The people of Paste' were dying of starvation, and no one knew what to do.

In my ignorance I said to Old Sarate, "See here, sir! You shouldn't give up. Try harder! It would be better if the magistrate sends out his principals and has them go from house to house. We'll find a good place for a meeting and see who wants to contribute and who doesn't. Those who don't—let them remain as leftovers."

"Lord, but that's a good idea, son. Let's follow his advice!" they all said.

Now I was at home in Zinacantán Center. My compadre, Little Manvel Promax, was in the midst of measuring out his yellow corn. And the people from Paste' were receiving the corn. Their mules were standing in front of Anselmo's house next door, waiting to be loaded. When I saw that he was selling stacks of corn, I said to my wife, "Lord, if only I had a lot of corn, I'd sell some too."

"How much of your corn would you sell? Could you feed the whole hamlet?" she asked. And then I woke up.

When I awoke this morning I said to myself, "God, My Lord, could that dream have been good or bad?" I think some of it probably had to do with Our Lord and some of it probably was persecution.

I Have a Drink, See a Plane, Our Clothes Drop in Church

I, Romin Teratol, dreamt when it was already light this morning, the second of July.

We were going to Great Carmen Ranch in the lowlands with Petul Peres from Zinacantán Center. "Let's go, Romin! Let's go have fun at Great Carmen. They say the country there is really beautiful. The car from the Cabaña is coming to pick us up right away."

My wife was terribly sick, but we quickly got ready. I had bought some medicine for her, a powder, like courbaril. She put a handful in her mouth, then drank some water to wash it down. She did it very hurriedly because the car had arrived. In no time we were at the foot of Muxul Mountain.

"Have you brought any cane liquor?" the driver asked.

"No," said Petul. "But we can buy a jug nearby."

They bought the jug at Petul Okotz's gate. Then they measured out the liquor with a large shot glass. They gave me a big shot, but after I swallowed it, my stomach felt awful. It was evil people tormenting me.

While we were drinking, a plane passed over. It had no wings. A corpse was inside it, completely shut up in a black coffin. The plane passed over terribly low. It was coming from Deer House and going toward Chamula. We could see the people easily because the plane had no hood.

After that, I didn't see how, but I was asleep in the church with my wife. We were guarding the Church of Saint Lawrence.

When I awoke, the worshippers were already kneeling. Their candles were lined up in rows. I got up quickly, but I couldn't find my sash. Who knows where my sash was. I was just clutching my pants.

"Romin, hurry up, please give us some candlesticks," said each of the worshippers, but there were too many people to serve.

"Hurry up and help them!" I told my wife, but she didn't have her sash either. Clutching her skirt, she went to fetch the candlesticks.

As for me, I found my sash beside Saint Matthew, near the font. But it was in front of the minor Saint Dominic where I had been sleeping. I finished tying my sash, but I was still a little embarrassed. I didn't see if my wife found her sash or not. I just saw her clutching her skirt, carrying her child, and passing out the candlesticks. The worshippers were simply packed in the old part of the church.

The candles were glowing.

And I woke up. The sun had risen.

Maybe Our Lord thinks that I'm unfit, or he thinks I never remember him, or he wants me to serve beneath the feet of Our Lord, or the shrine beneath the feet of Our Lord needs to be looked after. Who knows.

We Walk through a Deserted Village

I, Romin Teratol, dreamt just before dawn, Thursday, the twenty-third of July.

I was strolling across Muxul Mountain with my wife. We were all alone. Not even one of our children was with us.

We walked and walked. We reached the dry stream at the edge of the hamlet of Fallen Frost. There we started down the slope.

The place we came to had only Ladinos' houses, but all the owners had died, a Chamulan told us. Chamulans were living in a valley below the dead people's houses.

"What are you looking for, son?" a man from Five Pieces asked me.

"I'm looking for cane liquor, because there is sickness at home," I said.

"I have some at my house, son, if you'll go and get it."

"No, sir, I just came looking for it. I still have to bring a container." I was lying to him because I was scared, since there were dead people's houses where I was walking. Besides, it was growing dark.

Then two Ladinos appeared. Their faces were spotted. They came to shake my hand. "Spend the night here! That would be better because it's getting dark," the two "pintos" told me.

"No, we can still reach home! We certainly won't spend the night," we said.

On the way back we passed through Paste'. People were crying on the side of the road. They said they were crying because somebody had died. They told me the dead man's name. I knew him, but I didn't go in to see, since it was nighttime.

Then I woke up. I was terribly scared. What I had dreamt was evil. Besides, not a single one of my children was there. Maybe it's because they'll die. This is what it means when we travel at night—it means bereavement.

I Gather Snails, I Throw a Black Bull

Just before dawn today, Monday, the thirtieth of September, I dreamt again.

I was going to the lowlands with Mother Pil, my mother's older sister. She was driving her sheep to the lowlands. I was going to gather snails. We passed New Ranch. We arrived at Nantaburi'. The sheep followed in a flock.

Then I met up with Old Maryan Yemel. He was in the midst of gathering snails with his sons and his wife.

"What are you looking for? Is this your river?" he said to me.

"No, sir, I just came to get a few snails to eat. It isn't that I'm going to sell them, I'm just going to eat them." But he was still very angry. They themselves had already gathered plenty. Their burlap bags were full.

As for me, I only found a half cup of little snails. I waded in the river, but there weren't any more. They had collected all of them. When I looked up, they were leading a yoke of oxen along the riverbank. And behind the oxen's heads they had piled their bags of snails.

Suddenly I was standing inside a cattle pen. The oxen were gone. There was only one black bull. Its owner, a Ladino, was riding it.

"Domingo," he said to me. "Fight this bull. If you win, you'll be a real man."

"Well, I'll try, you bastard, if you think I'm so feeble!"

I grabbed the bull by both its horns. The horn in my right hand broke off.

I took out a long knife. I was about to stick it in its neck.

"You can't do that! Catch it with your hands!" he told me.

I grabbed the bull by its one horn and with the other hand I grabbed it by the legs. Ooh, the bull collapsed.

Crowds of people appeared. They began pushing the bull and trussing its legs with a rope. I was pushing it too.

But I was pushing my little child with my hand. His crying woke me up.

I was terribly scared.

"A devil is tormenting you," my wife said.

It's probably true that a devil was trying to trick me. The bull was a person who had transformed himself into a bull because he wanted to try me out to see if I could win. Thanks to Our Lord, I was able to catch the bull and throw it to the ground. The others suddenly came swarming in because they were going to kill it for good. So it's dead.

I didn't get very sick from that dream, since it was he himself who died. I was just a little scared when I woke up.

And that's all there is.

Mikel Tzotzil

What a leap my dream makes
from the moon into the wind!
—Federico Gárcia Lorca

I remember Mikel Tzotzil squatting every morning in the dusty street
in front of his brother-in-law's store at the entrance to Zinacantán
Center, shooting marbles with a bunch of schoolboys. By the age of
thirty he had fathered seven children. Three he had already buried.
He was the first Zinacantec, I recall, who wore no hat. His brow was
permanently furrowed with worry. He seemed hesitant, bemused,
strangely innnocent and youthful, soft for a Zinacantec. I had always
had difficulty in understanding his Tzotzil. Mikel doubled the pre-
fixes, adding more "*li's*" and "*shi's*" than appeared in any of the
grammatical tables I had seen. As he tried to tell me his dreams, I
discovered the solution to the linguistic mystery— Mikel was a
stutterer!

Mikel used to travel with his father, selling salt. At that time his
younger sister was being courted by the son of a shaman. Mikel's
father rejected the suitor and returned the brideprice. In revenge, the
shaman sold the soul of Mikel's father to the Earth Lord, and so,
when Mikel was eighteen years old, his father died.

Mikel then became a shopkeeper in his brother-in-law's store
and even invested money in his brother-in-law's truck (the first in
Zinacantán). His investment, however, was never returned. He became addicted to the cane liquor that he was selling daily. Mikel's
brother-in-law sold the store. Now Mikel raises flowers at home and
plants corn in the lowlands like most of his countrymen. He lives in a
demonstration house donated by the government.

The recording of Mikel's dreams predated his financial difficul-
ties. Unique to Mikel's narrative is the towering influence of his late
father, whose ghost appears regularly in his dreams.

Our Salt Is Ruined, We Fight, We Are Jailed

We were going to sell salt in the place where we always used to sell it.
I was with my late father. We had our mules.

The market was crowded. Chamulans came to buy.

I sold some salt for twenty centavos, just as we always used to sell it. All of a sudden a rainstorm came. Our salt was ruined.

We couldn't pick it all up since the rain came so suddenly. We tried to do our best. The rest of our salt was washed away. "Let it be ruined," I said to myself.

We went into a big house where we bought cane liquor. One of our friends was there.

We were drinking. We got drunk. They were playing records. We paid for the songs.

It was just like when we drink in stores.

We got stirred up. We were hitting each other. Blood was streaming from our noses, our faces.

The local townsmen seized us and put us all in jail.

We spent the night there. We bought a little meat for our meal. We got some firewood. We got some pine.

I lit the fire. There was a yard where we lit it.

Then my eyes opened. It was gone.

But that was a good dream, of course. Nobody dies from that. No! No!

I Am a Shepherd, I Am Cut Open

I was walking along. I had some sheep with me. I was watching over them as they grazed.

An awful highwayman appeared. Or could he have been a passerby? I tried to flee. I tried to take his machete away. Quickly he sliced me. My ass was cut wide open. My arms had shooting pains. I felt terrible.

I jumped out of the way so that I wouldn't die.

I woke up. I felt the machete slicing me. I felt a sudden chill. Sonofabitch, it was a terrific scare!

Who knows if a devil is tricking me. I simply couldn't get back to sleep before morning came.

I prayed. "In the name of God, could it be that I'm going to be murdered?"

My Father Is Dressed in Red

Beyond our house there is a steep hill. There was a horse and my father was riding it. His clothes were entirely red from head to toe. He was dressed like the Grand Spanish Lord in the Fiesta of Saint Sebastian. He was holding his banner aloft. He was riding on horseback over the hill to our house.

In the morning I told my father my dream.

"Maybe it means that I'll die," he said.

He hadn't been sick. He was just fine.

Two days later he was dead.

I let him know about it. It came true. His clothes were red from head to toe.

He just died. Yes!

I Am Offered Tassels by a Pretty Girl

There are many bad dreams. Have you ever dreamt of sleeping with another woman besides your wife?

That's what I've done. It seems they really desire us. They seem to be so beautiful. Yes!

The girl was really pretty. I had seen her before in Zinacantán Center. She passed by to talk to me. I was inside my house with a worker of mine, a Chamulan, flailing corn.

"Won't you buy tassels for your tunic?" she asked me. "Won't you buy the cords?"

"I'll buy some," I said. "Where are they?"

"My younger sister has brought them." Her younger sister is named Matal.

"Go and get them, then! Bring them on the sly, quickly!"

I went out to watch her. She was standing by Savel's house with her sister. They were choosing the tunic cords. I waited at my door.

She came to give them to me. "You've come," I said. I hugged her. I gave her a little kiss. Yes!

She was laughing and laughing. She gave me three cords for my tunic.

"How much are they?"

"You'll find out later," she said. "My sister doesn't know what price to ask."

She left. I went in to flail my corn.

"She's a pretty sexy girl! She wants to be taken," I said to myself. "Why else would she come purposely to give me the fastenings for my tunic? The cords for my tunic mean that she wants to be taken. She wants to be taken whenever I speak to her. I'll speak to her as soon as I can!"

I was flailing my corn.

Then I woke up. "Could it be that she loves me?" I said to myself. "Or could she be a devil?" If she's a devil, there's no way of knowing.

Of course I didn't tell my wife. If I had told her, she would have gotten upset. She'd say, "Then it's true! It's because you have a mistress." Yes!

Anselmo Peres

No one shall cast grains of corn for divination, nor
tell dreams, nor wear any marks or ornaments of their
heathendom, nor tattoo themselves.

>   —*The Ordinances of Tomas Lopez*
>   *of the Royal Audience of the*
>   *Confines* (1552)

Have you ever believed in dreams or bird calls, or
other abominations?
Have you ever worshipped the devil in images of stone
or wood?

>   —*Confessionario en lengua tzotzil* (18th century)

He was the handsomest Zinacantec I had ever seen, kin to a peacock, the day he appeared in court to defend himself against what might be termed a "morals" charge. Anselmo Peres' youthful self-defense before the magistrate and justices of the peace was so eloquent and his self-assurance so manifest I could not resist asking him to be a chief collaborator in what was to become *The Great Tzotzil Dictionary of San*

Lorenzo Zinacantán. Despite only three years of schooling, after little over a week of training by Romin Teratol, Anselmo learned to write Tzotzil almost flawlessly.

Then twenty-one years old, he had been brought up in poverty. His father had died when Anselmo and his younger brother were boys. Anselmo's mother remarried and moved from their home in Pat Osil to Zinacantán Center. There two more sons were born before Anselmo's stepfather abandoned them, forcing them to move once more, now to a borrowed house nearby. Still a teenager, Anselmo was appointed sacristan, a post he served for three years. The stewards gathered together and built his family a new house. It was there that he returned one evening with a friend to find that a man had broken in and was assaulting his mother. The two rushed to her defense, beat up the intruder, and tied him to a tree in the yard where, during the cold winter night, he died.

Anselmo supported his family by the customary corn farming in the lowlands, and by roadwork.

According to the gossip, when still a sacristan, Anselmo began sowing his wild oats in the meadow behind the Church of Saint Sebastian. The shepherdess went home happily to inform her parents, who advised her to tell the man to come ask for her hand. They waited and waited in vain, until finally they took their daughter to Anselmo's mother's house. "I never spoke to her!" he said. And so the girl who had thought she had found a handsome husband went home with a severe scolding.

When Anselmo recounted his dreams he had just, unbeknownst to us all, become a shaman. We learned this at Romin Teratol's house-dedication ceremony when the shaman in charge, after offering all the wrong prayers, passed out. Anselmo volunteered his services and proceeded through the ritual with extraordinary speed.

Shortly thereafter, he accepted without a blink, my proposal to join Romin Teratol on a trip to Santa Fe, New Mexico, even though he was in the midst of his engagement to a beautiful young woman from Magdalenas who was said to be possessed with dark powers. We learned that Anselmo's gay, debonair manner, his hearty laugh and sparkling eyes could cloud over. For weeks at a time he wore a morose mask, never sharing in the jokes, irritated with every intrusion on his person.

Four years later, living once again in Pat Osil, married, and the father of a girl, Anselmo left behind his melancholy and eagerly joined us on a second trip to the United States, combing the beach for conches at Chincoteague, Virginia, marching down the Mall for peace, in Washington, D.C., and storming the doors of the Pentagon. Upon returning to Zinacantán, he became director of municipal improvements, engineering roads and water systems.

For all his efficiency, Anselmo's life has not run the straight and narrow. While tending to the spiritual needs of a neighbor (Maltil Tulum's son-in-law), Anselmo became enamored of their daughter and she, convinced by his promises to seek a divorce, returned his affections. Every time Anselmo tipped the bottle and struck his wife she would run to their neighbor to complain that it was their daughter's fault. The neighbor was so worn down by the constant quarrels that he abandoned his house in Pat Osil and borrowed a house in Zinacantán Center.

Anselmo was also accused of witchcraft by a man who, not wishing to reveal that he had visited a spiritualist in Chiapa de Corzo, maintained before the magistrate that he had learned of Anselmo's evil doings from the bishop of Chiapa. Anselmo replied with assurance, "Let's go ask him!" and, accompanied by a justice of the peace, he went to pay the bishop a visit. They soon discovered that there was no bishop in Chiapa. When they returned to confront the man, he denied making any such statement. Anselmo threatened to have the liar thrown in jail and urged the justice of the peace to take him back to his town to administer the appropriate punishment. This was done. And so, Anselmo was freed of the accusation of witchcraft.

Unfortunately, Anselmo wrote down only five of his dreams. They reveal a self-assurance in the midst of traumatic experiences that seemed characteristic, but I had not foreseen their violence. Anselmo weaves a complex pattern in his dreams. They are like tapestries with a parade of extraordinary events winding in labyrinthine progression.

I Am Chased by Snakes, Saved by a Man,
Given a Cross and a Drink

They were taking me across a river on a tree trunk. In the middle of the river they began rolling the log and trying to push me off.

I didn't fall. I was able to grab onto a tree. Clinging to the tree, I crossed over.

There were snakes on the bank. They were trying to bite me. I caught one snake and threw it in the river. Now they were going to kill me.

I ran into a house. The owners of the house hid me. The snakes were circling around outside, waiting for me to come out.

I left by another door. The snakes didn't see me. Then I met a stranger on the path.

"Why did you come here? Where did you go?" he asked me.

"I don't know where it was I went. I don't know who it was who blocked my way. They were trying to kill me."

"Let's go see who it was. I'll find out!"

We turned around and there were those devils!

But the man defended me. "Why do you have to get him? What did he do wrong?"

"He killed one of our friends," said the snakes.

"Where? Let's go see!"

"He threw him in the river. We looked for him, but we never found him."

"I won't let you get this fellow," the man told them. "If you have to get him, get me instead!"

Those devils who were gathered there stayed behind.

The next thing I knew, I was in the church. There was a fiesta and great crowds of people. The man who had been with me appeared.

"So you're here now," he said. "Let's go over to my room." We went to his room.

"Here's a chair. Sit down!" he told me. I sat down.

A gentleman entered. "Have you come to visit me, son?" he asked.

"I've come indeed, sir." I bowed to him.

"Who brought you here?"

"A man brought me. But I don't know who he is."

"Where did he find you?"

"I met him on the path. They were trying to kill me. That man saved me."

"Who was trying to kill you?"

"I didn't know them. There was a pack of them."

"Lord, but why were they trying to kill you?"

"I don't know, sir."

"Never mind, son, take this with you. It will keep you company."

He gave me a little cross. The cross was beautiful. It was solid gold.

The next time I looked, I was walking past the courthouse door and somebody was asking me where I had been.

"I was in church," I said. "I went to pray to Our Lord. Now I'm going home."

"Don't you want to drink a shot of cane liquor? One shot won't hurt!"

We arrived at Old Nacha's store. The man asked for a half pint of cane liquor and a coke. He mixed them.

"Let's drink!" he said.

He was holding the half pint. I was holding the glass when I woke up.

That was three and a half years ago. The devils were tormenting me so badly long ago. I don't know why.

We Are Chased by Cows, We Kill Them, a Chamulan and I Take a Leg

I was going to the lowlands to look for a place to plant my corn. There were four of us.

We passed Thunderbolt Lake. We passed Masan. We reached Nandayapa. We were walking along on level ground.

Then we met up with two cows. Sonofabitch, the cows were trying to gore us. We climbed into a tree.

Now the cows were uprooting the tree. I hacked at them with my machete. I cut off their noses. Sonofabitch, they kept bleeding. Then they died.

The owner ran up. "Why did you kill my cows?" he shouted.

"Because they were trying to gore us," I said.

"Why didn't you run away?"

"As soon as we fled, they chased after us." I was chatting with him in a relaxed way.

I turned around. Sonofabitch, more Ladinos were coming. They were going to kill me.

I fled again. They kept chasing me. I ran into a cave. Sonofabitch, they sent their dogs in after me.

I was bent over at the back of the cave, watching those dogs run by. "Where did he go?" they said. I was crouched there, listening.

I came out of the cave. I looked for my friends. I went back to the place where I had killed the cows.

But my friends had been murdered. They were lying there now.

Then I met a Chamulan who was coming back from the lowlands. He had two mules. One was loaded with packs, the other had none.

"Won't you let me rent your mule?" I asked.

"What are you going to have it carry?"

"Three of my friends were killed."

"Where?"

"Under that tree."

"Who killed them?"

"Some cows were trying to gore us. We killed the cows. The owner came. He killed my friends."

We went to look. They were already being eaten by dogs and buzzards.

We took a good look. They weren't people. It was those cows. There was still one foreleg.

"Why don't we remove its foreleg?" I said. "Since your mule hasn't a pack."

"Let's remove it, then!" he said.

We were in the midst of taking it off when I woke up again.

I Get in a Fight, I Hide, Am Given a Drink, Find a Snake, Behead a Man

I was drunk. Maryan Buro and two of his friends were hitting me.

I was all by myself. But I gave them a beating.

The constables came to seize me. They were going to jail me. Sonofabitch, I hit the constables too.

I fled into the woods. There was a Chamulan on the path. I found him sitting at the foot of Horned Owl House shrine.

"Where are you going?" he asked me.

"I'm not going anywhere. I'm hiding, because the constables are chasing me. Didn't you bring along a little cane liquor?"

"I did," he said. "Will you drink a little to sweep away the fear?"

"Thank you," I said. "Sell me your half pint! Let's drink a little!"

"Do you mean it?" he said. "You shouldn't bother to share it."

We were in the midst of drinking when, sonofabitch, a herd of horses came galloping through the trees. Soldiers were chasing them toward us. I was completely dazed.

Then the constables who were trying to catch me ran by. I was hiding behind the Chamulan, watching them go past.

I started home. I was walking across the ranch. Then I saw a snake at the edge of the river.

I was terribly scared. I simply retraced my steps and started on the path again.

Then I met Old Xun Komis. "Pass on by, sir!" I said.

That Old Xun Komis was carrying some meat. Sonofabitch, a dog jumped out of nowhere and landed on Old Xun Komis' net. The old man was knocked way off on his back.

"You bastard, why did you push me down?" he screamed.

"When did I push you down, sir? Wasn't it the dog?"

The old man was furious. He grabbed me and hit me.

I found a stick and whacked him with it. His head flew off.

Two men were coming along. I hid behind a tree.

Old Xun Komis' head was lying in the middle of the path. Those men were filled with fear. "What happened to him?" they said to each other.

"But it's still all right. What if we take it along?" one of them said.

"Forget it, leave it be," said the other. They continued on their way.

As for me, I kept walking too. I was coming along by the bridge. I sat down for a minute. I was sitting there when I woke up.

My dream came true. I was beaten up on the earth's surface after all.

I Am Buying Sandals, I Hug a Girl, Kill a Cow, See a Corpse, Catch a Horse

I was standing in the market in Chamula. I was waiting to buy some sandals.

A girl came up to me. "What are you looking for?" she asked.
"I came to buy a pair of sandals."
"What do you need the sandals for?"
"I'm going to wear them to see my fiancée," I told her.
"You make me laugh!" she said.
"Why are you laughing at me? Am I naked?"
"No, I'm laughing at you because you say you are looking for a fiancée."
"So you are making fun of me because of that? If you don't like what I was saying, then it's you I ought to marry."
"Maybe so, if that's what occurs to you," she told me.
I hugged her. She was laughing and laughing.
Then her father arrived. I didn't know that it was her father. No! I realized it when he was about to hit me. The girl fled.
Then the constables came and seized her father. He was guilty of something.
I was left standing there in the market.
Finally the sandal seller arrived. I looked at the sandals. All the sandals were bad. "Forget it, then," I said to myself. I started home.
The next time I looked, I was sitting in Old Chep Tzotzil's house, drinking cane liquor. We got drunk. I was watching Old Chep slump over.
I left. I never saw how I went. Before I knew it, I was at Treasure Ridge. "But what am I doing here?" I said to myself. I came back by way of Old Maryan Hili'at's house.
Then I met four people on the path, pulling along a cow.
Sonofabitch, their cow went berserk. It kept bucking and standing stock still. Then its rope broke.
Sonofabitch, it tried to gore me. I ran, but it chased after me.
There is a big rock above Old Chep Kontzares' house. I climbed up on top of that rock.
The cow was circling around and around. Now it was climbing onto the rock!
But it toppled off and landed, rolling. It simply couldn't pick itself up. While it was thrashing about, its soul departed. That cow was lying there, ass up.
Two people came along. "What happened to the cow?" they asked me.
"It died because it rolled down off this rock. It was about to gore me," I said.

I was chatting with those two people. The next time I looked, a corpse was lying there.

"Let's go and bury it," the two men said. They tossed the corpse over their shoulders.

We came to a ravine. They threw that corpse down into it. Then they went on.

I climbed up the mountain of Our Holy Lady Saint Cecilia. I came out in front of Calvary.

There was a beautiful horse standing in the meadow.

"Why don't I catch the horse?" I said to myself.

I was able to catch it. I put its blanket on. I put its saddle on. I was about to mount it when I woke up.

Who knows what it means. Nothing has happened to me. No, nothing at all.

I Find a Corpse, We Bury Him, The Women Attack Me

I was going hunting in the woods on Great Mountain. I planned to look for squirrels.

There was a body lying on the path. Yes!

He had died of the cold. The poor guy got drunk and had fallen to the ground. The corpse was lying next to the cross.

I went to report it at the courthouse, but none of the authorities were there. I was standing on the churchyard wall, waiting for the authorities, when Maryan Chiku' came along.

"What are you doing?" he asked me.

"I'm waiting to talk to the authorities. I'm going to tell them that somebody has died."

"Where?" he asked.

"He's lying by the cross beyond your house."

"Lord! Who could it be? Didn't you recognize him?"

"Who knows who it is," I said.

"Let's go see!"

On the path we met a constable. "Where are you going?" he asked.

"I'm just going to take a quick look at my yard," Maryan Chiku' told him.

"Well, I was sent out to look for two or three men," said the constable.

"What for?" we asked.

"Because there is a body."

"Where?" we asked.

"There on the path."

"Who is it?"

"It's Old Palas K'o. He died of the cold, because he was drunk," said the constable. "Please, let's go bury him."

"Sonofabitch, I don't know. We were going to take a quick look at our corn field because it's being ruined by dogs," we said.

"Please, let's go bury him!" the constable kept saying.

"Oh, let's go bury the poor guy!" we said to each other. "He isn't the only one to die. It could happen to us too."

We went along with the constable. We arrived at the house where the funeral party had assembled. There were a great many people gathered together.

They gave us some chairs. We sat down. They gave us a meal. We ate. When we finished eating, they gave us a shot of cane liquor.

Then we went to bury the body. But the dead man wasn't put in a coffin. That corpse was carried off on a tumpline— the way we carry firewood!

They were going to bury him in the meadow near Five Springs.

"Why are you burying him in a place like this?" I asked.

"Because it's the right way to do it, so that he won't bring his wife's soul here," they said.

They never dug a grave. They were just pulling up a rock. But the rock was too heavy. "The bastard won't come out," they said.

"Never mind, we ought to bury him in another grave," said the dead man's wife.

"All right," said the gravediggers.

They just threw him into a gully.

People got terribly drunk. The women took off their blouses and came staggering toward me. I tried to leave, but the women kept grabbing me and pulling me back.

After I beat them all off, I came along to the east. I passed Old Nixyo Kontzares' house.

There by the cross I sat down for a minute. I was sitting there when I woke up.

Romin Tanchak

Sleep is the dew of the sky,
the yellow flower.
    —*Chilam Balam of Chumayel*
    Book XI: The Book of Enigmas

Romin Tanchak comes of a well-to-do family in Stzellehtik (Ridge),
where their houses have a sweeping view over the Pan American
Highway as it winds through the mountains. He is the youngest
brother of Romin Teratol's wife, and ever since their marriage has
been the friendliest member of the family. When he told me his
dreams he claimed to be twenty-five, but he scarcely looked twenty.
He is short but well-proportioned, with regular features, a dazzling
smile, and a deep laugh. At fiestas he walks tall in his high-backed
ceremonial sandals, his clothing immaculate, his shorts gleaming
white. Despite his family's hostility to gringo anthropologists and
other "new-fangled things," he always treated me with consideration
and, I like to think, warmth.

Our first encounters, though, were guarded and formal, since I
was his brother-in-law's employer. I only had occasion to visit him
when Romin Teratol had a matter of some importance to broach to
his awesome in-laws. It was a revelation to me, then, as the three of
us made a six-hour trek to buy corn in the lowlands, to see this
Lowell or Peabody of the Zinacantec world tearing down the mountain trail hurling after the mules, with great gusto, a constant barrage
of the most horrendous Spanish oaths. I had not realized that Spanish
was the language used to address Ladinos and mules.

Romin earned the funds to pay the brideprice for his wife by
working on a neighboring ranch, felling pine trees and manning the
saw. Since then he has devoted his energies to corn farming, in
anticipation of his entrance into the Stewardship of Saint Dominic.
When I asked Romin Teratol to tell me the gossip about the various
dreamers, Romin Tanchak alone emerged unscathed by the least
suggestion of human weakness.

Romin could not recall many dreams of his own, but with no reservation he described the model dreams of shamans, midwives, and bonesetters. He shows how dreams are a natural, integral part of life and knowledge, not merely isolated pieces of exotic information.

What Shamans Are Shown, What They See,
How Animal Spirits Are Fed

Whoever sees, dreams well.

Whoever becomes a shaman is summoned in their dreams to Calvary.

"We'll give you some work," the elders tell them. "Do you want to accept the responsibility of shamanhood, or don't you want to accept it?"

If they say, "I'll accept it," then it's fine. If they say, "I don't want to," they'll get a beating. They die.

If they do what they're told, they are given a little gourd for cooling flower water, the pot for their flowers, and their half gourds for the ritual bath. They are given laurel, wintergreen, peperomia, and savory. They are given whatever medicines are needed to cure sickness. They are given the bamboo staff—the dog frightener.

After they receive their powers, they are eager to feel the pulse, they are eager to cure. In their dreams they are shown what to give for the illness.

"Watch over the young and the old," they are told. "Do not rebel! You musn't refuse the request when the patient's family comes to escort you. If you rebel, you'll be punished for not accepting the command."

All the shamans are assembled in their dreams at Calvary, the old men and women and the young who have not yet been initiated.

The ancestral gods are sitting there, the way we see the elders sitting at the Chapel of Esquipulas.

Candles are offered.

There is a meal. Bottles of liquor are bunched up on the table.The food is set in rows. Chicken is brought to the head of the table, pork is placed in the middle, and beef, at the foot of the table.

The beef isn't snatched up. Don't you see, chicken is valued the most.

Now when the shamans arrive and their offerings are accepted, the elders eat right away. If the elders eat right away, then the patient will recover right away.

If, on the other hand, the offerings aren't taken, the elders don't eat. "No, not yet," they say. "We'll see," they say.

If the elders watch over the patient, little by little he will recover. If they eat on the third day, he will still recover. But if they don't eat at all, the sickness won't pass.

We'll die at the first opportunity.

Those who are shamans see well. They see the meeting place inside Great Mountain.

All our companion animal spirits are in the corral at Great Mountain. It is a big corral, they say.

Our animal souls need to be fed. Every night the hunters go out with lassos to catch the animals' food. Sometimes they bring back cows. Sometimes they bring back deer. Sometimes dogs. The animals, there, eat dogs.

The little animals that can't wait for their food get the dogs. The big animals that are patient get the cows.

One night it happened that the hunters couldn't find any food. There were calves, but their mothers gored the hunters. "What can we do? We can't catch anything," the hunters said.

Now there was a Chamulan looking for work at the house of one of our countrymen. He was spending the night in the sweatbath. He was sound asleep.

"Sonofabitch, but a Chamulan will do!" said the hunters.

They carried him off. The poor Chamulan was dead the next morning. He slept very well. His soul went to feed the animals.

The catchers' souls are powerful. But it's in their dreams that they catch their prey.

If there isn't a cow or sheep, then sometimes a human being is caught, a worthless person as we say.

The Lords of Great Mountain are watching.

The animals are cared for by the guardians. Those that wait properly for their food do well. Those that bite, that scrap and send their friends rolling, are tossed out. "Go on, you're no good—you quarrel too much with your friends!" they are told.

Those who have been put out are no longer watched over. They simply look for their own meals, until they are shot. We die if our companion animal spirit is thrown out.

That's what they dream, those who see. They see the truth.

The rest of us dream about any little thing. We see where we are working, or whatever trivial thing we are doing.

What Midwives and Bonesetters Are Shown

Midwives, too, are summoned to Calvary. They are right behind the shamans.

They are given gourds, pots, containers for their flowers.

"Do not scorn, do not spit on the baby that is being born. Watch over it. Bathe it carefully. Don't scorn it, for our sake!" the elders say.

Then they are given herbs, savory, "ghost flowers."

When the bonesetters are shown, a tree is felled for them in the forest. They say it is a big tree. It lands in smithereens when it falls.

"Set it!" they are told.

They pray over it! If they are able to set the big tree upright, then they will be successful setting bones. They acquire their powers that way. Even if our bone is badly broken, it will mend in three days.

Long ago my older brother, Maryan, broke a bone. Our father had just come home from the lowlands. He had brought back some fruit. Ooh, when Maryan jumped up to get the fruit, he landed face down. The bones in his arm were sticking way out. So they went to bring the bonesetter, who lived in Elan Spring.

He came to set it. "It should be bound for only three days," he said. "Untie it on the third day, in the evening! Have him toss a stone right away."

My mother didn't follow his advice, since it still seemed to be broken. On the fourth day that gentleman passed by on his own. "Is the patient's arm unbound?" he asked.

"Not yet," my mother answered.

Quickly he untied it. "Toss a stone now," he told my brother. My brother pitched it. He couldn't throw it high anymore. Now he pitches with his left hand.

"See, I was right! It wouldn't have twisted if you had unbound it. It should have been unbound after just three days."

They are able to mend bones quickly. If they are able to set the broken tree, they go on healing bones successfully.

I Am Carried from a Cave

Long ago, when I was very young, I used to be a shepherd.

Then I got sick. Blood poured from my nose. Ooh, I was dying. For two weeks I didn't eat. No tortillas, nothing at all. I lost my senses like a drunk.

My father brought a shaman. They held a curing ceremony for me.

I saw that I was in a big cave. The cave was damp, dripping with water. "Oh, why am I here?" I cried and cried.

The shaman arrived to take me out. "Now we are going," he told me.

"But you'll have to carry me," I said. "I can't walk."

"I'll carry you," he said.

I showed him the tiny path out.

The bearer carried me home. He set me down. I woke up on the earth's surface. I recovered my senses.

I saw that flowers had been offered for me. Flowers and air pines were lying on my bed.

"Eat some chicken!" my mother told me. "Eat!" But I had no desire for it.

I told my mother my dream. "Could it be that I'm coming back now?" I asked her.

"No one knows," she said.

The shaman continued curing. But the pain didn't calm down. My legs were aching. My toes hurt terribly. He drew my blood. He used lots of broken glass for the bloodletting.

Gradually the sickness passed. Gradually I ate, one little piece of tortilla, then another.

I started to get back on my feet. They strung up a rope for me. I clung to it. I was terribly thin and weak.

We had an old pig. It was good and fat. "Let's kill the pig, mother!" I said.

"We'll kill it when you get good and strong. You can help kill it," she told me.

I believed her. I got well.

"Now where is the pig?" I asked.

"We already sold it to pay for your curing ceremony," she said. The pig was gone, gone. Yes!

My Sister Was Underground

My mother dreamt that my little baby sister was lost. She was lost in her dream.

"Lolen!" she called. "Lolen!"

My baby sister was underground. She answered from inside the earth. My mother tried to look for her, tried to see her, but she never found her. No!

She called to her. Far off she heard her answering from underground. "Come on out!" my mother tried to tell her. My sister answered back, but she didn't come out.

Three or four nights later she got nausea and diarrhea. My mother brought a shaman, but the sickness didn't pass. My little sister simply died. She died at the first opportunity.

Dreams sometimes come true. If she can't be reached in her dream she's lost forever.

Mal Montixyo

They say the body is like a chest where the soul
is stored. But at times the soul is so big that
the body, like an anis seed, has to be stored in
the soul.

—Ermilo Abreu Gomez
Canek

I have only seen Mal Montixyo once in my life, the day she came in to San Cristóbal to tell me her dreams. She spoke Spanish with a fluency equalled only by Tonik Nibak and was surprised that I would want her to speak Tzotzil. She had a business-like air, no humor, suspicious eyes, a gravelly voice that seldom strayed from a monotone.

As the gossip has it, Mal was born in the coffee plantations, the child of a Guatemalan laborer. She was adopted by Lol Montixyo who, at the time these dreams were recorded, was the oldest living Zinacantec, a man with a gnarled cane and snow-white hair. When she was young, Mal used to spend all her days at the foot of Saint Cecilia Mountain, tending her sheep. There she found a lover, but their marriage was short-lived, for as the story goes, she was too "difficult." In time she married a man who came to live in her father's house, since her father had no sons. Mal's husband became a school teacher and then, town clerk. He changed into Ladino clothes and bought his wife a dress and a pair of shoes. When Mal's husband was fired from his job after demanding a pay raise, they both reverted to Indian clothes. Once again Mal picked up her tumpline and gathered firewood for the family hearth. Mocking tongues in the town made great sport of her past pretensions.

Mal related her dreams with a minimum of expression and self-involvement. She was careful never to reveal the identity of her dream characters. And more than anyone else, she denied meaning to her dreams. Those that Mal enjoyed telling most were dreams in which she was prominent in her shaman's role. Despite her nightmarish encounters, the strength of her ego is formidable.

I Am Chased, I Fly Away

I was being chased. Ooh, I was flying.
I flew to the edge of a wide ravine.
I landed in a tree, perched like a bird.
I was afraid of the ravine.
"Would it be a good idea to fly across?" I asked myself.
"As for me, forget it," I said. "I'll know when my pursuer
    comes."
I was waiting. He was approaching.
Ooh, I flew again.
I reached the other side of the ravine.

Ah, but this morning I was aching badly.
I didn't land properly. No!
It certainly was a bad dream. Yes!

I Go on a Curing Ceremony,
the Sacrificial Rooster Flies Off

I was going to pray with my patient. My patient was a man. I didn't
know his name. He was different—like the people from San Antonio.

I prepared his substitute. I carefully wrapped up his sacrificial
rooster before leaving.

But on the way, it came out of the candle basket that had been
slung over my assistant's back. It had been dead. But it flew away.

Oh, we did our best to chase it, but we never caught it. The
rooster fled.

It never reached Calvary. It never reached even one of the holy
shrines.

It simply left us behind on the trail.

It's just a torment. Just a torment. Yes!

A Spook Gets in My House

It came to my house while I was asleep.

It was scraping along the foot of the wall. It was looking for a
way to get in.

It reached the eaves. It came right in. It never gets big. It came in
under the eaves quickly.

I was frightened. I was simply lying there helplessly.

The Spook was groping about, looking for some coffee. Now he
was drinking coffee and whatever else he was doing inside my house.

I did my best to wake the children. I shook them, but they didn't
wake up.

I hardly moved at all, because I was so terribly scared.

But it doesn't mean anything. It's a devil, a witch, whoever hates
me. They come from underground to sell our souls to the Earth Lord.
Yes!

I had that dream two months ago. I was frightened by it. That's why I still have it on my mind. That's why I'm telling it to you.

A Charcoal Cruncher Comes to My Door

I had a horrible dream. The awful Charcoal Cruncher was rolling about next to the house. It was rolling around, rolling around, knocking about, over and over.

I went out to look. It was dark. I lit my lamp. There was a head outside my door.

It was the head of a woman.

Then it moved!

"Ah, but this isn't anything. It's only a skull with a dead woman's face. Never mind, I won't look at it," I said to myself.

It was just rolling about. It didn't say anything to me and I never spoke to it either.

It could be a devil or my soul's madness. Or nothing at all.

I See a Fallen Flesh

I was on my way home from Pat Osil. I had paid a visit there. Now I was walking along in the dark, holding my flashlight.

Past the graveyard, on the ridge at Sok'on, there was a cross. There hadn't been a cross when I passed that way before.

A skeleton was hanging on the cross. Hanging. Hanging. Its flesh was in a pile on the ground.

"This is bad!" I said to myself. "But never mind. It's probably a devil." I made the sign of the cross on it.

There are evil people who torment us wherever we are. They hold us up on the path like murderers.

Xun Min

> We only come to sleep, we only come to dream,
> It is not true, not true that we come to live on the earth.
> —Tochihuitzin Coyolchiuhqui

Xun Min apppears to be a gentle man of few words. Occasionally a shy smile plays around the corners of his mouth, but most often he wears an impassive face that grows even more wooden when he is cracking an outrageously funny joke.

There was nothing easy about Xun's childhood. His father died before he can remember. He was the youngest of four children. From an early age he was out seeking jobs. Together with Romin Teratol he worked on a ranch at the edge of San Cristóbal, carrying garbage for one and a half pesos a day.

When Xun was only fifteen, his mother died and he had to grind the corn for his own tortillas. As he describes it, a widow took pity on him, proposing that he marry her daughter. The unfortunate girl's husband had ordered her to have an abortion and so she had fled home to her mother. After a brief courtship of only a month, and a bride price of a mere one hundred and sixty pesos, she became Xun's wife. Xun remembers that he was so young that he still could not hoist a ninety-five pound sack of corn onto a mule's back. After his marriage Xun was employed as a gardener by the National Indian Institute, did roadwork, and raised corn. He also learned to build houses and to play the fiddle, guitar, and harp.

At the age of twenty-two he went to school, but gave it up after two weeks. Yet five years later, at the time he was telling me his dreams, Xun was a member of the school board.

Xun is now a man of moderate prestige, having held office for a year as justice of the peace and continuing his service as musician for the stewards and stewards-royal.

Xun is the only member of this company of dreamers who had the opportunity to report to me periodically his soul's wanderings. Once a week he detailed his latest adventures and related some of the dreams that had haunted him in the past.

After watching Xun's inscrutable face as he described his soul in action—dancing, fiddling, praying, fighting, victim and culprit, visited by devils and by saints, an innocent and a trickster, now a hero, now a cuckold, summing up his soul's wanderings with an embarrassed neigh—the question repeats itself, "Who is Xun Min?"

Whoever he is, he believes in his dreams, if only he, too, can figure them out. When he does, the consequences on the earth's surface are startling.

I Commit Murder and Am Covered with Pooh

I was traveling on the trail to the lowlands. Below Elan Spring, under the madrone trees, that Old Maryan Seto appeared. He swung a machete at me.

I ducked way down. I grabbed his hand. I wrested the machete away. I cut off his head. He collapsed.

Then his son, Lol K'obyox, appeared. I seized his machete and cut off his head too. It was still holding on a bit. Even so, he collapsed.

I was going to cut it off for good. But Maryan Seto revived. He was about to stand up and grab me.

I didn't attack him with a machete now. I just stomped on his guts. He fell over backwards. I stomped on his stomach. I jumped and jumped. I stomped and stomped.

His belly burst. Ooh, I was covered with it.

I woke up sick. I simply couldn't see. It seemed as if it were dusk.

I came to buy some medicine in San Cristóbal. I told the druggist what had happened. "I'm sick. I can't see. I dreamt I met a murderer on the trail. I killed him. I was covered with shit. I can't go on."

"Drink some neshito!" he told me.

I don't know what it was he gave me in a shot glass. I drank it. It made me well.

I still dream about meeting murderers, but I never get sick from it now. I flee.

When I was younger and my soul was attacked, it took to the skies, but now my soul can scarcely run. Maybe it's because I've aged. Maybe sickness has found a way in, as we say. If I run, it's with fear now. My arms and legs grow numb. Sometimes I slip way into the woods, but the paths turn into open streets. I'm always seen. Sometimes I walk on all fours now. They always catch up with me. I'm carried off.

More Pooh

I dreamt that I was drunk. I didn't see if I fell, or how I got the shit on my hand. It was human shit.

"Sonofabitch, but how could it have happened?" I said to myself. I was able to wipe it off, but then I touched it. I couldn't find any water to wash myself, none at all.

I dreamt it in the lowlands.

It came true, indeed, on the earth's surface.

It was the very next night that my younger brother, Maryan, came to my house when my wife was asleep.

"Are you in bed?" he said.

"Have you come back?" my wife asked.

"I'm not him, I'm Maryan. Open the door. Let me warm up. Light your fire!"

In my dream I foresaw it. Me, I touched shit. That's what shit means. Yes!

"Why should I let you in when your older brother isn't here? Why are you doing such a thing! What have I let you see?"

"Nothing at all, but it's so cold. I collapsed on the ground, because I got drunk. I've sobered up now. Light your fire and let me in!"

"I won't light my fire. I won't let you in. Would your older brother be pleased?"

"Forget it, then, I'm going."

But he crept back quietly. He threw three big clods of dirt in under the eaves. My old harp was standing next to the wall. It was hit by rocks. Its belly was split.

My wife scolded him away.

Then I came home from the lowlands. I had cut my hand. The bone was split. My arm was in a sling.

As soon as I arrived, my wife started to cry. "Your younger brother tried to break in and get me. 'Open your door!' he told me."

I had been hungry before, but I couldn't eat anything now. I was furious. "I'll get even," I said to myself. "He didn't come in, but even so, I'll pay him back as soon as I can. I'll get his wife, the bastard!"

We saw each other in San Cristóbal three days later.

"When did you come back?" he asked me.

"I came back the night you tried to break into my house to get that wife of mine."

"Why would I break in? Don't I speak honestly? It was because I had sobered up. It was because I was so cold. It was because I wanted to warm up."

"Would you like it if the door to your house were opened to warm someone up? Would it make you happy? Then I'll do it to your house!" I told him.

"Oh, fine, since we are brothers," he said.

"I'm not playing games, since you did what you did. If you had been let in, I wouldn't say another word. We would be friends. Now, if we were traveling far away sometime, I'd leave you dead. I'm just telling you in good faith, since you'd be happy to be let into my house, then you'll be happy when I grab your wife. I'll grab her the next time I see her!"

"It's up to you!" he said. He simply strode off.

Three nights later he got drunk with my next-door neighbor, Maryan K'ohcho'. They arrived screaming and waving their machetes. "We'll kill you, you bastard!" they were shouting.

"What have I done? Why would you kill me?" I was standing at the door, clutching my pants. I hadn't tied my sash.

"Come on out, it's you I'm talking to, my older brother, Xun, you bastard! Come on out, I'll kill you! You have no shame. You think you're rich because you have a tile-roofed house. And me, I don't know if I can support my old woman."

Ooh, I came out. I came out without my machete. I was still clutching my pants. I thought if they tried to hit me, I'd just take off my pants and fight.

Maryan K'ohcho' swung his machete. It just missed my leg. "I'll kill you, you bastard!" he screamed.

"Kill me, but first, tell me in a few words what I'm guilty of."

"You aren't guilty of anything," he said. "I'll kill your younger brother instead."

"Don't kill my younger brother for me. Let him come close and see if I don't kill him myself. I'll kill him with my bare hands."

"No, I'll kill the bastard!" He went chasing after my brother.

I picked up several rocks, circled around, and went out my other gate. I thought I would meet up with my younger brother on the path and lob rocks at him.

But he ran to the house of Old Petul Votax. "Come on, you bastard, don't be scared," he hollered.

I prepared myself. I took along my good double-edged machete. I was going to kill him once and for all.

But he didn't come out. He didn't make a sound.

"All right, then, we'll talk together tomorrow when I return." But I didn't leave. I was hiding.

"I guess I'll go. My older brother, Xun, has probably gone," I heard him say.

"Watch out for yourself when you leave!" he was told.

"You'll hear where I've died," my brother said as he left.

Ooh, I chased after him. He didn't see me until I was right behind him. Then he started running.

"Don't run, you bastard, if you're still a man!"

He turned around and faced me. He was flourishing his machete.

I let mine drop. I didn't want to commit murder. I hadn't gotten drunk. I was sober.

I watched to see which way his arm was coming. I caught him by the arm and kept twisting it until his machete fell. I didn't throw him down on his machete, though. I threw him to the left.

He landed with a crash. I knelt on his stomach. I hit him with my knuckles. I bashed him in the face.

Ooh, his face was terribly cut up, covered with blood. He was hanging on to my clothes while I was beating him. I clamped my teeth down on his fingers.

His machete was left lying there. His hat was left lying there. I had satisfied myself. But he threw his arms around me and tried to pull me to the ground.

"You bastard, do you want some more?" I said. I gave it to him again.

The next morning the constables came right off. They took me to the courthouse.

"Why do you hit sacristans?" asked the justice of the peace. My younger brother was a sacristan.

"Even if he is a sacristan, why does he come to my house to kill me? He was lucky. He came back alive. If he had found me drunk, I would have killed him for sure. But you saw that I was playing music," I said in court.

I had played for Antun Lopis, the steward-royal, that Sunday afternoon before the Fiesta of Esquipulas. I didn't drink a single glass because I was sick with a fever. I made an effort to play.

Afterwards we went to escort the tithing man from Five Pieces. We were caught by the dark at the three great crosses. On the way back we stopped at the house of the steward-royal. We ate. The others, who were well, drank. As for me, I poured mine into a bottle. It was probably around nine or ten o'clock when I returned. As soon as I came home, I threw myself on my bed. Then my brother arrived. I was sober!

"I never tried to kill him. If I had killed him, then you would have gone to pick up the body, of course. Since he was going to kill me, why shouldn't he get what he deserves?"

"But you can't hit sacristans," said the justice of the peace. "You should have told him to sober up."

I looked at my younger brother. "Do you remember what you did?" I asked him.

"I remember that you said you would grab my wife. Yes, I remember that!"

"But it was because you went to my house first."

"Ah, you asked for it, then!" the justice of the peace told my brother.

"I asked for it, yes. But why? I'll quit the sacristan's post, because that's how I get presents of cane liquor. That's how I get into trouble."

"What do you mean? Do the stewards torment you? Do they send you on errands? Do they order you about?"

"Of course not!" my brother said.

"Sonofabitch, it's your fault, then," the justice of the peace said to me. "Why did you hit him? Your poor younger brother gets presents—he didn't buy the cane liquor.

"We'll see when the magistrate comes. I'll let you go free now," he told me. I was free, then, at dawn.

But my brother's clothes were covered with blood, completely wrecked. One of his eyes was closed and his head was bandaged.

"If it's ruined, you have to pay damages for the eye," I was told.

At the end of the Fiesta of Saint Sebastian he still had his head wrapped up. His eye had barely healed by Candlemas Day. It was a month, then, before that dispute was settled.

My younger brother caught it good!

"I'll divorce my wife!" I told the magistrate. "I'll divorce her because they've been seeing each other. Make my younger brother confess it once and for all!"

"But I've never slept with her! I was acting with good intentions. I never thought that he would be jealous of me. I thought I could warm myself since he's my brother, she's my older brother's wife."

"Would you want the same done to you—that your door be opened for your older brother when you're not there—that happily he warm himself with your old woman? Would you be glad?" the magistrate asked him.

"Of course it's fine. He's my older brother."

"You bastard, you don't know what's right!" the justice of the peace told him. "That harp—you'll pay for that harp you broke. That woman you're going to take—think it over if you'll take her. Think how much money you will have to give your older brother so that he can find someone to take her place.

"You'll spend the night in jail. You'll carry rocks!"

But Old Chep Kontzares, the church president, interrupted. "Don't say that! It wasn't the poor guy's madness. In this case they are real brothers. I'll stand up for him until it happens a second time. Don't stick him in jail, because this was really the fault of the cane liquor."

"Beg forgiveness!" he was told by all the stewards.

They pulled out their bottles one after another and gave them to my younger brother. The magistrate took half the bottles and I took half. My brother was kneeling, asking my forgiveness.

Sonofabitch, that Chep Kontzares upbraided me. "Why don't you forgive him? If you won't forgive him, you'll certainly regret it later. You'll see what I'll do to you."

"What will you do to me?" I asked. "Would you be glad if the same were done to you?"

"But you are real brothers, man! I'll stand up for him. Don't stick him in jail, not till he does the same thing a second time."

I forgave my younger brother.

But you see, my mother-in-law interfered. "Why did you tell him?" she asked my wife. "If you hadn't said anything, if you had just looked Xun in the eye when he came home, there wouldn't have been any trouble. You opened your mouth wide. Now I don't want to speak to you. Don't try to remember that you have a mother!"

My wife told me about it. Hell, I lost my temper.

The time came when I got drunk and went to have a word with her. "You have no shame, you whorish old woman. You're in on it together. You want my younger brother to drop in on my wife that way. Hell, what kind of reasoning is that—that you want me to be looked in the eye with nothing said?" I was sober enough to know what I was saying. It was just that I was enraged.

Ooh, she went off to tell lies in the courthouse. She told the constables I had said, "You have no shame, whorish old woman. You've given your ass to my younger brother."

The next day the constables came for me. I was put in jail. I got out at two o'clock.

"Is my punishment over, sir?" I asked the magistrate.

"I don't know. Ask your mother-in-law if your punishment is over."

"I won't speak to her, by God! Not a word, not a syllable."

"Hand over the two pesos, then—the cost of your sweatbath!"

"I'll give it to you the next time I come here to play for the stewards-royal."

"Remember to turn it in! Don't expect to be asked for it."

"I won't run away because of two pesos." I bowed to the magistrate and left.

My mother-in-law was standing at the door of Old Nacha's house. I passed by without speaking.

Why did she lie about my offenses? I was sober enough to remember a little of what I shouted.

I dreamt about it first when I was in the lowlands. I touched shit. A little landed on the middle of my hand. That was what the shit meant.

I used to be on good terms with my mother-in-law. Whenever she came by, I would break open a watermelon squash, give her some firewood to carry home. Happily we would visit often. My mother-in-law used to seem pretty nice.

But you see, we broke apart, my wife and I. If there was the least fault, my meal wasn't cooked. "Why are you behaving like this?" I would say to my wife at noon or in the evening or whenever there was nothing for me to eat.

My wife meant to keep looking for trouble, because that mother-in-law of mine made suggestions to her. "Don't do what he says!

They say he has a mistress. They say you have offered yourself for nothing. They say he has found another."

I had never heard such a thing before!

One day my wife said, "Buy me some thread for my shawl! Pay a weaver for me!"

I bought thread for her shawl. I bought wool for a tunic for my little boy. I bought thread for a shawl for my little girl, Tinik.

But no weaver had been found. And we quarreled. "Can't you weave them? If you keep weaving, little by little, you'll finish them yourself," I told her.

She wove her shawl. She wove the woolen tunic for our little boy. She wove the shawl for our little girl.

" 'Pay a weaver,' you said. 'I can't weave it,' you said. Look, you were able to weave it!"

"But it was because our mother came to give me her advice. 'Let him pay for a weaver! Don't let him see you are weaving, because he'll be spoiled. You won't be here always, because he will divorce you. They say he has a mistress,' our mother keeps telling me. That's why I didn't want to weave."

It was our mother's fault that we quarreled so. We would live together for two or three weeks. Then we'd separate. Sometimes we'd separate for a day, sometimes we'd separate for two days. Once it was for ten days.

We took it to the courthouse.

First I went to talk to the magistrate, Old Telex Tzotzil.

"Didn't you meet your mother-in-law on the path? She was just here," he said to me as soon as he opened the door. "I'm leaving for the courthouse now. Wait for me there!"

"I just want to say a few words to you. It will only take a minute."

While the magistrate finished eating, I told him how we separated.

"My wife got sick with 'wind' in her shoulder. She couldn't carry her child. She asked for a prescription. I don't know what medicine it was. It was liquid. The bottle was in a little box. 'Rub it on,' I was told in writing. It was Old Rutilia who wrote it down on a piece of paper. I gave it to my wife.

"But that mother-in-law of mine gave her some advice. 'Don't drink the medicine! That's poison, because he doesn't love you,' she said.

"I have a boy named Petul. My wife gave him the medicine in the box to fiddle with. She gave it to him to waste. That box had contents in it. It was lying on the hoed ground.

" 'What happened to the medicine?' I asked her.

" 'I don't think I ever took the medicine. Will medicine cure me right away?' she said angrily.

" 'You bitch, you've some nerve! Since when do we say that it will cure us right away? Are we gods? After we've done our best—seen whether we get well or don't get well—then we try something else. You bitch, you act as if the medicine weren't paid for.' Then I slapped her."

"That isn't the way she tells it!" said the magistrate. "They say it's because you separated her corn, you've separated her beans and put them in a different place. There are burlap bags where you hide your corn when you go to the lowlands. 'You bitch, you eat too much! The corn runs out too fast,' you tell her."

"I never told her there weren't containers for my corn. I have a corn bin by the wall."

"How about it," said the magistrate as we walked to the court-house. "Will you still live with your wife?"

"But it wasn't me who separated. I didn't send her off. I struck her, but she was at fault. She threw out the medicine even though she was sick."

"But won't you live with her now?"

"Maybe not. It seems she doesn't love me, acting as she does. She talks back very haughtily."

"Don't believe that she doesn't want to live with you! You say she doesn't want to because it's you who's scared. It's you who will turn into a woman for sure!"

We arrived at the courthouse.

"If you want to accept it, I'll give you some advice," said the magistrate.

" 'You bitch, who would hit you, who would scold you if you didn't talk back that way? You bitch, you have no sense of responsibility, treating the medicine like a toy. Let's go now! Light our fire! You remember we have a home. Let's not come exposing ourselves to shame in the courthouse!' Tell her now," he told me.

"And apologize to your mother-in-law!"

"I won't apologize to her. That's all there is to it."

The elders were sitting there now, the grand and petty alcaldes and the prefects. Old Maryan Komis, the prefect, gave my mother-in-law a good scolding.

"What are you good for, you bitch? How did you ever serve in office? How can your child, born of woman, born of man, serve in office the way you keep behaving? Where is your sense?"

My mother-in-law didn't answer.

"If you learn that she keeps giving meddlesome advice to your wife, take care to knock the old woman down. Don't be afraid!" he told me.

For two weeks she was angry. Then the old woman came by quietly. "How are you?" she said.

The dispute ended then. We haven't separated since. It was all the fault of that mother-in-law of mine.

She is beginning to interfere again, until the time when we quarrel for good.

I Am Offered a Fiddle, I Am Excused from Playing

It was Old Chep Kontzares, the church president, who first asked me to play for the stewards.

"What instrument shall I play?" I asked. "I don't know how to play the harp or the fiddle. I can only play the guitar so long as there's someone to tune it for me."

"It can be tuned," he said. "Please play!" There were no other musicians.

I took up the fiddle even though I didn't know how to play it. I was embarrassed because it is the fiddle which strikes up the tune. It is the fiddler who leads with the words, since the stewards' names are sung in a special order.

I was able to do it in the end. But when Old Chep Kontzares came to ask me another time, I told him that I wasn't free. "I'm going to the lowlands," I said. "My tortillas and my posol are ready." I was just telling him a story.

But after he left, I said to myself, "Sonofabitch, what if God punishes me for refusing? What if I get sick, what if I die?"

I bought a five centavo candle and I went to pray. "Please pardon me, my sainted Mother, it isn't out of madness, it's because I don't know how to play. I'm ashamed. I feel the shame in my back, in my side. Forgive me! Don't reject me! I'll just expose your laborers, your contributors to shame."

I returned home. I was exhausted. I fell asleep.

"Are you there, Xun?" said the lady when she appeared at my house. "You came to talk to me earlier today." I realized she was Our Holy Mother.

"Yes, I went to tell you that I simply can't play. I just expose the stewards to shame. I don't know the songs. The songs all have their own special features, but I can't remember how they go."

"Well, don't give up completely!" she said. "Forget it for awhile. Later, when the rainy season is over, you will serve again. Until then, don't despair utterly!

"I just came to tell you this quickly. I'm going now, Xun."

I woke up then. It was raining.

"When the rainy season is over, then you will serve!" Our Holy Mother told me.

I was afraid of playing for a long time. Now I go again. I play for the stewards, I play for the saints.

I Die and Am Buried

I dreamt that I was stretched out inside the house, my head to the west. I tried to move. But I couldn't move because I was dead.

They were playing music for me. I was nailed up inside the coffin and carried to the graveyard.

"The grave is deep enough now," they said. "Toss it in! Bring the dirt!"

They lowered me down.

"Sonofabitch, now I'm going to rot here." I couldn't breathe. There was no air. I couldn't even yell. "I'm going to die from this!" I said to myself.

I tried to move my hand. I scratched at the coffin lid. I kept scraping and scraping.

"There's noise coming from the coffin," they said.

They opened it up. They lifted me out.

"I'm alive!" I said in my heart.

All the men and women who had come to bury me were crying. "I thought he was dead!" they kept saying.

I came back home. I woke up.

I was terribly frightened. But I haven't died.

I Am Offered a Flute

Long ago, when I was learning to play the flute that accompanies the drums, I had a dream.

I was summoned to the courthouse. The elders were sitting in a row, as the elders always do, their heads bound in red turbans. A big basket was sitting in the center of the table. There were flutes inside the basket.

"Would you like to play the flute?" I was asked.

"I'd like to," I said.

"Play, then! Pick one out!"

There were brand new flutes inside the basket, but I didn't choose them. The flute I picked out for myself was old and had been used already.

Now I can play the flute for the ensign-bearers!

It was its soul I received. Yes!

I Clobber a Stallion and a Shaman

We were celebrating Cross Day. Maryan Krus was the shaman. While he was praying, the musicians started to quarrel amongst themselves.

"You bastards, see how you're fighting!" the shaman said. He got disgusted and left.

"Why are you quarreling? It's your fault that the shaman rebelled," I said.

"What business is it of yours? It's you who's come to mess up the affair!" they told me.

"How did I mess it up? It was you who ruined the celebration."

Now it was me who was taking the blame.

The musicians went to catch up with Maryan Krus and bring him back. He forgave them. As for me, I went home. I refused to stay, since I was blamed for the shaman rebelling.

That very night I dreamt. I was still standing next to the house where the candles were being offered for Cross Day.

Ooh, a fat black stallion appeared. It came galloping after me across the field. I tried to hide behind a white sapote tree. But the stallion kept chasing me around and around.

I found a long stick lying on the ground. "What else can I do?" I said to myself. I was worn out from running.

I swung the stick at it. The stallion landed way off, rolling. I kept clobbering it with the stick. I was about to kill it when it turned into a man. It was Maryan Krus!

"Don't kill me!" he said. "Here, take my bamboo staff. Take it!"

I grabbed it from him. I whacked him on the back again and again.

"Stop! I won't do anything more to you," he pleaded.

That was the end of it. I returned home. I was able to finish my dream.

Maryan Krus' soul was tormenting me. But nothing has happened, since I paid him back. I attacked him with his own staff. I don't know what he would have done to me if I had taken his staff home. I clobbered him good. He was going to sell my soul. Yes!

My Dead Brother Tells Me How It Is
and How It Happened

I used to have an older brother, Antun. He died.

The second week after his death I dreamt I was standing by the church door in Zinacantán Center. It was on a Sunday afternoon.

There I met my older brother, Antun. He was weaving palm.

"What are you doing here?" I asked.

"I'm just relaxing, because it's Sunday. They let me out for a little while," he said.

"Where have you been?"

"I've been working at Little Tuxtla," he said.

"Where is Little Tuxtla?"

"I'll show you!" He led me up Old Savel's path.

"What kind of work are you doing?" I asked him as we walked along.

"Weeding sugarcane. Watering flowers. Any other little thing."

"You were sick on the earth's surface. Are you well now?"

"I'm really pretty well now," he said. "I never died. I was sold to the Earth Lord. But I can do the work."

I followed him. Water was gushing in the irrigation ditches. There were fields and fields of sugarcane.

"This is where I weed," he said. "Return right away, now that you have seen it! If they catch you, they won't let you go."

"But I want to learn before I leave, on whose orders you died. Who sold you?"

He had a mistress when he was alive. Tonik was her name. "Yes, she was the one who sold me to the Earth Lord," he said.

"Because of her you died. Then how could you be alive now?" I asked him.

"It seems that I died, but I'm not really dead. I'll die again, and the next time I'll die altogether. I'm only sold to the Earth. I came here intact."

"What would they do if you asked permission to send for her—if you had the woman who sold you to the Earth come here and join you?"

"I did my best to tell them. But they wouldn't authorize it. They told me she would come later.

"Return right away or they'll see you!"

Ooh, I jumped back. I was scared because I realized he was dead.

She had told him on the earth's surface when he started to speak to her, "If you want me, come and petition me. If you don't come to ask for me, then we'll see for sure! I am a shaman. I can pray. You'll die as soon as possible if you don't marry me!"

You see, he was trying to ask her for a "meal," as we say. Gradually she gave in. Since he wouldn't marry her, she prayed to all Our Lords.

"You pray yourself!" they told my older brother. But he never prayed. And so the saints took him.

"It was because she was offended," his soul said to me.

"I was freed for a little while since it's Sunday. On week days, of course, I work."

That's the way it ended. I reached home and I woke up. "Lord, it's true that Antun was sold," I said to myself.

He told me the whole story in my dream. And besides, he had said when he was still alive, "She'll probably eat my soul if I don't marry her."

That dream was the truth, it wasn't just my soul's madness. My brother was sold to the Earth.

How We See Whether It Will Be a Boy or a Girl

When a child is about to be born, I am given a water jug in my dream. And I am given a deep tortilla gourd.

"Take this! Set it aside. Treat it well!" I am told.

Then it will surely be a girl.

If it's to be a boy, I am given a hoe, a billhook, and a digging stick. They are a boy's soul.

That's what I dreamt when my eight-year-old boy was born. It came true. Yes!

The deep gourd and the water jug are for a girl.

That's what they surely forecast!

I Am Dancing Like a Steward

I dreamt that I was wearing worn-out clothes. I was getting drunk. The music was good. I felt like dancing. "Come on and dance!" my friends told me.

"But how can I dance looking like this?" I said. I tried to leave.

"Dance!" I was told.

In a second I saw myself dancing spiritedly. I had on a ceremonial robe and fine ceremonial sandals. My friends who were dancing were stewards, and I was dancing like them.

"Which steward am I?" I asked myself, "Steward of Saint Anthony, Steward of the Holy Sacrament, Steward of Saint Dominic?" I couldn't remember what my office was, but I was dressed up in my ceremonial robe. My sandals had fine high backs.

I was dancing like a steward. But I haven't seen it come true.

I Am Eating Laurel

In the first dream I had long ago there were laurel trees that had been chopped down. The trees had sprouted leaves.

That's what I was eating. I hung on to the limbs with my forelegs. I was chomping down on the leaves with my teeth.

My forelegs slipped down. I landed on my side. My ribs were aching.

I was sick the next morning. I recovered with the help of a shaman.

I keep seeing that dream. I'm always in a corral, but now I never fall. I just go about eating leaves. I'm loose in the woods when I wake up.

It's my companion animal spirit, wherever it is hidden.

I Discover Some Little Candles and Destroy Them

I was walking on the path that runs along my back fence.

At the end of my land was a little bank with an overhang. Underneath it there were piles of candles, black, green, and red little candles lined up in rows. There were ribbons of blue and ribbons of many colors cut into lengths.

"Hell, but what is this?" I said to myself.

I called to my wife, "Bring a machete!"

I cut them like this. I cut them like that. I slashed them to pieces with my machete.

Then I pissed on them. Waddling along, I pissed on rows of candles. They were soaked.

Sonofabitch, I pissed a good long distance!

After I pissed on them, I came home and I woke up.

"Hell, could somebody be tormenting me?" I said to myself.

Maltil Tulum

If a man could pass through Paradise in a dream,
and have a flower presented to him as a pledge
that his soul had really been there, and if he
found that flower in his hand when he awoke—
Ay!—and what then?

—Samuel Taylor Coleridge

Maltil Tulum looked much older than the forty years he claimed to be. He was skinny, with spindly legs—not in the least bit handsome or prepossessing. With a serious air and total conviction he would spin out his dreams. As he warmed to the subject, he lovingly stacked repetition on repetition, his voice rising to a shrill falsetto squeak with dire comic effects.

Maltil had once been a salt seller but had given it up for corn farming. He had been a sacristan, a scribe, and Senior Steward of the Holy Sacrament.

He was a respected shaman who participated in the communal offerings at the mountain shrines. In times of sickness it was to Maltil Tulum that Romin Teratol turned for aid.

It was also from Maltil Tulum that Romin, in his youth, learned many myths and legends while helping in the corn fields. Romin recalls that Maltil would be the spokesman for a group of Zinacantecs going to rent land in "hot country." But unlike most of his country-men who would hurry back up to the mountains as soon as they could, Maltil would take along his first wife and stay for many weeks at a time. So pleased to have money in his pockets, he would hire himself out to all his friends while his own corn field would grow choked with weeds. Romin remarks that Maltil's harvest was only half as large as his own, which must be a record for crop failure! Maltil also did roadwork at four pesos a day until he became foreman at six a day.

Maltil had a craving for cane liquor, as did his wife. Town gossip had it that if his wife passed out on the trail, Maltil would sit down and wait for her to sober up; but if his wife was alone when she collapsed, she was fair game for any man who passed by. These incidents led to much marital strife, Maltil's wife often seeking shelter for the night in a neighbor's house. Whenever she spent the night at the Teratol's, she would urge Romin to marry her daughter, but he was too poor to take her offer.

Two years after Maltil recounted his dreams to me, he was of-ficiating as shaman at a celebration of Holy Cross Day. Pork was served at the banquet. That, they say, was the cause of the diarrhea that ended only with his death.

Maltil's dreams show a man in constant communication with the denizens of the supernatural world, whether they be ghosts, devils, or deities. Maltil's conviction that dreams "always come true" was fortified with the following examples: (1) He dreamt of digging up big potatoes. Four months later his first wife died. (2) He dreamt that he lost his horse's lead rope. Three of his horses died. (3) He dreamt that he was chased by dogs. He fell ill. (4) He dreamt that he received a bowl of corn. He had a poor harvest. (5) He dreamt that he was stained with excrement. His wife was unfaithful. (6) He dreamt that a plane crashed at the shrine of Saint Christopher, burned the crosses, and hurled pieces of wreckage over his house and the entire town. He had sickness in his house all that year.

Maltil was possessed by Bosch-like visions of witches and demons. Several times he dreamt of walking a tightrope while the witches stood below watching and shouting. He has taken to the air, with his wings under his arms like the Plumed Serpents of the Fiesta of Saint Sebastian, soaring to a safe haven in the mountains and then returning home. But not all his dreams are of torments. Just as often he is given the special protection of the gods. Through Maltil's dreams the deities are cast into view as jealous, but conscientious, defenders of the righteous.

I Search for My Patient in a Cave and See What It's Like to Be Sold

I had a patient on the earth's surface. The sickness was severe. I dreamt that I went into a cave to find her soul.

The cave had a huge entrance. A Ladino opened the door.

"Will you come in?" he asked.

"I'll come in," I said. The door closed behind me.

A man was standing in the middle of the room.

"Was it you who prayed?" he asked.

"It was me," I said.

"Look over there, then! She's in the kitchen."

I reached the place where the kitchen was.

"Was it you who prayed?" asked the master.

"It was me."

"The woman who has come won't leave now," he said. "Look at those three!"

The poor things were already sold. They were sitting with their feet dangling. They had come there to wash dishes. We die from that because we swell up from the water. It can't be cured with medicine.

"The person who delivered the patient will be right back," the master said. "Wait awhile. She'll come before long."

There was another Ladino around the corner.

"Have you returned?" he asked.

"I've returned," I said.

"Was it you who prayed?"

"It was me."

"But she won't leave now. They've already buried her. Wait, the boss will come."

A Ladina was stirring a pot of boiling water. I don't know what she was cooking.

"Have you returned?" she asked me.

"I've returned," I said.

"Was it you who prayed?"

"It was me."

"But she won't leave now. They buried her yesterday. Wait a little while, the one who delivered her is coming."

The Ladina stirred her pot. "When you're dying with chills and fever, it's the boiling water," she told me. "Oh, many, many have come already. Many have come already."

The boss arrived. "She won't leave now," he said. "She won't leave now. Wait, the witch is coming!"

I saw two women at the door. I couldn't tell who they were since they had changed their faces. One was still a girl. The other was old and wrinkled. She was the real teacher!

I grabbed her by the arms. "Where are you going? What are you doing?" I shouted.

"Don't hold on to me!" she said. "I'm going down to visit for two days."

But there two days are two years!

I wanted to hit them, but I was afraid the Ladinos would scold me.

I let the women go. They are there in the underworld now.

Then a Zinacantec came up to me. He had a leather apron on, the kind we wear when we are working or weeding.

"Are you returning?" he asked me.

"Of course I'm returning," I said.

"God, how do you know how to return? Me, I came a long time ago. I'm here for good."

He was working as a carpenter.

"We never rest for a single day. Not even a minute. Not even on Sunday. It's terrible when you are sold.

"Oh, many of us have come already. Many have come already."

"But I'm returning, of course."

"Return then, since you know how!" He came to talk for just a minute, but he had to go back. He was scared, since he had a boss.

When we go to the caves we suffer so. We have been sold like slaves.

"Are you leaving?" asked the Ladino who guards the door.

"I'm leaving," I said.

He opened the door. I simply came out.

I had a friend now. Surely it was Our Lord.

I Am Offered Flowers, Pencils, Gourds, a Bottle, and a Staff

When I came out on the earth's surface, when I obeyed the command, Our Lord arrived.

"Let's go! They say you are to learn your orders," he told me.

He led me to the house of Our Holy Father Esquipulas. The elders were there in their red turbans. I bowed to them.

"Son, you will serve," they said. "Here is your little present. Receive these, please!"

I was given many Easter lilies. They were beautiful.

"Here is another bunch." They were pencils. "With these you will walk!" they said.

Later, as they escorted me, they gave me two ceremonial gourds for pinole. They were wrapped in a cloth.

Two gourds and a quart bottle of cane liquor.

Then I was given the bamboo staff.

I arrived at the courthouse. But it wasn't the courthouse. It was Calvary.

"Wait just a second, son! Soon you will pray."

I had already seen one or two patients. Their sickness passed. The gods heard about it. I hadn't been properly installed on the earth's surface. I had never bowed to them. I had never prayed. I was anxious because I might get a beating.

I simply prayed. I've been pretty well to this day. That's the way it is when I walk, where I walk. Our Lord gave me my power.

I received flowers, two ceremonial gourds, a bottle, my staff, and a bunch of little pencils. The pencils meant that I would become a scribe.

I was a scribe for two or three years. Then I became secretary of the band committee. That's what the pencils were for, since we draw up the records.

That's what I dreamt when Our Lord installed me. It was nearly twenty years ago. I was still a boy.

I See an Underground Mass

There are saints inside the world. There are priests. And there is Mass. The saints are lined up at the door of the church. The altar is exactly the same as the altar for Our Lords, but it is underground, of course, underground.

"Come in!" the acolytes command us. "Kneel down!"

"If I want to, I'll kneel. If I don't want to, I won't kneel," I told them. I knew it had to do with the earth.

"But why are you so strong-hearted?" one of them asked. Quickly, from behind, he touched my prick. "You bastard!" he said. "You are still so strong!"

Since I refused to kneel, I survived. Otherwise the Earth Lord would have taken my soul. If you kneel, you are theirs!

When the patient's illness is grave, his soul is seized and dragged under the earth. We shamans must wrest him away.

We are tormented. We take the blame. Yes!

I See Dancing Buzzards

I was coming to San Cristóbal in my dream. I had some salt that I'd come to sell.

Ah, God, the awful buzzards—they wouldn't let me by!

The buzzards were dancing. They were playing strange instruments. They weren't harps. They were like bass viols. They were like bows and arrows.

The buzzards were plucking away. They were banging on a little drum. Ooh, the buzzards were puffing up their tails as they danced. They had crests. Their faces were hideous.

The next day I was frightened when I was coming toward San Cristóbal on the earth's surface. "Could it be that something is going to happen to me?" I said to myself.

Then I reached the place where the buzzards had been dancing in my dream. Blood was spilled there. Human blood.

Could it be that some people had been fighting? Could it be that somebody cut himself? I don't know. A lot of blood had flowed. It was in the very middle of the road. They do a dance on our blood, the bastards! They're some jokers, the witches! They're tricky!

If you have some salt, sprinkle it on the blood so the witches won't come in. If you don't do anything, they'll take your soul. They grow strong on our blood, since blood is our strength. That's so!

Those buzzards were witches. The musicians were witches. They had crests and hideous faces. They had bass viols, not real harps.

They were thumping on their drum so they could dance.

I Am Given Two Drinks

I dreamt I was going to work. I met a man and a woman on the path. The man gave me a hoe.

They had a bottle of cane liquor with them. "How much are you going to give him?" they said to each other.

"I'm going to give him a large shot glass," said the man.

"I'll just give him a small one," said the woman.

"Well, serve it, then!" he said.

She poured two drinks. I drank one large shot and one small shot.

Then I took the hoe and went to work.

The next day, on the earth's surface, I went hunting.

A little rabbit appeared. It just popped out of the ground and ran into the underbrush.

"Bring the rifle!" I said to my son. I drilled the rabbit right in the spine.

"Ah, but I was shown this!" I said to myself.

At dusk I went hunting again. I walked on and on through the woods. I saw more rabbits, but they didn't wait for me.

It was almost midnight. I started home.

Suddenly there was a big rabbit on the trail. Its eyes were shining.

I stopped to change the batteries in my flashlight. When I looked up, the rabbit was gone.

I circled around. The poor thing was lying flat. After all that, my gun didn't fire.

But the rabbit doubled back. It was a present now. It was that big shot glass. Yes!

I flung a rock at it. I thought I missed it. But it was stretched out, the poor thing.

It didn't die right off. When I grabbed it in my hands, it scratched me.

"That's what I dreamt about," I said to myself. I got that little rabbit in the afternoon and the big one at night.

Our Lord treated me with two. I think it was the Earth Lord who favored me.

That's the way it is when we go hunting. We dream about it. Yes!

I've only dreamt that once. Now if I go hunting, I don't hit anything. Sometimes I get a bird. But bigger animals, no more.

I See My Dead Wife Drunk

I dreamt about my late wife.

Sometimes she drank a little cane liquor. She drank a lot of cane liquor.

I saw her exactly the way she was, the way she walked. She was wrapped in a basket-weave shawl, prettily checkered. That's what she had taken with her.

Her soul was drunk. Her soul was buying cane liquor in a house. I don't know where the house was. She was drinking one drink after another.

I dreamt that she finished drinking. There was a little rise, a little path. I came along right behind her. But she never spoke to me. She was drunk. She was staggering about just as she did when she got drunk on the earth's surface.

"Could it be that she hasn't entered the afterworld yet?" I asked myself. Who knows. She never spoke to me. I don't know why.

It was soon after my wife died. It's when they have recently died that we dream about them.

I never saw her again. Never!

I Watch Dogs Ferry People Across a River

We were high on a hill. The river below was wide. The dogs climbed down to the river. One dog was black, one was white, one was gray, and one was yellow.

"Who will be the first to go in the water?" they asked one another.

"You go in first!" the awful black dog was told.

So the black dog jumped in.

People were crowded on the riverbank. "Climb on!" said the black dog.

A man mounted him on the spot—the way we mount horses. The black dog swam rapidly across the river. He came back to take another person.

"Help me!" he told the other dogs.

The gray dog helped a little. The yellow dog helped a little. But the white dog was no help at all. He tired on the way. He had a terrible time getting out.

I was standing on high ground, watching. Many people crossed over. The awful black dog was strong. He ferried many people across.

I saw it in my dream. Who's ever heard of such a thing on the earth's surface?

They say there are rivers when we die. Dogs are the ferrymen, they say. Our Lord shows us so we won't harm dogs.

We musn't kill awful black dogs.

But the others can be killed occasionally, of course.

Petu' Nibak

> For hope is but the dream of those that wake.
> —Matthew Pryor
> *Solomon on the Vanity of the World*

When I first knew Petu' Nibak she was already considered a "left-over woman," but she was still pretty, lively, bold, with remarkable self-assurance and a throaty laugh that would give any man the shivers.

Petu' ran off with Mikel Tzotzil's brother-in-law, the truck driver, but after a month, disillusioned, she returned home. Her mother was so angry at the truck driver that, rather than take the truck to San Cristóbal, Tonik, carrying her market goods on her back, would walk half way to flag down a passing truck from Chamula.

Petu''s problems had only begun, for when a suitor came to ask for her, Tonik demanded that her daughter, though scarcely a virgin, be married in style. Despite the constant flow of gifts from the suitor to her, Tonik would not relent.

Though it is said that Petu' loved her fiancé, she did not dare risk a second elopement, for if it were to end as abruptly as the first, her mother's wrath would not subside. Petu' would be left homeless, with no one to turn to for shelter. Only after Tonik was brought to court did she give away her daughter. Convinced that Petu' would be murdered if she moved to her husband's house, Tonik insisted that the man come live with them so she could see how hard he beat her daughter. Petu''s husband endured his mother-in-law's company long enough to give her a grandchild and then sadly returned alone to his hamlet.

But the story is not quite so simple. When she was engaged, one of Petu''s neighbors fell in love with her, and she with him. After Petu''s husband left, the neighbor would come to spend the night, bringing beers for them all. Even Tonik was delighted and promised to give him her daughter, but she wouldn't let him sleep with Petu' before they were married. Considering Petu''s past history, the magistrate determined that her neighbor should be required to pay only a token bride price. This reasonable decision was rejected outright by Tonik, thus dashing her daughter's hopes for marital security. Today, her beauty lost, Petu' is still living in her mother's home, alone.

Petu''s dreams reflect her preoccupation with her unmarried state. Again and again she is the victim of unwarranted attacks. Unlike Maltil Tulum, she is seldom the subject of divine attention. Indeed, because she is so fastidious, Petu''s one gift is reclaimed by the gods. But few dreams reveal such dramatic finesse as Petu''s playing the toreador!

My Fiancé's Father Brings a Barrel of Cane Liquor,
I Am Chased by Dogs, I Hide Under the Blankets

Dogs were chasing after me. They were snapping at my leg. But they didn't bite me. I climbed a tree.

There was a table. It was standing in the house of Old Chep Hili'at. I was sitting at the table with my mother, when Old Petul K'obyox from Deer House hamlet came looking for me. He had a barrel of cane liquor stuck in his net.

"I want to speak to Petu'," he said. "I'm going to the courthouse to see about settling their dispute. I want to know, once and for all, whether she will still marry my son or not."

"She isn't here," said the lady of the house.

The old man addressed my mother. "Please be so kind as to receive this barrel of cane liquor. The quarrel can't drag on and on. Take this barrel for my sake."

"Talk to my daughter," my mother told him. "It isn't my affair."

"How can that be? My son asked me to come and leave it with Mother Tonik."

"As for me," I said, "I don't want to accept anything more from your son. And I'll return the money for whatever gifts he's given." The old man left in anger. He carried the barrel of cane liquor in his net to the cantina.

I started home. The dogs came swarming toward me on the trail.

I ran to the house of Maryan K'obyox, "Avocado" we call him. He's a marimba player who often comes and plays at our house.

It was there that I hid. They piled lots of blankets on top of me.

Then a man arrived. He was chasing me too. "Haven't you seen a woman?" he asked.

"I never saw her," said the mistress of the house.

"But she came in here."

"No, come in and look!"

I was rolled up in the blankets. Ooh, I was scared. "If they have fleas, I'm afraid I'll get the fleas," I said to myself.

"Oh, never mind! Ooh, but I feel something wet now. It feels as if water's been spilled here." I tried not to move.

Then Maryan's wife shook me. "The man who's looking for you has left. Go home now!"

As soon as I went out, the dogs chased after me.

I reached home. I closed myself up in the house. The trouble ended.

Who knows what it means. Maybe Old Petul K'obyox will come to witch us, we told ourselves.

"What if he sends something, what if it drives you mad?" my younger sister, Loxa, said to me. "What you dreamt is ugly. Those dogs you dreamt about were sent from Totolapa."

"But he won't send witchcraft from Totolapa if I return the money," I said.

"But if you don't marry his son, he may still send it."

"Who knows. I'll see what turns out," I said. "Do dreams have few meanings? Do we dream of just one or two things?"

I Am Attacked by a Cow, I Play the Toreador

I'll tell about that big cow I dreamt about.

It was there on the trail to San Cristóbal where the spring wells up and it's swampy. The cow was standing in the middle of the path. Her baby calf was sucking, but the cow was tossing her head up and down.

"The cow is going to gore you!" my mother said. She threw her shawl to me. I waved it at the cow.

I climbed onto a little house. The house was made of palm fronds. It was swaying back and forth.

"Dance! Dance on top of the little house," my mother told me.

The cow was moving this way and that. I dangled the shawl and kept covering the cow's face with it. The little house was rocking.

I was dancing with the cow!

The cow never gored me. I climbed down off the house and crawled under the fence. The cow went off to Ravoltik Ranch.

It's a witch, the people say.

"Who could have seen you yesterday?" asked my mother. "Who did you meet at the mill?"

"There was just the young widow, Kavilan, Loxa Koko'on. She was the only one who saw me. She was pulling along her little girl."

"Ah, that's who it probably was if she was angry and making fun of you at the mill," said my mother. "And the little calf is her little girl."

In the middle of the path I met her. The same way the big cow stopped me on the trail to San Cristóbal. Its teats were hanging down. The little calf was sucking.

As for me, I'm smart. I climbed up on the house. I kept using the shawl to cover the cow's face so she wouldn't gore me. I was playing the toreador!

I Am Cooking a Wedding Banquet

Last night we were dancing at a wedding.

The wedding was in a meadow deep in the woods.

Musicians were playing. Women were singing. Me, I was fixing the meal inside the house.

"Hurry up with the meal! Is the food ready yet? The bride and groom are ready to eat," said the ritual tutor.

"When the bride and groom have finished dancing, then the bride and groom will eat," I said.

"They've finished dancing," the people came to tell me. "Dish out the food! Bring the bowls!"

I served the meal. The music played. There was lots of laughing. People were dancing. After they danced, they ate. When they finished eating, the fiesta ended.

Who knows what it could mean. Maybe I'll die. A wedding is a bad sign.

My Mother Is Shot Dead

There was a murder. It may come true, because I dreamt I was at home. Remember when I told you you were shot, mother?

I was on my way to the spring. Maryan Chobtik, my older sister's husband, shot my mother. He committed the murder and left her dead.

"My mother's dead! My mother's dead!" I ran to tell my older brother.

"She's dead? Agh, you're lying! Our mother won't die," my older brother said.

She was lying face down on the path to our spring, there where the elderberry tree is growing. She was lying face down in Old Pinto Sarate's yard. The witch!

My older brother took his gun. Maryan Chobtik was gone. My mother had disappeared. I was all by myself. It was dark.

"What could it mean, mother? What if Maryan Chobtik comes to kill us another time?" I said.

Who knows if he's planned to murder us. Who knows.

I Am Given a Chicken, But It Is Taken Away

There was a little chicken. It came out of a cleft in the rock.

A man and a woman appeared. "Take this home!" they said.

But the chicken had dirtied itself. Its little rear end was covered with shit.

"Why is it so filthy? I don't want this one," I said.

"But this is the one we are giving to you."

"No, I want the yellowish one, because it's pretty. Its little head is crested."

"When you reach home, stick it in a chest! Burn incense for it!" they told me.

We were walking along the trail to Five Pieces.

But my little yellow pullet disappeared on the way.

"I wonder why it was taken from me," I said to the owner.

"It's because you didn't ask me for the one I gave you first. See for yourself, you didn't want it! You wanted the yellowish one. That's why it was taken away."

There hadn't been any sickness. There hadn't been any chicken disease. I had that dream and then my chickens died. They were dying in large numbers.

"Why would my chickens be dying, mother?"

"It's probably because there are so many droppings under their roost," she said.

"Ah!" I said.

I Am Told to Make a Sash for Saint Anthony

I was lining up to bow to the gods in church.

"Why would it be raining so much?" I asked while I was waiting.

"It's raining because Our Holy Father Saint Anthony needs a sash cord," I was told.

"What kind does he want?" I asked.

"He wants it to be striped like your sash cord. He needs it because his leg came loose in the earthquake."

"Is that so?" I said.

I went to bow to Our Holy Father. I went to see if his leg had come loose.

It hadn't come loose. It was fine. Our Holy Father Saint Anthony wanted a sash striped liked mine.

"And you will make it for him," I was told.

I lined up to bow to all Our Lords. Then I came home in the rain.

I know he wants to be given something.

But I haven't any money.

I had that dream a year ago, when it was raining all the time.

Tonik Nibak

On what day? In what moon? In what year
did this story happen? As in dreams, as
in nightmares, everything happens at once,
everything is here and now.

—Rosario Castellanos
Ciudad Real

She hoisted a huge bundle of daisies onto the truck and set herself down complacently on the bench, giving the Ladinas a bright smile and a cheery "Buenos dias." All the bumpy way to San Cristóbal she added her worldly wisdom to the Ladinas' excited accounts of all the ghosts and buried treasures they had known in their brief lives.

She may be seventy-seven years old now, but that is only a guess because Tonik's confident calculations of her age at the time of personal crises and historical events simply do not agree. Her early childhood was spent in Zinacantán Center with her mother and her younger sister. Her father was deceased. When Tonik was seven her mother died, and she was adopted into a Ladino household in San

Cristóbal, paying her board and keep by the performance of small chores. Two years later she returned to Zinacantán. There she learned to weave. By the age of twelve she had become a regular helper and protegée of the resident priest.

Tonik attended school for three years with Romin Teratol's late stepmother and three or four other Zinacantec girls. Tonik recited to me from memory the verses she had had to deliver at her graduation from third grade, and even the lines that one of her classmates had declaimed. She alone learned to read and write. "And what do they know now? Ha! How many tales have *they* told you?"

Engaged to be married, Tonik rebelled and willfully rejected her suitor—an act that obliged her to return to San Cristóbal to work as a maid in order to earn the money needed to repay her suitor's court-ship expenses. Tonik's younger sister then jilted her fiancé and skipped town, "forcing" Tonik to take the marriage vows in her stead. During their twenty-eight years of marriage she bore her husband ten children, only five of whom survived into adulthood.

Restless at home, Tonik became an agent of the National Indian Institute. According to women's gossip, she wrapped her belly in a straw mat so she would look more pleasantly plump. Her husband finally grew tired of all the rumors that were bound to stick to a woman who would leave her husband to earn a wage, consorting with Indian schoolboys and teachers from many towns. He accused her of carrying on with two men, grabbed her pigtails, and hit her about the shoulders with a firebrand. Not one to submit in silence, Tonik evicted her husband and marched off to complain to the direc-tor of the National Indian Institute in San Cristóbal, then to the director of the Department of Indian Affairs, and finally to Don Erasto Urbina, local defender of the Indians. She explained that if she didn't work, her family would be dressed in rags, for her husband offered no support, that half her earnings she gave to her husband, "And since when has a wife been obliged to do that?" She had been married in the Church, had respected and obeyed her husband as she should. After listening to Tonik's tale of woe, Don Erasto summoned her husband to San Cristóbal. "Old Black Joe," as he was known, was ordered to provide ten pesos a week to support his children. But since then, says Tonik, he has provided "not ten centavos a week."

In recent years Tonik has carried on an adventurous flower trade, selling her products in far-off Tuxtla, the state capital. In her spare time she has taught weaving to a number of American guests at Na Balom, and has been commissioned to weave exceptionally fine blankets.

Despite a never-ending series of squabbles with her children's fiancés, husbands, and wives who never seem to live up to her high standards or even to respectable community standards, she has managed to live so free of sickness that people ask her, "Are you a pillar of the world?"

No one denies she is a "strong-hearted" woman. Her sharp wit, whether expressed in faultless colloquial Spanish or in Tzotzil, is both feared and relished by the men whom she engages in lively banter. Intensely righteous, pretentiously Catholic, vicious in gossip, her gaiety still commands affection, and her nimble mind earns grudging admiration from the men of the town.

Tonik's gift of the gab, lively wit, and forceful personality are evident in all her dreams. Even the ancestral gods take offense at her forwardness. Tonik's religious devotion pervades her dream life. Her frequent contact with the Ladino world, particularly as a merchant, is another dominant theme. Nevertheless her conviction that "dreams always come true," and her recollection of dreams that were experienced as many as thirty-eight years before reveal a woman solidly embedded in her own culture. The standard Tzotzil motifs are simply put into action with greater attention to detail and with more elaborate dialogue. Tonik's powerful self-defense when summoned to court on false charges gives witness to the strength of character of the woman named Tonik.

Saint Lawrence Asks to Have His Face Uncovered

I dreamt, because there had been so much rain. It is because Our Holy Father Saint Lawrence is unhappy when his face is covered.

He summoned three prefects.

"What is wrong, son?" asked the prefects when they arrived at the church.

"I am very upset that you have covered my face," said Our Holy Father. "I've told you all along that I don't want a glass front to the casement. I want my face to be in the open."

"Why, son? That's the way it should be. Your face will get covered with dust," the elders told him.

"It isn't your responsibility. I know how to look after myself. My face won't get covered with dust because I know how to dust it off. I have a neckerchief."

His neckerchief was beautiful. It was pure silk. The down was thick, of velvet, and it was bright white.

He held it in his hand. "This is how I dust my face," he said. He wiped his cheeks and forehead with the neckerchief. "See, there's no dirt left on my face!"

"But your face is supposed to be covered. The altar needs whitewashing. It needs to be looked after."

"If you will, leave my face uncovered. I am unhappy that I can't see what people are doing here in my home.

"When I see what's happening, then I give orders. I detain the workers' hands if they work poorly. It's awful your covering my face. I can't see how they're doing whatever they're doing!"

"Wait then, the magistrate will come. Let him settle it," said one of the elders.

Two constables were sent to the courthouse to bring the magistrate.

"What is it, sir?" asked the magistrate.

"I'm tired of having my face covered like this. It makes me sad," said Saint Lawrence. "Please be so kind as to remove the glass."

"The three Maryans will have to be notified," said the magistrate. It was the Maryans who had covered Saint Lawrence's face.

The three sacristans were summoned.

Then my dream was cut short. I woke up. Rain was pounding on the roof.

I Find a Pile of Money

I was coming back from San Cristóbal.

There is a stone on our path that fell from the sky.

Beside that stone was a pile of money.

"Oh, My Lord, there is money here! I guess I'll pick it up," I said to myself.

I scooped up the money. I stuck it in my shawl. I had a hard time getting home clutching all the money.

"Look here!" I said to my daughter. "I found it piled up at the foot of the gully."

"But it isn't right if you put it in our chest, mother. It isn't good. The money will corrode," my daughter told me.

"No, I'll put it in the chest," I said. "No, it's better if I put it in the little baskets that I bought today."

They were filled to the top. They were filled with money.

"Cover them! Tie the tops well! Store them away!" I told my daughter.

She took the baskets inside my house. She put them on my little table and covered them with a cloth.

At nine o'clock the next morning I woke up in my dream. "Is the money there, mother, or has it gone?"

"I'll see what it is, daughter. It may be some kind of snake. Or it may be 'wind.' I don't believe it's money."

I was delighted. The money was all in coins. There wasn't a single bill. Just round pesos, round twenty centavo pieces, round fifty centavo pieces.

"Now I won't suffer," I said to myself. "I have lots of money. I'll be able to live on it for a long time.

"Store it away, daughter! Just get it out when I go to buy our corn."

The next morning the money was gone! It was just a trick. It was just a dream.

The rains hadn't started yet when I dreamt I had a basketful of money. What more could I want? Now it's gone.

I Attend a Requiem Mass for My Mother

The priest arrived, Father Lusiano Martines. He died a long time ago, but in my dream he was still alive.

"Daughter, hear the Mass!" he told me when I met him at my gate. "A Mass will be celebrated for your late mother. She used to be my maid. I'm giving a Mass for her this morning."

"Fine!" I said. "Ring the bell for Mass a bit early."

"Early of course, don't worry! I'll direct the sacristans to ring the bell."

They rang the bell for Mass. "Change your clothes, girls! Let's go to Mass!" I told my daughters.

But you see, the church wasn't Saint Lawrence's church. I don't know where the church was. It seemed to be far away. It was small and gray, and its friezes were completely different.

The cathedral isn't like it, nor Saint Francis nor Saint Nicholas nor Saint Dominic. There is no saint who has a church like it.

There were three altars and three priests celebrating Mass. "Why would it be like this?" I said to myself.

"Perhaps Our Lord wants a Mass to be celebrated for my mother. It may help her soul to be freed."

God, Jesus Christ,
    Spirit,
Finality,
    Extinction,
Now the priest whose tortillas you made
    Is celebrating a Mass for you.
Now he remembers your soul, your spirit.
    Kneel before Thy Lord and ask,
What were your sins,
    What was your evil that you should have died so young.
You did not suffer long.
    You did not see three sunsets before you died, mother.
Now that your Mass is being sung,
    Pray to Our Lord.
What were your sins?
    What poor person's hatred consumed you?

I bowed to the Virgin.

Heavenly woman,
    Heavenly lady,
Free her soul for me,
    Let her spirit go,
My mother,
    My saintly mother.
She is suffering,
    She is downcast,
Since she did not speak to me
    When she expired.
She suffered.
    She grew mute.

What did my saintly mother wish to say?
How was her little plot of land to be left?
Ask her for me, heavenly lady,
Then show me in my dream, in my spirit.

The Mass to the east ended. The Mass by the cross at the church door ended.

I turned around. The Mass was over.

"Let's go, girls! Cross yourselves!" We came outside.

Now the entrance was all brick and tile. Cars were standing on the road.

"Where am I, My Lord? I know this isn't my home."

I was scared. I roused myself. I woke up.

It was midnight. I was lying in my bed at home.

That dream was very strange. I seemed to be so far away. Where could my soul have been traveling?

I woke my daughters up. "I dreamt that I was far away, listening to Mass."

"It's because you ate too much before you went to bed," my daughters told me. "Your beans have a lot to say!"

"No, I just ate a little bit of jerked meat."

"Go to sleep! Stop gabbing!" they told me.

I had that dream a month ago. But I'm not so troubled that I have to talk about it wherever I go.

I Gather Firewood and Am Rebuked for Praying at a Shrine

I was gathering firewood on the earth's surface.

I stopped to pray in front of the cross on Great Mountain.

My Holy Father of White Cliff,
My Holy Lord of White Cave.
May Thou not hurl me away,
May Thou not toss me out, My Lord,

I prayed, and me, just an ignorant person. How would I know it wasn't right?

That night I had a dream.

A gentleman appeared before me.

"See here, young lady, don't cross yourself all of a sudden. Don't kneel all of a sudden at the door to our house. Only the elders, only the shamans can cross themselves there. You are a little puppy. You are a little piglet. Don't cross yourself in vain.

"Don't you see, we aren't all of us sitting there every day watching who passes by. It may be that you will come across a strong-hearted person there. Then you will get a beating. While you are walking about carrying your firewood, you may slip and fall. Or you may come upon one of our little servants, the snakes. Our servants come out every Thursday, every Sunday. They relax by the door to our house," he told me.

"I just crossed myself like a poor little dog, a poor little pig, sir!"

The gentleman had a long white beard. He was leaning back in his chair.

"See here, young lady, you are right indeed to respect me, but don't pray at length like that. Just say 'God, My Lord,' as you pass by."

"I'm just exceeding my authority by crossing myself," I said.

"You see, young lady, it isn't always me who is watching over you at dusk and at dawn. Sometimes I go to visit my other friends. If I'm not there, you'll just get a beating. Don't pray in vain as you go by. Forget it! Continue on, minding your own business! Why do you have to talk to me, speaking as you do? How would you know how to pray?"

"All right, sir. Thank you for letting me know. I had thought it was possible for me to pray, as I say. It was just that I passed right by the door to your house.

> May I pass before Thy beauteous face,
>   Thy beauteous eyes,
> My Lord,

I said as I passed."

How would I know that he would be displeased? It's because I'm not a shaman. I'm just a little woodgatherer. I just crossed myself the way we cross ourselves before Our Lord in church. I don't know the proper way. I'm just an ignorant person. My soul saw it clearly. It's probably because my soul is clever. Who knows. I know he told me.

I talked about it with my neighbor, Mother Akux. She was still alive then.

"It doesn't want to be visited," she said. "Who knows what the Earth Lord's heart is like. Did you remember the cane liquor for them, you stupid loafer? Forget it, you don't have to pass by in front of the cross."

"It was because so many pines had fallen there. The wood was good and dry. I like to have the dead ones."

"Do you think firewood is so scarce, you stupid loafer? Do you want to break your leg or one of your arms?"

I don't cross myself anymore. I pass by like a fool. No fuss. What if I were to make a mistake!

I never carried firewood from there again.

I Am Getting Married and
Leave Him on the Trail

You've seen Maryan Chiku''s yard? There used to be two paths that ran through the middle of it. I was standing where the two paths crossed, under the pear tree.

I was getting married. I had a fine new feathered robe. My shawl was the shawl that I was to be married in, of course. My outer skirt was brand new. But the skirt I wore on the inside was old and faded.

"Oh, My Lord, if the hem of my outer skirt turns up, people will see that my inner skirt is faded. This isn't good at all, My Lord! It's better if I don't walk.

"Stop!" I told my fiancé.

I didn't recognize the man I was supposed to marry. "And where is the house I'm going to? Why am I standing in the middle of the path, My Lord? I'd better go home.

"Stand aside!" I said. I abandoned my husband. I left him standing in the middle of the path.

I hoisted up my robe and arrived home in a rush. My mother wasn't there. I was alone. How could I imagine that my mother would be there, since she was already dead?

I called my neighbor. "Mother Akux, Mother Akux, please come and unbind my hair for me. My head is terribly tired being bound up like this."

"Why is your hair bound? Who are you marrying? Where is your husband, Chep?" she asked me.

"He's gone to work," I said. "I don't know why I need to marry someone else. How many men do I want? I'm just so disgusting!"

"That awful husband of yours is just skin and bones, daughter, skin and bones. Is your nose still as pink as a baby's that you are looking for another man? And you with two children! Where are the children?"

Now I was worried about the children. I had put them to sleep in the place where I was getting married. But in the end it wasn't on the earth's surface. It was in my dream.

I unbraided my hair. I took off my headress. I wrapped it up in a white cloth. I took off my robe. I folded it and put it away. I took off my outer skirt and kept the faded one on.

My husband-to-be was left standing in the middle of the path, in his new pants, his new shirt, his black hat, his shawl.

They say it's bad if we dream we are getting married. "Why do you dream such awful things?" my neighbor said. "Who knows if you won't get divorced sometime?"

It was no lie. I never thought I would get divorced. My children are grown. How could I know that man would slowly get jealous. If I were chatting the way I'm chatting now, Holy Mary, I couldn't do it! The old man is very wrong-headed.

It was thirty-two years ago when I had that dream. I had two children already. My mother had died. And I was going to have her take off my robe!

That husband of mine had gone to the lowlands. I was sleeping alone with my children. But I was getting married to another man!

I Go Selling and Am Left Behind

I went to San Andrés. I went to buy beans. I went to buy chayote roots. I was going to sell them in Tuxtla.

I finished buying all my beans. My bag of beans was ready. I had a basket of chayote roots and a crate of passion fruit.

But I never found a truck that would take me. The driver of the truck wanted to charge me for making a special trip.

"But I know you. It isn't the first time you've taken me," I told the truck driver.

"That may be, ma'am, but you have to pay fifty pesos for the trip. That's how much it costs."

"But I won't make any profit if I pay you fifty pesos. Forget it! It's not worth it. I'll go tomorrow if you'll take me when you go."

Do you know Old Manuel? He's very fat and he has a few black spots on his face. He arrived.

"What are you doing, Tonita?" he asked me.

"I'm not doing anything, don Manuel. I'm waiting for the truck. Do you think it will leave early tomorrow?"

"Early! It leaves at four-thirty in the morning."

"Please wake me up then, if you hear it coming."

"All right. Don't worry!" he told me.

I spent the night by the courthouse door. I didn't have my straw mat with me. I was rolled up in my blanket. I made a pillow of my beans. I stacked my passion fruit on top of my chayote roots.

I slept. I didn't ever sleep for long. I woke up early. I heard the hum of the truck coming.

"Please take me!" I said.

"All right, hand up your things!" said the truck driver. My things went up. I climbed up.

"How much will you take me for?"

"Fifty centavos for your things, a peso for you."

"Let's go, then!" I said. "Please!"

"Where are you getting off?" he asked me.

"I'm getting off at the market in San Cristóbal," I said.

"Aren't you getting off here at the fork?"

"No, I'm not getting off at the fork. I'm going to Tuxtla. Don Ramiro is waiting in San Cristóbal. He will drive me to Tuxtla."

But instead of letting me off in San Cristóbal, he stopped in Chamula.

"But how could Chamula be my home? Didn't I tell you to take me to San Cristóbal?"

"Then you'll have to pay six pesos more," he told me.

"All right. I'll pay it," I said. I gave him the other four pesos.

I arrived in San Cristóbal. I got off at the edge of Merced Market. They left my box and my bags in a pile.

Then that old car of Old Margarito's came along.

"Well, don Margarito, are you going to take me to Tuxtla?" I asked.

"All right!" he said. "Hand up your things!" My things went up. They were stacked.

As for me, I was left standing there. My things went. But I, myself, was left behind.

"My Lord, my money, my chayote roots, my beans, my passion fruit! I've lost a lot of money this way, My Lord! What can I buy now to take with me?

"Ah, never mind, it's Old Margarito. They won't be lost. They'll arrive at his house. My passion fruit will rot. My chayote roots will rot. But nothing will happen to my beans."

And I left at noon on the second-class bus.

I arrived in Chiapa. I went to Old Margarito's house.

"Don't worry, Tonita, here are your things," said Old Margarito's wife. "Margarito unloaded them here, since I saw you weren't coming."

I was delighted now.

"Tomorrow, then, you'll take me to Tuxtla in the truck," I said.

Where was the truck? It was in my dream!

And where were my beans?

They were gone. There was nothing. My dream was probably that way because I worry when I get my load, wherever I go.

I didn't even have my money. Who knows where I'd find the money. Where would it appear? It was my dream!

It's probably because I'm worried. If I had some money I'd go buy beans to sell. I'd see if they bought the runner beans or not. Sometimes they buy the kinds of beans that grow in San Andrés. They are being harvested now.

"It won't be long before they appear here, since I dreamt about them," I said to myself.

I Am Falsely Accused in Court
and Am Finally Vindicated

I dreamt the principals came to put me in jail. They said I was stealing corn, stealing chickens, stealing beans.

"You are going to enter the house of darkness," I was told in my dream.

"But I never steal corn and beans. I never steal chickens. Why do I need chickens? I have my own chickens. Even if there is just one, but I have my own chicken."

"Ma'am! You are supposed to come and hear the command, says the magistrate."

"What might he say? The magistrate is like a father to me. That's where I gained my understanding. Is someone there who has accused me?"

"Old Nixyo Kontzares says you stole his chickens, you stole his corn. You went to steal his beans."

"I'm not like his sons who steal!" I replied.

"That's right, ma'am. You have nothing to be afraid of, nothing to be ashamed of if you haven't stolen anything. But if you have carried off stolen goods, then of course you'd be afraid!" the awful principals told me.

"Let's go!" I said. "You go on ahead, I'll come along right behind."

But I didn't arrive at the courthouse. It was an ordinary house. Six prefects were sitting there. But my friend the magistrate wasn't among them. In my dream the grand alcalde was the magistrate.

There was a row of hands to be met in greeting.

"What do they say is my crime, sir? What do they say is my evil, sir?" I asked the magistrate.

"Old Nixyo says you broke into his house, young lady. He says you took his corn and his beans."

"So now that my hair has grown white I go opening houses! I never opened a house when I was a girl. You can laugh if there is a witness, if somebody saw me."

"What better witness is there, ma'am? That corn of his is your witness. Those beans of his are your witness, since you took them!"

"Have them search my house!" I said. "If they are found there, then, yes, indeed, he can say such things about me. Let me have one or two of your constables and one of your justices of the peace. Have them go see what I've stolen!"

"Old Nixyo says you have covered up that chicken in a basket."

"God, My Lord, Jesus Christ, Saint Lawrence, but I have never stolen anything. I'm not yet a pauper, a beggar to be coming to steal from my father or my mother."

"Old Nixyo! Go along with the lady. Have her hand over that corn and those beans of yours. Because of course they're there," the magistrate said.

"That's right! Have her carry them back here!" said Old Nixyo Kontzares.

"But compadre, do you realize what you are saying about me? Is this the first time that I say, 'my holy companion, my holy compadre?'—that you come and accuse me falsely of robbery?"

"Of course not, comadre! Of course not! Even though you probably haven't stolen anything, just let them look in your house for my things that are missing. Because I found my house open," he said. That time he made a slip!

We left in a procession. In front were the principals, the justice of the peace, and right behind, the owner of the corn and beans.

They looked in my house. But they didn't find anything, not the least thing, not even a needle.

"Is this yours?" he was asked about my corn.

"My corn isn't like that," he said.

"Are the beans yours?"

"These are San Cristóbal beans," he told them. "My beans are round beans. My corn is round-kernelled corn. This corn is from the lowlands. And besides, this corn is white corn, but my corn is yellow."

"Is this your chicken?" he was asked. I had a speckled hen then. It has died since.

"That isn't it!" he said.

"What you want is a good beating! What you want is a good jailing! Have the lady give you a few clouts. She had to take the trouble to come here for nothing."

"What if my heart were the same as yours, coming to shame me, coming to mortify me? You hair is white, you stupid old man. You are good for nothing. Shame on you, you red-whiskered old man coming with your white thighs to accuse me falsely of robbery! Your face is like your old woman's ass.

"Shame on you, you stupid old man. You're acting like a baby, you're acting like a child. You are just a pimp for your daughter! I don't steal things. I don't do anything bad. If I find what I need to live on, I find it. But if I don't find it, if I have to die of starvation, then I die of starvation, rather than go stealing from my father or my mother."

"But Old Chep K'o told me, 'That's where your corn went. That's where your beans went,' when he looked in my divining basket."

"Ah, of course, you asked your basket! I don't look at baskets," I said. "Only Our Lord knows. Our Lord alone has seen if my things are lost. My chickens disappear too. My turkeys disappear too. I lose my things, but I've never picked fights. I've never accused another person falsely. You've lost your senses over this, you stupid old man. Your old woman has made you lose your wits."

"Forget it, ma'am. Forget it, young lady. Don't lose your temper. It's not worth it. He's just maligned you," said the magistrate.

"Please put him in jail for me or he will get in the habit of coming to lie about my crimes. I want him to have a week of punishment. Have him clean the ditch next to the Chapel of Esquipulas."

"Stick him in jail!" said the magistrate.

Old Nixyo was put in jail. I came back home laughing.

My Child's Carrying Cloth Is Covered with Caterpillars

I went to the stream. I did my wash.

I came back from the stream. I spread out my child's carrying cloth at my neighbor's gate.

But the cloth was completely covered with caterpillars.

I shook the cloth. I flicked a few of them off. But the cloth was black with poisonous spines.

"I'd better get my cotton shawl," I said to myself. "I'll carry my child in it."

But my shawl was crawling with horrible lice. "My Lord, why are my shawl and my child's cloth covered with caterpillars and lice? How can I carry my child?

"I guess I'll simply get my worn-out gray blanket." I ripped the blanket in two.

My child woke up. I held it. I changed it.

I carried my child in the little old torn blanket.

"Forget it," I said to myself. "I'll go boil my cabbage. My husband will come back soon to eat."

I cooked my cabbage. My beans were ready. I added the salt and the leeks. I ground the chili for my beans. Then my husband arrived from gathering firewood. I gave him his meal.

"Why are you carrying your child in that, wife?" he asked me. "It looks like an old Chamulan woman's blanket."

"Oh be quiet, the child's cloth is all covered with caterpillars and my shawl is all covered with lice. How do you think I'm to carry my child if I haven't a good cloth?"

"Boil some water! Scald those lice or our bugs will multiply. They'll surely say we live like beggars," my husband said.

I boiled some water. I scalded them. But the awful stinging caterpillars wouldn't come off. They had simply ruined my baby's cloth.

"Since my shawl is free of lice, I'll spread it out, and when it's dry I'll carry my child with that. Later I'll weave a replacement for the carrying cloth. The trouble is, I haven't the money to pay for the thread."

"Never mind, I'll earn it by working," said my husband.

I simply carried my child in the little old blanket and in my shawl. That's how I raised him.

When I woke up the next morning, I went to cry in the Church of Saint Lawrence. "Saint Lawrence, Saint Dominic, what could my soul, my spirit be saying? Could it mean that my child will die?" With a five centavo candle I went to cry to Our Holy Father, Christ.

"Don't be anxious, foolish one!" he told me in my dream that night. "It's because the gentleman above the spring is tormenting you." That's the way he answered me. Yes!

The gentleman above the spring was tormenting me.

I know who is above the spring!

I Try Crossing a River, Am Covered with Lime, Am Given Food, I Fall

"Let's go to San Cristóbal!" my mother told me.

But there was a river pouring over the trail.

"I'll never get across this, mother. Never! I don't know how to swim. The only thing that will happen to me is that I'll go and die."

But the porter on the riverbank kept shouting, "Cross over! Cross over! I'll lead you."

I tried crossing over, but the water was too deep. I reached the middle of the river and then waded back to shore.

When I climbed out, the river mud didn't look like mud. It had turned to lime. My legs were bright white.

I went into a house. I climbed the stairs to the second floor. No one was there. When I reached the third floor, I heard a voice.

"Come in! Sit down! Would you like to eat?" a Ladina asked me.

"No, I didn't come because I was hungry," I said. "I was just coming to sell my chicken eggs. But I met an old man on the trail. He told me, 'Come on! Cross over!' I got half way across the river—look how my legs are from it! Both my legs are simply caked with lime."

"You were foolish to have gone into the river. You should have grabbed the old man and pushed him down," the Ladina told me.

"But you see, I lost my head. I should have picked up a stick and whacked him. It's not as if he was my father, coming to order me about. He forced me to cross the river. Now it is his fault. I washed my legs with water, but the lime wouldn't come off. Now my legs are going to split open. They will bleed."

"Don't be afraid! They won't bleed. Here is some medicine for it." She gave me a clear liquid in a bottle. "Rub it on! You'll see tomorrow. Your legs won't be white anymore like the lime that is covering them now.

"Don't go yet! Stay! I'll take your chicken eggs," she told me. She said she'd give me six pesos for fifteen eggs.

"No, I'll give you a new price. The cost of your meal will be deducted."

"Why should I pay for my meal?" I said. "If you give it to me, then give it to me! But as for paying for it with my chicken eggs, no! I still have to buy corn with them."

"There's no reason for you to go to San Cristóbal. I'll give you a lot of tortillas. For two or three days you'll be eating the tortillas I give you."

"I won't be satisfied with the tortillas you give me. I won't get full on them," I said.

But you see, I ate her food. My stomach was full. And she gave me more to take with me, wrapped up in a tortilla cloth. Besides the tortillas, there were some sausages and meat. That's what I was supposed to live on for a long time.

After I took my food, I opened a hatch in the loft and fell into a hole. I landed sitting down, with my legs doubled under me. "Now I've broken my leg," I said to myself.

I didn't feel as if I had fallen. But when I opened my eyes I saw that I was sitting deep inside the earth.

"How am I going to climb out of here? My children will suffer indeed, My Lord!" I prayed.

Then I saw a rope. I held on to it and I climbed up.

"Huh! Disgusting reeking cunt, horrible stinking ass of a Ladina! You never wipe your ass! That's why you are tormenting me like this. Why did you toss me down that hole? Do you think I have any use for your tortillas? Here, eat them!" I picked up my tortilla gourd and my shawl and I left.

I was still gabbing when my son, Antun, woke me up. It was late at night. "Oh, oh, oh!" I was saying in my sleep.

"What's happening to you, mother?"

"I was dreaming that I was being thrown down inside a great big house," I said.

"Who did you see earlier today? Who did you meet on the trail? She certainly hates you!" my boy said.

You see, there was a fiesta yesterday. And so I changed my clothes. I don't have many skirts. This one is patched. The other is new. I put on my new skirt, a new blouse, and a new shawl. Of course people probably resent it.

Throwing me into a cave like that!

It wasn't a witch. It was a Ladina. The disgusting people in San Cristóbal resent my not asking them for anything.

They resent it if you eat. They resent it if you have money. They resent it if you own a house. They want you to be naked. They don't want you to have anything. It displeases them.

They want to be the only ones who can eat!

My Hair Falls Out, I Gather Firewood, I Fly

I went to the stream to wash my hair. I came back home to comb my hair.

The next time I looked, I was bald. "Why don't I have any hair, My Lord?" All I had was my scalp.

I turned around. I looked behind me. Now I had hair! "I'm probably going mad!" I said to myself.

I started to comb it. Holy Mary! It was coming out in my comb. I used to have lots of hair. It wasn't a little pig's tail the way it is now!

Oh, my hair was coming out in clumps. My head was as smooth as a ceremonial gourd.

"But what can I cover this with, My Lord? Even if I covered my head with my shawl, people would make fun of me. 'Why does she have a gourd for a head?' they would say about me," I said in my heart, in my dream.

I picked up an old rag and wrapped it around my head. I covered the rag with my shawl. Then I took my tumpline, my ropes, my pad and I went off to gather firewood. But when I returned with my load, my neighbor said to me, "Why is your head bald?"

"Because all my hair fell out," I said.

"Oh, get out of my way, stupid loafer. Go to bed!"

"Of course I'll go to bed! The sun's set," I said.

I ate, and then I went to sleep. I dreamt I was gathering firewood at Little Muxul Mountain. I found a pine stump there. I dug up all the roots. I stripped off all the rotten bark. Just the red heart of the wood was left. I bound up my wood and carried it back. I climbed over our fence and set the pine down by the live oak tree.

Then I flew off. I landed in the live oak tree on the side of Muxul Mountain.

"Tonik, why in the world are you flying?" I was asked. "Why did you leave your pine in a heap?"

I flew back to get my pine. Then I woke up in my dream. It was already light.

I picked up my load and carried it home. I made a tiny corral of my pine. I stacked it four-square by the side of the house. Then I woke up on the earth's surface.

I told my mother the next day, "I dreamt that my hair fell out. I dreamt that I flew."

"Oh, I'm about to perish, daughter! I'm about to die for sure! Be happy! You'll be left alone. There won't be anyone to scold you. There won't be anyone to criticize you," said my mother.

God, I started to cry when my mother told me that. I felt terrible that my mother should die from that dream.

For exactly six months she was fine. In the seventh month, on the ninth of January, my mother died. It was the little cold, the little chills. My mother would warm herself by the fire. She had no strength left. She kept vomiting. After she vomited, she fell over next to the fire. Her nostrils were buried in the ashes. God! My mother's time had come. We gave her purges for three days. It did no good.

You see, the dream came true. I flew a little. All my hair fell out. My mother died. I became an orphan. Whatever I dream always comes true.

My Tooth Falls Out

I dreamt that one of my teeth fell out.

I was cupping it in my hand.

I stuck it back in. It grew firm.

"My tooth is fine. My tooth hasn't anything wrong with it now," I said to myself.

I was eating well. I had nothing to worry about.

My tooth was fixed like that. They've been fine ever since.

None have come out again.

Who knows why we dream that. It's said that our husbands will die. It's said that our children will die. But nobody of mine has died yet from that tooth falling out. No one!

I Am Naked, My Skirt Disappears

I went to the river to soak my laundry. I took off my blouse. I took off my skirt.

I changed my skirt. I tied my sash. I was wearing my skirt properly.

I finished washing my clothes. I finished wringing them out. When I climbed up the riverbank and reached the trail, I saw that one side of my skirt was torn and flapping.

"Why is my skirt like this?" I said to myself. I felt my waist. No skirt now! I was naked.

"Thank God my blouse is long! The awful men will stare at me, naked as I am, My Lord."

I tried to pull my blouse down. My blouse was too short. Now my blouse just came down to my middle. My left breast was poking out. I wrapped my shawl around me, because I was ashamed.

Then my old godfather, Maryan K'ohcho', came along.

"Why are you wearing your shawl that way? What's the reason?" he asked.

"Don't mention that, father! I don't know how—while I was just standing on the bank—my skirt disappeared. That's why I wrapped myself in my shawl. If you think I have my sash, it's the poor cord of my shawl that I'm using to tie around my waist!"

"Lord, what in the world is the matter with you, daughter? Where did you put it? Who stole it? Could you not have seen who stole it from you?"

"I didn't notice where it went. I changed my clothes properly. I tied my skirt properly. I shampooed my hair carefully. When I finished my wash, my skirt was gone. I was walking around naked."

"Go get one, then! You must have an old skirt at home. Is this the time to be walking around naked? People are abroad now. It's late afternoon. I'm going to bring in the mules," my godfather told me.

I hurried home.

I spread out my wash. I combed my hair. I had an old skirt, covered with patches. The trouble was, I had no sash.

I picked up my son's little sash. It was too short. I fastened a leather belt around my waist, but it wouldn't do.

"I'll simply go to Mother Loxa's house and ask her to weave a sash for me. How could I get along without a sash?" I said as I left.

Then my husband woke me. "What are you saying? Gabbing away, you loafer! Get up! It's growing light."

One of my children had died recently. I was carrying the baby. She was six months old.

"What are you doing, gabbing away? Get up! Grind the corn, you loafer!'

I got up to light my fire. I was crying now about being naked.

"What could it mean, My Lord? Are my children going to die? Why was I without my skirt?" I said to myself at dawn.

"Hurry up, you bitch, with the tears streaming down your cheeks! I'm going to gather firewood. Fix my tortillas."

My firewood gatherer went off to the woods. I was left to cry by myself. Sitting at the foot of my metate, I prayed.

God, My Lord,
   What could my soul, my spirit mean?
Will another of my children die?
   Which one of my children will die?
I am suffering,
   I am wretched, My Lord.
I can't bear the loss,
   I can't bear the bereavement.
If my children die, My Lord,
   It feels as if I myself were dying.

Then my crying subsided.
   "Never mind," I said to myself. I finished grinding. I went out to feed my chickens after he left me with a scolding because of what I dreamt.

I Go to Chenalhó, I Am Cheated on the Bus,
Stranded on the Road

I went to Chenalhó the day before yesterday. I went to buy oranges, to buy sweet lemons, to buy guavas, to buy bananas.
   The thing is, it's a help if there's a bus.
   "Oh, I know what's missing—it's my sugar. I don't have the sugar for my corn gruel," I said to myself.
   I left the spot where I was waiting for the bus. I retraced my steps and went to get the sugar.
   The sugar looked like little cakes of wax. I didn't want it like that. How would I know how to measure it? How big a piece should be put in my pot of gruel? The sugar was in hard brown blocks. "Ah, forget it. I'll buy some in San Cristóbal," I said to myself.
   The Chenalhó bus appeared.
   "Are you going to San Cristóbal?" I asked.
   "San Cristóbal," said the driver.
   "Please take my things, then." I had my bag of oranges, my sweet lemons, my basket of bananas, and my passion fruit.
   "How much will you take me for?"
   "Six pesos," he told me.
   "Do you think San Pedro Chenalhó is as far as Tuxtla?" I said.

"It's six pesos from Tuxtla to San Cristóbal. But this is from Chenalhó to San Cristóbal."

"It's the same. It's eighteen leagues or so," said the driver.

"Why is it eighteen leagues? Tuxtla is further away. San Pedro is nearer."

"Is it of no use your being old now?" he said. "Don't you remember? You know that San Pedro is further away, that Tuxtla is nearer."

"Are you harrassing me like this because you see I'm an Indian? Tuxtla has always been further away than San Pedro!"

"Forget it, then! With your baggage you can go for five pesos."

"Well, that'll probably be all right," I said. I got into the bus. But you see, he left me off at the fork.

"How are my things going to get home, with me at the fork?" I said to myself. "Now that Maryan Ok'il had a fight with my son, he'll never pick me up. Who could I send off to tell my daughters, so that one of them will come and meet me?

"I'll simply go to the house of the Chamulan who lives at Window Pass. I know him. I'll leave my fruit there for safekeeping, because I won't speak to the truck driver."

I left my sacks of fruit at the Chamulan's house. I was walking along on the other side of the ridge with my little basket of bananas.

I never reached home. The river had flooded. The bridge had collapsed. I couldn't cross over. I woke up.

I thought it over on the earth's surface. "If I go to San Cristóbal now, just before the Day of the Dead, the road will probably be flooded. Then I'll have to go the long way around.

"This is not a good thing. Trucks and cars won't get through. And it's terribly roundabout on foot. It's impossible for us to travel," I said in bed. "That's why I dreamt that."

"Ah, don't keep fretting! Do you have anything important to worry about? Are we going to eat lots of sugar, just the two of us?" my Petu' asked me.

Just like when she worried when you left, Lol. "Can you get over that part of the road where it's bad? What if you have to spend the night alone?" she asked you.

"What if something happens to him, mother? If Lol spends the night there, what if someone kills him in his car?" That girl frets too much. Yes!

"No, he won't be killed. He'll get by, of course!" I said.

She went outside to listen. "You hear, mother, the car sounds as if it's stuck. If he has to spend the night there, when is he going to get his coffee? When is he going to get his food?" she kept saying to me.

"If we had someone to keep us company, daughter, we'd go down to look," I said. "But listen, he's gone around the bend now."

She went out to watch for you, to see if you were coming back, to see if anything happened to you. She just worries too much. That's why she said that to me. She saw I wasn't fretting over my sugar.

I dreamt it the day before yesterday. I was worried because I need my fruit. I need all the things that are necessary for the Day of the Dead.

That's what our custom is. We buy bananas, oranges, sweet lemons, passion fruit, peanuts, sugar, meat. Everything we eat, the spirits of the dead eat too.

We wait for the spirits' souls. Yes!

I Am Attacked by a Spook or Was It Saint Michael?

I don't believe what they say in our town about the talking god.

My husband went to play music for him on the earth's surface. "I'll be back. I'm going to play at our compadre, Manvel Okotz's house," my children's father told me. That's where the talking god lives.

"Go on, what do I need you for? The devil's your father!" I said.

"Wait and see, he'll come to grab you in your bed, talking that way against Our Lord! He's Our Lord, he's not the devil," he told me when he left.

He was right. It was no lie.

"Flap, flap, flap, flap," went his horrible wings next to my house.

"That's the Spook, daughter. You'd better see if our door is fastened tight." My house just has a stick to hold the door shut.

"It's firmly in place, mother. Don't worry! Go to sleep!" my daughter told me.

First he tried to open my door. Then the awful Spook was standing at my little window. He was thrusting his ugly hand in. His horrible fingernails were this long! "Open the door!" he told me.

He was walking into my house now. He came to grab me in my bed. He was scratching me with his horrible fingernails.

"Get your horrible fingernails off me, you disgusting thing! You're the devil. How could you be god? You are temptation." I spat on him. "Stinking, stinking, disgusting witch, devil, temptation!"

I started to say the prayers, "Ave Maria Purisima!" I said the catechism, "Our Father who art in heaven." You could hear me saying the catechism so the Spook wouldn't grab me.

But it wasn't the Spook—it was that horrible talking saint. He was offended because I called him a devil.

I don't believe in him. That's why my husband told me, "He'll come and grab you."

When he went to play at the house, he prayed.

> Señor San Miguelito,
>   How are you?
> I've come to play Thy tunes.
>   I've come to play Thy songs.
> Wilt Thou give me Thy grace?
>   Wilt Thou give me Thy blessing?
> Because I have come from quarreling,
>   From fighting with my wife. My wife said,
> 'Go and see your father, the devil.
>   Go and see your father, the demon.

He said that when he arrived at the house of the talking saint. That's why the talking saint came to startle me. That's why he pushed against my door and frightened me in my bed.

He's nothing less than the devil!

Thatch-roofed house and corn fields of Zinacantán. Photograph by Robert M. Laughlin

Crosses at La Ventana (Window Pass), at the entrance to Zinacantán Center. Photograph by Marcey Jacobson

Anselmo Peres, a shaman, offering prayers and incense during a curing ceremony. Photograph by Jeffrey Jay Foxx

Spook at the Fiesta of Saint Sebastian. Photograph by Frank Cancian

Stewards in the Church of Saint Lawrence, Zinacantán Center. Photograph by John Swope

Young woman making tortillas. Photograph by Jeffrey Jay Foxx

Zinacantec women gathering wood. Photograph by Jeffrey Jay Foxx

Procession of musicians and stewards leaving the Church of Saint Lawrence, Zinacantán Center. Photograph by John Swope

Xun Vaskis and his wife, Paxku, in their backyard in Naben Chauk (Thunder-bolt Lake). Photograph by Jeffrey Jay Foxx

Robert M. Laughlin sharing a drink with Petul Vaskis, the son of Xun and Paxku Vaskis. Photograph by John Swope

The Burden of Days

TALES

Holy heaven,
   Holy glory,
Holy earth,
   Holy ground,
Holy king,
   Holy angel,
Holy serpent,
   Holy Thunderbolt,
My beauteous Father,
   My beauteous Lord.

When the Guatemalans Were Blown Sky High

Long ago the people of Guatemala used to be very evil. Long ago the people of Zinacantán went there to trade. They went to Tabasco to buy tobacco. They went to sell it in Guatemala.

The people in Guatemala seized all the traders and stuck them in jail. They were given cane liquor to drink.

When the Zinacantecs drank all the cane liquor they could drink, they collapsed in a heap.

Then their balls were cut off. In their drunkenness they didn't feel their balls coming off. They were turned into eunuchs, they were turned into oil.

That's how a tremendous number of people disappeared. They were fattened up in jail.

Four elders discussed it together, since they saw that people just vanished in Guatemala.

They thought it over to see if they could do anything—if each one of them had something in his heart.

"How can it be that all our countrymen perish in Guatemala? You, don't you know something? Can't we defend each other? Can't we find out why they die?"

"Well, I know a little," said one.

"But what do you know?" asked the others.

"Me, I'm Whirlwind."

"Ah!" said the others.

"As for you, don't you know something?"

"Me, I know a little. I'm Thunderbolt of course!"

"And you, what do you know?" they asked the next one.

"Me, I'm Hawk."

"Well, it can be done with that," they said.

"And as for you?" they asked the fourth elder.

"Me, I can be Blowfly."

"Hell, it's fine for playing with them now! We have nothing to worry about! Let's go see if they're eating them, or what in the world they're doing to our countrymen that they keep disappearing."

It was a serious affair now. The four elders went off together to look for a good spot. They found a big cave under a cliff. The cave took the place of their house.

First they sent off a butterfly. "Go, Butterfly!" said Thunderbolt and Whirlwind. "See what they have done to our countrymen."

Butterfly flapped by the barracks door. He saw the soldiers.

He looked through the jail door. All our countrymen were packed in prison.

He flew back.

"What did you see?" asked Thunderbolt.

"The soldiers are just scattered about, enjoying themselves. Our countrymen are there, indeed! They're packed inside the jail."

"Nothing's happening? There's no war?"

"No," said Butterfly.

"Now you go, Hawk! Pick out the fattest hens and roosters. We'll fix a meal. We'll eat well before we leave," said Thunderbolt and Whirlwind.

Hawk went to each house to pick out the biggest roosters and very best hens. He kept on catching chickens and carrying them back to the cave. Thunderbolt, Whirlwind, and Butterfly prepared the feast.

The Guatemalans weren't too upset. They hadn't figured out yet that they had enemies—only that Hawk had stolen their chickens.

After the elders had eaten, Blowfly was sent to see what the soldiers were doing.

He arrived, buzzing, at the barracks door. Pots of food were boiling.

Blowfly laid his eggs in the cauldrons where the meals were cooking. When the cooks stirred the broth in the cauldrons, maggots came floating to the top.

They couldn't eat now. They were mad. The soldiers blew their bugles and sounded the alarm. They shouted to each other, "The enemy has come!"

Blowfly returned to the cave to tell Thunderbolt and Whirlwind. "The soldiers were happily scattered in the open. Their food was cooking. Their minds were at ease. But I laid eggs in the broth. The cooks stirred it. The maggots came rising up. Maggots. Then they went mad. They blew their bugles. All the soldiers gathered at the barracks. The whole town has assembled. They're ready," said Blowfly.

"Well, we have nothing to worry about! Let's go!"

Thunderbolt and Whirlwind entered Guatemala. "What did you come looking for?" they were asked by the guards.

"We're just taking a trip," said the elders. They had brought along a little something to sell so they would look like traders. "We want to speak to our friends whom we see shut up in jail."

"Okay, talk to them!"

"What's the matter, friends? What happened to you?" they asked when they arrived at the jail.

"We're shut up here because we're going to be killed, we're going to be turned into oil. Our balls have been cut off. And as for you, you'll die here with us, because it's too late. Every one of our countrymen who comes dies here. They are castrated before they die."

"Don't worry, we'll get out!" said Thunderbolt and Whirlwind. "They've had their way persecuting us so much."

"But what can you do? We haven't been able to win. Who knows if you can!" said the prisoners who were packed inside the jail.

"You'll see what kind of game will be played today," said Thunderbolt and Whirlwind. "Just watch the spectacle. Don't be afraid."

"As for you two, you're going to jail!" Thunderbolt and Whirlwind were told.

"Are we guilty of anything?" they asked.

"You aren't guilty of anything, but take a rest, join your friends anyway!" said the soldiers.

"All right, then. But first we want to sell our things."

They sold them. And for as long as they could they chatted with their friends.

Then they were stuck in jail.

A jug of strong cane liquor was set down in front of Thunderbolt. He drank and drank until he had drunk the entire jug. Another jug came. He finished it. Another one. He finished it.

"Why doesn't he get drunk?" said the soldiers. "He must know something special."

They gave him another jug. Thunderbolt thought to himself, "But that's enough. It looks as if I'll collapse." He toppled over.

The soldiers came. There was a hole dug way down where Thunderbolt had been sitting. When he drank the cane liquor, it ran right through him. He pissed into the hole.

"Look what kind of trick this Indian was pulling! It isn't as if it stayed in his belly—it poured into the ground!

"But it makes no difference now, because he's gotten drunk. Now we'll cut off his balls."

Since he had collapsed on the ground, Thunderbolt looked as if he hadn't heard.

The soldiers brought a pocketknife. When those balls of his were grabbed, then he felt it very well. The soldiers were squatting next to him. The pocketknife was put against his balls.

Thunderbolt let go a fart, but a mighty one. Those castrators were finished! Thunderbolt was suddenly cracking. He smashed the whole jail.

Then Whirlwind came. He smashed the whole barracks. Whirlwind picked up all the guns. He picked up all the soldiers and tossed them and turned them high in the sky. They landed far off, face up. He scattered all the houses. The whole square, all the buildings were ruined.

Our countrymen were free.

They came back home together, but they had started to swell. Nothing could be done, since they were already castrated.

That's how the affair ended. Since then there have been no more wars with Guatemala.

Today they don't do anything to us, because there were mighty elders who defended us long ago. That's why some still say that Zinacantán is so terribly strong—because Zinacantecs can be Thunderbolts and Whirlwinds. They know the tale about olden times to this day.

—Romin Teratol

War between the Cricket and the Jaguar

Once Cricket spoke. Wherever it walked, face down on the path, in the fields, in the woods it couldn't be seen. It was little.

Jaguar came striding along.

Cricket was face down on the trail. Lord, Jaguar's paw stepped on the cricket.

Cricket spoke. "Don't you have any eyes that you just stepped on me and left me very ill?"

"Hell, what big deal are you? You can die, you can perish. Don't you know this is my trail?" said Jaguar.

"It's hardly your own path. All of us who travel share the path. But no, you wanted to punish me. Well, all right, thank you for squashing me. But are you as strong as a man?" said Cricket.

"I am as strong as a man," roared Jaguar. "How could I respect you? You're a good-for-nothing size. You're useless. You're tiny!"

"Never mind my size. At least I see what I'm doing!"

What can you do—Jaguar squashed him again.

"Now that's the second time you squashed me," squealed Cricket. "You don't care about me.

"We'll set aside a day, then. Get your troops! We'll have a battle. We'll wage war."

"We'll do it!" said Jaguar. "Where will we meet?"

"I'll wait for you here on the trail. I'll show you how many of my troops I can muster. We'll see if you can win."

"I'll win!" said Jaguar. "Hell, why wouldn't I win. Our Lord made me strong. I'm the strongest there is. There's no one else as strong as me. As for you, you're terribly little. Your little mouth just goes 'squeak, squeak' when you call at night, but that's nothing. Me, I roar loudly wherever I go."

"You're brave because you have a deep voice. You don't respect me because my tiny mouth just squeaks when I call. But I sing a pretty song. I don't scold. I don't say anything mean. I'm good-natured," said Cricket.

"You just wake up people, calling in their ears. 'Squeak, squeak!' That's all you're good for."

"Well, they think it's worth it that I sing my pretty song. You're brave when you roar, but you only roar in the woods, far away. All right, we'll wage war!"

They set aside a day. When Jaguar arrived with his troops, little Cricket was waiting all alone on the trail. His army was hiding.

"Come and kill me!" said Cricket. "If I'm killed, my troops won't come out at all. If I'm killed, they won't have a leader."

"If you die, forgive me when our souls talk together. You'll surely die!" said Jaguar.

"You'll die!" they told each other.

Jaguar's troops advanced. They were snakes. The snakes came

slithering with their jaws gaping. When they rushed to swallow Cricket, little Cricket jumped.

One snake would come, Cricket would jump quickly, the snake would pass straight by.

Who knows how many times they tried. "There's nothing we can do," said the snakes. "He won't die. He's too little. We can't grab him."

"Can't you coil around him?" asked Jaguar.

"It's impossible to coil around him. He's too little."

"If he stood up a bit, I'd wrap my tail around him. I'd kill him," said one of the snakes.

"It's not possible," they all hissed.

"Go another time!" said Jaguar.

All the snakes raced toward Cricket with their jaws wide open. Just as they were about to bite him, little Cricket jumped!

"Well, you won," Jaguar told Cricket. "Let your troops come, I'll see how I do."

Cricket called his troops.

Oh, his troops covered the earth. Yellow wasps, black wasps, bumblebees. Everything that stings.

They were swarming in black clouds on Jaguar's body. They were crawling all over the snakes. The snakes were thrashing. Jaguar was rolling down the slope. His old tail whipped around. Lord, Cricket's troops didn't let up. The awful wasps, the stingers, stuck on.

Jaguar reached a steep cliff and thudded to the bottom of the gully. He stretched out straight. He died.

The snakes stretched out. They died.

"I'm the strongest!" said Cricket.

The wasps and bumblebees gathered.

"Thank you for defending me," said Cricket. "We won indeed! Now no one will bother us, no one will pester us. Build your nests. Hang them up in a hollow tree. Let little ones be born!" That's why yellow wasps hang their combs in trees. "Hang there, be happy. No one will squash us now. The terrible angry one is dead."

"Now we're good friends," they said to each other.

"I won't try to talk anymore," said Cricket. "When I talk, I make enemies. I'll just sing."

Cricket became mute. He just goes "cheel cheel" at night. That's the only voice he has.

So the world was left in good shape.
Except if a wasp gets you!

—Petul Vaskis

When Christ Was Crucified

When the world was made long ago, the holy father walked. He made the rocks and sea, corn and trees, everything there is on earth.

When he was chased by the devils he ran. But the devils were right behind him. They saw that there were trees already, peach trees, white sapotes, everything.
"Hurry up, you bastards, he's here now, he's near now.
He's planted everything already."

Our Lord ran around the world. Ooh, he was tired out. He hid under some banana trees to rest.
"He's near now," said the devils.
The magpie-jay was there. He was a human then.
"Is it Our Lord you're looking for?" asked the jay.
"He's here now. Seize him!"

They captured Our Lord. They made him carry a cross. Our Lord bent low to the ground.
They hung him on the cross. He cried. He bled.

"Let's eat! He's dead now," said the devils.
Our Lord was left hanging.

A rooster landed on the arm of the cross.
"Tell me if they are coming," said Our Lord.
"I'll climb back up the cross right away.
I have more work to do. You call out!"
"All right," said the rooster. "Cock-adoodle-doo!"
Quickly Our Lord climbed up the cross.

"Where are the devils?" he asked.
"Nowhere, they aren't coming," said the rooster.
"What are you good for?" said the Lord.
"This is what you're good for!"
He wrung the rooster's neck until it was dead.

A sparrow appeared.
"You sing out," said Our Lord.
"I'm going to work a little while."

The Lord came down from the cross. He looked for a blue pebble.
He threw it into the air. The sky was made.

The sparrow called out. Our Lord climbed up the cross.

All the devils arrived.
"He's still hanging here," they said.
"We killed him. Let's bury him."
He died. He was buried.
"We'll come back three days from now," said the devils.

"They thought I died, " said the Lord.
"But I'll revive in three days."

Living he rose to heaven. He left a substitute here on earth.
"The rooster is no good. He can be sacrificed.
The sparrow musn't be harmed," said Our Lord.

So, living, he rose to heaven.
He arrived at the right hand of the judge.

—Romin Teratol

A Visit to the Underworld

There was a man whose wife died. The man cried and cried. He went to the graveyard. He went to weep.

A man appeared. "What are you crying about?" he asked.

"I'm crying because my wife is dead."

"Do you want to see your wife?" asked the man.

"Of course I want to see her," said the husband.

"Close your eyes, then."

The husband closed his eyes. He arrived in the afterworld. There was his wife.

"Why have you come?" asked the woman.

"Because I miss you so," the husband said.

"But you aren't supposed to come yet," said his wife.

A lord appeared. "What have you come looking for?" he asked.

"I came because I miss my wife."

"I'll give you a pair of new sandals," said the lord. "When your sandals are worn out, you can return to the earth's surface. Now go catch the mule and bring it!"

"Where is the mule?" asked the man.

"There at the edge of the brook."

The man went to look for the mule. He looked hard, but he couldn't find it. He came back.

"It's not there, my lord," he said.

"Of course it's there. How could it not be there? Ask the women washing clothes. Tell them it's the priest's mule."

The man went off again. He asked the women who were washing, "Have you seen a mule anywhere?"

"What does the mule look like?" they asked.

"It's a white mule, the priest's mule."

"Oh, that's me!" said one of the women.

The woman was called the priest's mule because at her wedding, long ago, the priest snatched the groom's hat and went inside the house, shutting the girl up with him. He knelt on the hat and gave it to the girl. That's why she was called the priest's mule when she died.

"How about it, shall we go? We are supposed to haul firewood," the man said.

"But it's bones you must look for, not real firewood," said the woman. "Give me three whip lashes!"

He gave her three whip lashes. The white mule landed way off. Now it wouldn't carry its load. He gave it a good whipping.

The man returned with the firewood. But it was bones, rotten bones for warming the ghosts who had committed the worst crimes. That's why Hell is called "warmed by bones."

Soon it grew dark. "Too bad, husband, we can't sleep together," said his wife.

The man slept apart. In the middle of the night he reached out to touch his wife, but there was just a pile of bones lying there. The man was terribly frightened.

The next day his wife spoke to him. "Don't be stupid, husband, rub your sandals on a rock. Then you'll return immediately."

He rubbed his sandals on a rock. He traveled about.

There were many toilers. Whoever dies in infancy comes to suck sap. Whoever is a little older sucks on tree roots, but the blood pours from their mouths. Whoever is lazy at work goes to herd goats among the rocks, but the blood pours from their feet. Whoever longs to die has lice appear on their flesh. They are seated under a tree that is nothing but lice.

The man saw everything. The sandals wore out.

"Go back," he was told. "Go back!"

—Romin Teratol

How Rabbit Won His Hat and Sandals

Once a traveler was coming along.

He saw a dead rabbit lying on the trail. "What happened to the little rabbit?" he asked himself. He picked it up and put it in his shoulder bag.

He found a stump. He hung up his shoulder bag and went hunting. When he returned, he discovered that his rabbit was gone. Ooh, then he heard it tooting on its gourd. The rabbit had come back to life.

It went on, tooting on its gourd as it went.

Then it met a coyote. "What are you doing, little rabbit?"

"We are holding a meeting because we are going to die. If you want to be saved, I'll tie you up."

"Eh, I don't think so," said Coyote.

"I'll tie you up with a good strong rope. You'll be saved for sure!"

"All right, tie me up, then," said Coyote.

Rabbit tied Coyote to a tree trunk. Who knows how, but Rabbit had taken the man's axe with him.

"Look how sharp the axe is!" said Rabbit. "I'll try it out to see if it can cut down this pine."

He took a big chunk out of that coyote. He killed him. He pulled out his teeth.

He went off tooting on his gourd again. Then he met a woodsman. The woodsman caught Rabbit, tied him to a tree, and left him there.

A jaguar came along. "Why are you tied to that tree, little rabbit?

"It's because they want me to marry a girl. I don't want to marry her. What's more, the girl doesn't love me because I'm too little. If you would like to marry her yourself, I'll tie you up instead. The girl is very beautiful. You'd make a wonderful match."

"Why not marry her? I'm man enough!" said Jaguar.

When the woodsman returned for the rabbit, Jaguar was tied to the tree. "What are you doing here?" he asked Jaguar.

"The little rabbit tied me up. He said I could marry your daughter. I'm his successor."

"Then it's your ass I'll burn!" said the man.

In a second he stuck a red hot metal poker up Jaguar's ass.

As soon as the woodsman left, Rabbit came out from behind a bush. "Will you forgive me?" Rabbit asked Jaguar.

"I won't forgive you. A red hot metal went up my ass."

"If you will forgive me, I'll make amends."

"But I won't forgive you. My ass is punctured."

"If you'll calm down, I'll bring some ripe mangoes for you to eat."

"Go and bring them, then!"

Rabbit went up the tree. "Open your mouth wide!"

Jaguar opened his jaws wide. "But why aren't the mangoes falling down?"

Rabbit shook the tree. A hard green mango landed in Jaguar's mouth. His teeth were knocked loose.

Rabbit climbed down. "Won't you forgive me?" he asked.

The moon was round and bright. The water was rippling.

"See the cheese rippling in the water," said Rabbit. "If you calm down, I'll let you drink the juice from the cheese."

"But I won't calm down," said Jaguar. "And I won't forgive you."

Rabbit kept stirring up the water with his paw.

"I'll drink it," said Jaguar. He drank the cheese water, but he couldn't hold it in. "It's because my ass is punctured," he said.

"Let's plug it up!" said Rabbit. He plugged it up.

Jaguar guzzled the cheese water until his belly burst.

He died. Rabbit pulled out his teeth.

He went on, tooting on his gourd as he went.

Then he met a crocodile. He thought that he would kill it.

"What are you doing, little Raa-bbit?" snapped the crocodile.

"N-Nothing, uncle!" Rabbit got scared and ran away.

Crocodile gathered his friends together. They all went chasing after the rabbit.

But Rabbit changed his clothes. He was standing by a stream, drawing water with his gourd.

"Are you the one who was going to kill me?" asked Crocodile.

"It can't be me. I'm kind-hearted," said Rabbit.

"That certainly isn't him!" said Crocodile. "Who knows where he went."

"That's him over there!" said the other crocodiles.

They went to search in the woods. Who knows what got into their heads. They killed each other.

Rabbit pulled out all their teeth.

He went along, tooting on his gourd.

He arrived at the sandal maker's. "Here is the money for my sandals and hat," he said. He gave the sandal maker the animals' teeth.

"But who knows if you can walk with them."

"I can walk," said Rabbit.

"Fine," said the sandal maker. Take them, then!"

Rabbit was dressed in his new hoofs and antlers. He went deep into the forest.

A deer came along. "How much did you pay for your hat and your sandals, brother?"

"Ooh, lots!" said Rabbit.

"They look a little big. Are they comfortable?"

"Yes, indeed!" said Rabbit.

"Do you want to make a test? Let me borrow them for a minute or so," said Deer.

"No, I won't give them to you. You'll just run away."

"Give them to me for a minute, I'll try them out," said Deer over and over. Rabbit didn't pay any attention at all.

"Give them to me for a minute. I'll try to jump over that gully with them. You'll see if I can jump it."

"Oh, take them, then!" Rabbit took off his sandals and his hat. Deer put them on.

Deer jumped over the gully. Ooh, he ran off.

Rabbit's hat and sandals were gone for good.

—Lol Sarate

The Priest and the Constable

Once there was a priest. He was a witch. He was a devil.

He bore a grudge against a constable. "Deliver this message. Come back immediately," the priest told the constable.

But the place was very far. It was late in the day when the constable arrived and delivered the letter. The clerk looked at it.

"Oh, this is worthless. You've been tricked, you've been abused. You'll see tonight, you'll meet a devil on the road."

It grew dark on the way back. The moon was bright. A devil appeared. He had long hair.

"Let's fight," said the devil.

He drew a circle on the ground. "You stand here!"

The devil rose up in a whirlwind. The constable tossed his hat in the circle. He himself stood back. The devil was descending now. The devil's sword sliced his hat.

While the devil was slashing his hat, the constable struck him with his stave. The constable's hat was left in shreds. But the devil died from the constable's beating. The constable skinned him and took the skin home.

He went to report to the priest. "Here is a message for you from the clerk," said the constable.

"So you've come back!" said the priest.

"I've returned. Why wouldn't I have returned?"

"Didn't anything happen to you on the way?"

"No, nothing happened to me," said the constable.

"Where's your hat, then?"

"The wind took it. It blew off because I went in such a hurry."

"Are you telling the truth? Speak plainly! Didn't anything happen to you at all?" asked the priest.

"No, nothing!" said the constable.

It was just before Carnival. The constable sewed up the devil's skin and celebrated Carnival in it. He went to show it to the priest.

"My poor devil, I knew he was killed!"

The priest died in a fit of rage.

—Romin Teratol

John Skin Slays the Sea Serpent

Once there was a man named John Skin. He was called John Skin because he always wore clothes made of animal skins.

He went out traveling to find a job. He met a friend on the road.

"Where are you going, John Skin?"

"I'm going to look for work."

"Do you have any tools?" asked his friend.

"No, I don't know what I can work with," said John Skin.

"If you want something good, buy a sickle and an axe," said his friend.

"All right, then, thank you for telling me. I'll buy them if that's the way I can earn money."

"That's the way!" said his friend.

John Skin bought a sickle and an axe. He arrived in a big town.

"Have you any work?" he asked at the first house he came to.

"What kind of work do you want?" asked the man.

"I want whatever there is. If there is thatch-cutting, that's all I want," said John Skin.

"There is, but just by the job."

"Fine, I'll try it out," said John Skin.

John Skin went to work. He didn't give a thought to how hard he worked. Who knows how many jobs he finished in a day. Every evening his grass was piled up. He earned a lot of money.

Little by little it was learned that there was somebody by the name of John Skin. A king sent for him because a huge serpent was preying on his house. At midnight it came out of the sea to eat his servants, his family. Half the townspeople had been doled out. That's why John Skin was summoned to a country down on the coast.

"What is your bidding, Your Majesty?" said John Skin when he arrived at the king's house.

"Nothing much," said the king. "I simply want to ask you if you wish to become my son, if you wish me to give you one of my daughters to marry."

"Ah! Where is your daughter?" asked John Skin.

"Wait! I will send for her."

The king's daughter arrived.

"Enjoy yourself! Don't you want me?" she said.

"I do!" said John Skin.

"Then I'll live with you, but only if you promise you will never leave."

"Agreed!" said John Skin.

The sun set. Night fell.

"I'm going to bed now," said the old king. "You can sleep with my daughter in a separate room."

"Fine!" said John Skin. He went to spend the night alone with his wife. The king let him sleep with her the very first night. He was overjoyed.

John Skin didn't get sleepy at all. He was pacing back and forth.

"Come to bed, Johnny! Come on, let's go to sleep! Come on, let's get together!" said the girl.

John Skin kept pacing back and forth.

"Come on, hurry up, Johnny!"

"Oh, I can't. Wait a bit! I'll be there in a minute."

"See here, Johnny, I'll tell you openly. Are you prepared? A serpent is coming to eat us. We are going to die."

"Ah!" said John. "Is a serpent coming, then?"

"A serpent is coming. It arrives every midnight. It comes to eat people and fill its belly. That's why I lured you in."

"Hell, so I was tricked, then!"

"Yes, but now we are both going to die." The girl cried and cried.

"Don't worry, child. We'll see if I'm up to it. If I win, I'll tell your father in the morning. Please don't cry!"

"But it has survived everything. Soldiers have shot it again and again, but it can't be killed with bullets."

"Just the same, I'll see for myself," said John Skin. "But only if you love me with all your heart."

"With all my heart, darling, if you mean you'll take me forever."

"Oh, we'll see. The important thing is—exactly what time will it arrive?"

John was ready. With his sickle over his shoulder he stood behind the door. "Now, child, you stay in bed, but keep an eye out for what I'm going to do."

When the serpent came poking its head in, John Skin grabbed it and cut off its head with the sickle.

Groaning, the serpent died.

At dawn he went to tell the king. "Father! Go look at the serpent! It's mine this morning. I cut off its head."

"What kind of a man are you? My soldiers shot it again and again, but it wouldn't die."

"But it was me who won out. Go see for yourself!"

The old man went to look. The serpent's head and rear end were lying on the ground.

"With all my heart I give you my daughter. Take her forever," said the king. "You will stay in my home. You will work here. You won't ever leave."

The king sent a messenger to tell the soldiers that one man, John Skin, had slain the sea serpent.

One day John took a trip to another town, dressed in his animal skins. "What are you looking for?" asked a Ladino whom he met on the way.

"I'm not looking for anything. I've found work already."

"Where do you work?" asked the Ladino.

"I work at the king's house. The king is my father-in-law. I'm married to his daughter."

"Go on, you stupid jerk! Would you be given a girl, you beggar? Is that the way you pose as a man?"

"I won't say whether I am a great man or not. But I'm some kind of a man."

"You say you can do a day's work. Then reap my wheat!"

"All right," said John. But first they made a bet.

"Do you have any money?" the Ladino asked.

"I do, why wouldn't I? I'll risk this much," said John.

"If it's true that you can cut my field of wheat, I'll give you my house, I'll give you my cattle, I'll give you my horses. I'll move to borrowed quarters."

"I'll be back tomorrow when the sun is high. I'll bring my father-in-law for you to meet."

John Skin went home to tell the king. "See here, father, a Ladino thinks I am just skinning him, just tricking him. 'The king is my father-in-law,' I told him. He didn't believe it. 'You're really a beggar, you idiot,' he told me.

"Now he made a deal with me that if I could do a day's work he would give me his horses, his house, his cattle, and he would go to borrowed quarters."

"Fine, let's go and talk to him, then," said the king.

"Is it true what you conversed about with my son-in-law?" the king said to the Ladino.

"Is it true that he is your son-in-law?"

"Yes!" said the king.

"Oh hell!" said the Ladino.

"Let him work!" said the king.

John Skin went to work. In a minute he cut a day's worth of wheat.

So the house was left to him, the land was left to him, all the cattle and horses were left to him. And that's how John Skin won even more.

—Romin Teratol

The Man Who Didn't Know How

Once there was an old woman and her son. The old woman had no husband, the boy had no father. Who knows if he died. Who knows if the boy was illegitimate.

The boy grew up. Now he was a full-fledged man. But he had no wife.

His mother saw that her boy was never going to get a wife. "See here, son, if you can't pay the brideprice for a woman, just go out and speak to some girl. Go into the streets. I'll stick some tortillas in a bag for you. Go for a few days and see if you meet someone to speak to. Take her! It's better if you have a wife."

His mother fed him before he left. She gave him his tortillas to take along. He wasted maybe a week or more waiting for girls in the street.

When he came home, his mother asked him, "Were you able to speak to a girl, son?"

"No, I was standing on the corner, but they passed right by. They didn't say a thing."

"Stupid, why did you imagine that they would speak to you? It's you who should speak to them! Now go out again for a day or so!"

She gave her son his tortillas to take along. He ate before he left. He stood in the street. He spoke to the girls.

When he returned home in the evening, his mother asked him again, "Did you find one, son?"

"I found one. She answered me. You are right that they have to be spoken to."

"Good. Take her once and for all if she speaks to you again," the mother told her son.

He followed it up. He spoke to the girl. They got married.

Night fell. The boy went to bed with his wife, but he didn't do anything. He just slept happily.

But the woman wanted to know the man. She shook her husband awake. She took his hand and put it on her thigh. She let him know what it is that girls like to give.

During the night the boy shouted, "Mother, my wife won't let me sleep. She grabs my hand. She sticks it up her thigh. I don't know what it is there. It has a beard. It has a mouth. It feels as if it has teeth. I'm afraid that it will bite me. I don't want my hand hurt. I don't want to sleep with her anymore."

"Stupid, it's because your wife loves you very much. Don't you give her anything? Don't you climb on?"

"No!" said the boy.

"Tomorrow night you climb on top, then. Don't be afraid of it. That's a good thing! Your wife longs to enjoy you," said the old woman.

The next day the boy got his ladder ready. He leaned it next to his bed.

"Climb on quickly when night falls!" said his mother.

Night fell. Quickly he climbed up the ladder.

Maybe the ladder wasn't leaning properly. Down they came together—he and the ladder. He landed on top of his bed, and on top of his wife too.

"What are you doing, crashing around?" asked his mother. "Don't give me such a fright!"

"It's your fault, mother! You told me, 'Climb on up when night falls!' I thought it was good advice. I put my ladder by my bed. I climbed up into the rafters to spend the night. See here, I fell down. It would have been your fault if I had broken a bone."

"Stupid, it's on top of your wife that you should climb! You should stick your prick in where you say she has that beard. That's where it goes in. That's what your wife wants so badly. So give it to her! Stick your prick inside her!"

The next night that's what he did. The boy became a bit wiser.

—Romin Teratol

Cinderella

Once there was an orphan.

The orphan suffered greatly. The master's children ate first. They drank first. The poor girl was given the leftovers.

She hadn't a blanket. She hadn't any clothes. The people weren't kind to her at all. When they slaughtered pigs, it didn't matter if she was covered with lard. It didn't matter how she slept. She just wrapped herself in her little shawl. The poor thing slept buried in ashes. She slept with the little dog and the little cat.

Her master was a pig killer.

"Maria!" said her mistress. "Go wash the tripe!"

For a long, long time she had done nothing but wash tripe, grind corn, make tortillas, fix meals.

Every day she washed tripe at the river's edge.

> God,
>> My Lord,
> I am suffering,
>> I am miserable,
> I am wretched.
>> I am worn out, My Lord.

A little old man appeared. "What are you doing, daughter, sitting on your haunches at the river's edge?"

"I'm washing my little bit of tripe, because I'm a poor orphan. The people where I live never take pity on me. I am suffering."

"Never mind, daughter. Because of me you will rest. If you have to fry the tripe when you reach home, do it, don't be unhappy. Tomorrow I will give you something to relieve your hardship. I didn't bring it today," he said.

The next day, "Maria, go wash the tripe!" said the awful old woman.

"Will one of your daughters go with me?" Maria asked.

"The girls never go. The girls go to school. As for you, go wash the tripe!"

Maria went, clutching her little old skirt, her little old blouse, her little old shawl. She carried the washtub on her head. "God, My Lord, it's hard for me to lower the washtub for the tripe at the river."

"What are you doing, daughter?" asked the little old man.

"I'm washing my tripe, sir."

"For a long time you have been tormented by this hardship. God has had enough of your suffering. Now you will rest. When the burro brays bow your head. When the cock crows scan the sky."

When the burro brayed she bowed her head. When the cock crowed she scanned the sky.

A star appeared. "My Lord!" she said when it alighted on her forehead.

She took her little shawl and bound it tightly around her head. But the star shone through her shawl.

She tore off the hem of her skirt. She folded it four times.

The little man appeared. "Don't keep covering it up! You didn't steal it. Uncover it! There's nothing to be afraid of. Don't keep tearing your skirt.

"If you like, I'll give you a little ring."

"But where shall I put my ring? If my master sees it on me . . . "

"It's none of your master's business. If you don't want the ring, I'll give you a sash for your skirt. With your sash you will have nothing more to complain about. When you are sent to wash tripe, it isn't you who will wash it. The tripe will wash itself."

"That sash of mine, what do I say to it?"

"Say, 'Please, sash, do my work because I'm terribly worn out. These lungs of mine are sick,' you tell it."

She didn't work hard anymore. She just sat down and rested her head in her hand like my daughter does. As soon as she set down her washtub, the tripe was already well-rinsed.

She took it back to the house right away. "See, here it is!" she said.

"Why, you haven't returned covered with dirt!" said her mistress.

"Maybe it's because I haven't soiled my clothes yet."

"Go on, go and cook! Sweep the kitchen!"

Maria sat down again. "Sash, please do me a favor, sweep my kitchen for me. I don't want to work at all."

It swept the house. It tidied up. It washed her plates, her bowls, her metate, her metate platform.

The sash made the tortillas. It fried the fatback.

"Now, go sell the fatback!" she was told.

Maria stood outside the door. One person, another and another came to buy the fatback. All the fatback was sold right there at the door.

"What kind of god favored you that your fatback was bought up in a second?" her mistress asked. "How much money did you get for it?"

"Look how much!" said Maria.

"Oh good, go and sit down a minute! When you are finished sitting, make some coffee, because we are going to drink some before leaving. There is a dance at the king's house tonight. The girls are going."

"As you wish." Maria fixed the coffee.

"Bring it!" said her mistress. Maria brought the coffee in a little pottery pitcher, and four little clay cups.

"Fill them up!" her mistress said. "Are the toasted tortillas well-larded as I told you?"

The fatback drippings had been ground and kneaded. She put in eggs. She put in sugar. She patted them carefully.

She brought them in, stacked high in a gourd. She served them to her mistress.

She took the place of a maid, you see. She was a grown girl, like my own adopted daughter, but her mistress didn't treat her as her child. I take my daughter with me when I go to see a movie or go to have a good time at a fiesta. Her mistress wasn't like me!

"The girls have finished drinking their coffee. Fix the dinner! I want to find dinner well-prepared when I return."

The poor girl stayed all alone in the kitchen. She talked to the little cat, to the little dog.

Then that sash spoke. "Daughter, you ought to go enjoy the fiesta."

"I'd like to go. The trouble is, there is no way for the meal to be fixed. And I still have to make the tortillas."

"Don't worry. If you want to go, go on! I'll give you a carriage. I'll give you fine clothes. I'll give you a pair of shoes. Go on, go dance! Dance with whomever you wish to dance!"

The poor girl didn't even finish listening to the sash. She ran out the door, where her little car was sudddenly standing. She stepped down.

The king's wife greeted her. "Come right in, Miss!"

Maria was seated immediately. You see, she was dressed as a Ladina.

"Where does the beautiful girl come from?" asked the prince. "I'll certainly dance with her!"

The prince didn't dance any numbers with anyone else during the fiesta. He danced with her alone, for she was the most beautiful girl. But it was Maria Cinderella, the stupid girl, the orphan.

When the fiesta was over, the guests were saying good night to the host. "I'm going now. It's very late now. My maid is at home alone. The little orphan is surely nodding away by now. She sleeps too much," said the mistress.

The girl overheard. She left on the run! She slipped into her carriage and hurried home. But one of her shoes fell off and was left behind. It was a little metal shoe.

The prince said, "Whoever's foot fits this shoe, that person I will marry."

"But who does it fit? Who has a shoe like this? There isn't anyone here with such a shoe." The shoe was nothing less than a charm.

"I will marry the person whose foot it fits," said the prince.

He went everywhere that girl might be. In one house after another there was no one whose foot fit it, until he arrived at the house where Maria lived.

"I'll slice off part of my foot!" said the girl's mistress.

Maria huddled in the kitchen. She didn't make a sound.

"Come here!" the girls were told. Their feet didn't fit.

"Haven't you any other daughters?" the prince asked.

"No, I haven't any more daughters."

"But your maid is in the kitchen," the prince said, as if he knew.

"Oh, uh, my maid . . . she's there, but, ach, she is an orphan, a little orphan. I took her in because her mother died."

"Even so. If it's her foot that fits, I'll marry her."

"How can you believe that sooty thing's foot will go in?"

Holy Mary, her foot slipped right into the shoe! Now she was in that prince's hands!

"Now even if you bawl me out, even if you get mad, I'm taking the girl away!" The prince didn't respect her mistress.

"The only thing I recommend to you is that tomorrow you come to the wedding and that's that, no arguments."

The awful daughters were left in anger.

"I can't believe the shoe fits that Indian. That loafer, covered with ashes."

"If only I had another orphan, then I'd see how to be married. I'd surely get myself a husband."

"Why wasn't it my foot that fit? It would be me getting married tomorrow," the sisters said.

I don't know if they published the banns. I don't know if they had a priest. They were married. They celebrated the wedding for two days. She asked the sash for music. She asked the sash for food. She asked for whatever was desired. It was a fine fiesta.

Now the girl was well-loved by the king, since she held the fiesta herself. "It's my own responsibility," she said.

"But how do you do it?" asked the king.

"I know how to look after things," said Maria.

"Fine!" they said. "Ah!" they said. "We're hungry!" they said.

"Eat!" she said. She served the meal right away. She and the prince ate too, even though they were newlyweds.

The maids were treated well. "I'll help you," she said.

"Don't bother!" said the prince. "Why should we mistreat you after you already have been mistreated?"

"She is my son's wife!" said the king.

Hah, in a minute she washed the dishes, but it wasn't her hands that washed them. As soon as she looked at them they were done. Plates, bowls, tortilla gourds were suddenly face down.

The king had some chairs. They weren't like the chairs of today. They were tall, wide, and thick and carved out of pure stone. She wiped them off, and in a minute they were dry. "How does the girl do it?" they said. They didn't want to complain about her at all.

On her own she would go to the kitchen to help the maids fix the meals.

"No, don't do that!" said her husband.

"But the poor things, I feel sorry for them. That's the way my hardship was."

"If it's like your suffering, for that very reason you should rest. Now that you are under my control you will stop. Before, because your masters were poor people, they were very satisfied having you go out to sell fatback or pork from house to house. But when you began to be favored, you didn't have to work so hard. I saw that your fatback was bought up right at the door. It was just when you got that wonderful star on your forehead."

It was true that then her hardship eased. When she had to carry heavy baskets of pork on her head and go sell it, her little shawl was covered with blood, covered with lard. The poor girl smelled rancid. You wouldn't ever marry her.

"Don't work anymore. Just sit next to me," said the prince.

Sometimes she would do what he said, sometimes she wouldn't. She worked because we get used to working.

She made quick trips when the prince wasn't noticing. She would come back and sit down. They would chat and chat.

"Let's have a party!" she said. "I'd like to dance. I'd like a fine dress. I don't want to suffer forever."

They had a good party, like the fiesta that had just passed. They danced and danced. The girl was well-loved.

The end.

—Tonik Nibak

The Spook and the Girl from Magdalenas

Once two Zinacantecs were sleeping in a cave. "I'm afraid," said one, "I don't know why. What if something should come!"

"What are you scared of?" said the other. "Are you blue-assed? Do you wear women's skirts?"

"Sonofabitch. You be brave!"

"I am brave, man. Put a lot of firewood on. You're blue-assed!"

The man was shivering with fear.

Late at night the Spook came whooshing down. He saw the fire gleaming in the cave. He set down his pack, entered the cave, and squatted by the fire.

The brave man pissed in his pants. His ass was sopping wet.

The Spook spoke to his trembling companion. "What's up, friend? What are you doing?"

"I'm not doing anything, sir."

"I'll warm myself," said the Spook.

"Fine, warm yourself, sir."

"Do you want a smoke?" asked the Spook.

"I'll smoke," said the man. He was given a cigarette. It crumbled up in his shaking hands.

"Bastard, what are you doing to your cigarette?"

"Well, sir, I'm smoking the way I always smoke."

The Spook gave him another and another. The man wasted three cigarettes.

"You bastard, this kind of act is no good. Do you want to fight?"

"Fight if you know how to fight, sir, but me, I don't know how. I'm just sitting here warming myself by the fire."

"You bastard!" said the Spook.

"Look here, whose bastard? Hell, I'm not your bastard, because your hair is so kinky, you bastard."

The Spook rose up. He took out his sword. He thrust the point straight down.

But he thrust it into the ground. The Zinacantec had a good stick. The man whacked him two, three times right off. What a man!

The Spook grew weaker and weaker. Now he was hovering like a bird. The man hit his legs. The Spook fell to the ground.

The "brave" man's piss was just pouring out as he watched the fight. He was helpless.

The Spook was dying. His teeth were bared in his horrible black mouth.

The man tied a lasso around the Spook's neck and pulled it tight. Turning blue in the face, the Spook died.

The man went out to look in the Spook's bundle. There, rolled up in a new straw mat, was a girl from Magdalenas.

"What kind of thing are you? Are you a Spook?"

"It's me, sir. Don't kill me! Untie me!" she said.

He untied her. Now a wife had come to the man. The girl was a lush babe.

The man shook his companion. "But what happened to you?"

Now that he had a woman, he was swishing a switch. He gave the "brave" Zinacantec a good beating.

"Never mind, if it's just a whipping. Don't kill me! Take her! I thought I was brave. I wasn't brave at all."

The man took the woman with him. He didn't return her to her home.

"Sonofabitch, it must be a Magdalenas man coming along!" said some men who were standing on the trail. "How did the bastard do it?"

"He wasn't afraid."

"But she's a devil. She has taken the devil's orders."

—Xun Vaskis

The Buzzard Man

Long ago there was a man who was very lazy. When he went to work he just ate his tortillas and went to sleep. Then he came back. He came back and he left. And he came back and he left. And that's how the year passed. He said that he had corn and that he worked. He just lied to his wife.

The poor woman's heart, God, My Lord! "My corn is about to be harvested," she said.

But how could her corn be harvested? Sleeping is what the man did! In no time he spread out his woolen tunic. He made a pillow of his tortillas.

"Holy buzzard, how is it that you don't work? You fly, gliding easily along. But it's hard with me. What agony I suffer! Look at my hands! They have lots of sores. I can't work at all now."

Maybe Our Lord grew tired of it. The buzzard came down.

"What is it you want with me, talking that way?"

"I don't want anything. It's just that you seem so well off. Without a care you fly in the sky. I suffer working in my corn field, and I haven't any corn. I'm a pauper. My wife scolds me because we have nothing to eat. So I borrow ears of corn or I borrow beans. 'My corn has been harvested. My beans have been harvested,' I tell her. I have so many debts now I have no way to return them. If you wanted to, you could take my clothes and I'll go buzzarding."

"I'll have to ask permission," said the buzzard. "I'll come, depending on what I'm told. Wait for me on Tuesday."

The man sat down to wait for the buzzard. "Holy buzzard, why don't you come to change with me? I'm so tired of working."

He had taken his axe and his billhook with him to clear the land. He felled two trees. Then he returned home.

"How about it, have you finished clearing your land?" his wife asked.

"Oh, it's nearly ready. I finished trimming all the trees I felled." All the trees? Two! The loafer!

"I'm going again tomorrow. Get up, please, and make me a couple of tortillas."

He went out to wait for the buzzard again. He sat down right off.

"God, I'm hungry already. I feel like drinking posol. I have too much work. There's no way to replace the corn I've borrowed," he said.

The buzzard finally arrived.

"Our Lord has given me permission. He says we can change places."

"But won't my wife realize that it isn't me anymore?"

"No, she won't know. It's by Our Lord's order," said the buzzard.

The buzzard shook off all his feathers. The man took off his pants, his shirt, his wool tunic. The buzzard put them on.

Then the man put on the buzzard's clothes. The buzzard's feathers stuck on.

"Let me tell you how we find food," said the buzzard. "When there is a dead horse or dead sheep or dead dog or dead pig, you'll see its fumes rising in the sky. If you are hungry, then look for fumes rising. Now go have fun!"

Three days later the "buzzard" returned. The "man" was clearing his land.

"God, it's true that I'm no good for anything. Look how much of your land you've cleared! It took me months just to cut two trees. Did my wife tell you I was good for nothing when you arrived?"

"'Why do you stink so? You reek!' she told me!"

"What did you tell her?"

"'Yes, I certainly do stink. It's because I'm working. In the past I lied to you. I just slept all the time. But now you can see for yourself. I'll take you along when I burn our land. You can help me watch the fire,' I told your wife."

When the time for burning came, the "man" asked his wife to accompany him. "Sit here. First, I'll clear a fire lane around our land."

The wife sat down. She lit a fire and prepared her "husband's" meal. Then they ate.

The smoke from the burning trees was curling up. The lazy "buzzard" thought it was his meal. He came whooshing down. The fool landed right in the fire. He burnt up.

"Could that awful buzzard be so stupid that he came and burnt himself up?" said the wife. "That's what the disgusting thing deserved."

"Yes, the order said that's what the lazy buzzard deserved," said the "husband." "Never mind! In a week we'll come to plant. You will plant the beans yourself."

They left. They each carried a load of firewood, one load of wood for the "man" and one load of wood for the woman.

They arrived home. "See here, I'm just covered with soot. 'You stink like a buzzard,' you tell me. Hand me some clothes. I'll change. Wash the others tomorrow," said the "husband."

"You're right. It's just your clothes that stink. It's your sweat," said the wife.

How would she know he was a buzzard? Do you know how she discovered that her husband was a buzzard? It was when he was weeding his beans, his corn, and his watermelon squash. He was lucky now.

"Now that you have corn and beans, return to me all that your late husband borrowed," a neighbor said.

"Isn't he my husband, the one who has always been with me? Do I have two husbands, then?" asked the woman.

"Oh, why don't you want to admit it? Your husband turned into a buzzard," said the neighbor who was asking to be repaid.

The lazy man had lived on stolen goods. They say he borrowed forty ears of fresh corn at one house, a quarter-measure of beans at another, thirty ears of dried corn at another. They all came to recover their loans.

"Come on! Get out! When we harvest our field, you can have your corn and beans if you're telling the truth. I don't know anything about it," she said.

"Why wouldn't we be telling the truth? When your husband went to work he went to sleep on the job. He told the buzzard, 'Oh, holy buzzard, give me your suit. You fly so well, gliding in the sky. But me, my hands hurt so. I can't stand it' said your husband." The people asking for beans told her the whole story.

"I was right that you aren't my husband, that's why you know how to work. You see, you used to be a buzzard," she told her husband.

"Oh, what concern is that of ours? That was long ago. What people won't come and tell you so that we'll repay them!"

"Hah, I was right that you stank like a buzzard!"

"Who knows. I never felt like a buzzard. Just because I sweat, I have a bad odor. That's why I ask you for clean clothes. I change so you won't tell me I'm a buzzard."

"Oh forget it, so long as you provide for me."

After they harvested, they had plenty of corn, plenty of beans. They repaid their debts and had a lot left over.

"Look how nobody is saying things to me now that we have corn and beans. There's no problem as long as my stomach's full."

Her "husband" wasn't a loafer any longer.

—Tonik Nibak

Journey to Irdivolveres

Three doves arrived to bathe in a stream. They took off their clothes, their feathers.

A man stole the clothes of one of the doves and hid them.

The doves who had their feathers flew away. The other dove was left behind.

The bird turned into a woman. She was the mistress of the river.

"I really would love to marry you. I have lost my heart to you," said the man.

"Fine," said the woman. "But I will only sleep with you at night. I don't want us to see each other's faces."

The woman was taken to his house. They slept together in the dark.

"Hell, why can't I look?" said the man.

When she fell asleep, he lit his candle. He looked at her face. Sonofabitch, the child's face was beautiful.

The woman felt the candle wax drip on her. She woke up mad!

"Now look here! There's absolutely nothing we can do after what you did to me. We had agreed that we would never look at each other's faces, we would just be together in the dark."

Lord, before they were even married, the woman changed houses. She went home to her parents. He was thrown over.

The man cried and cried over being abandoned. But he had been told, you see, what her father and mother's house was called. Its name was Irdivolveres. "If you go looking for me, go there!" the woman said when she left. "If you will still marry me with your whole heart, go look for me!"

He spoke to Mother Wind. She was a wild-haired old woman. "Won't you tell me if Irdivolveres is far away?"

"Wait, my son is coming! Pay him!" It was Whirlwind strolling along.

"Where do you think Irdivolveres is?" he asked the old woman's child.

"It exists, but my grandfather knows where. "If you want to ask him, I'll take you along. But you really stink!" that countryman of ours was told.

He was flown off by Whirlwind to Whirlwind's grandfather's house.

"My wife has left me," the man said to the Wind. "But she told me where she went—to her father and mother's house, Irdivolveres. That's where she is living."

"Well, I don't go there very often, but I've heard stories about it, of course. If you are going, I can take you," said Whirlwind's grandfather. "But shut your eyes!"

He shut his eyes. He was carried by the Wind.

"How big is the world now?" he asked.

"As big as a peso," said Whirlwind's grandfather. They went on and on.

"How big is the world now?"

"As big as a fifty centavo piece."

They went on and on. Gradually the world grew smaller and smaller. They had almost arrived.

"How big is the world now?"

"As big as a five centavo piece."

He arrived at her house. He arrived on the Wind.

"Is this the house of Irdivolveres?" he asked the old man.

"Yes," said Whirlwind's grandfather. "Their daughter is just coming out."

Sonofabitch, that countryman of ours was overjoyed!

He went to speak to his father-in-law. "If you aren't up to the work, you certainly won't have a wife!" said his father-in-law. "You're going to clear roads!"

His wife whispered to him, "You are to take the worst tool. The good ones won't work. Pick one that is terribly dull."

He grabbed the worst tool. He was assigned a job. Lord, he was to hoe a road through the mountain. He cried. He hadn't even pecked at it when the woman came to give him his tortillas.

"Sonofabitch, I can't finish it!" he said. How could he? He wasn't a tractor!

"Rest, then," she told him. Immediately she cleared the trail. Who knows how.

"It's finished," he told his father-in-law. "Go see for yourself!"

His father-in-law went to look at his work. "Clear the underbrush tomorrow!"

But it was heavy forest. It was to be flattened. It was to be burned. When his wife came to bring him his tortillas, Lord, that gentleman hadn't felled a single tree.

Who knows how she worked. It wasn't with her hands. The trees just fell by themselves.

She set them on fire. The land was ready.

The man returned. "I've cleared the forest, I've burned the trees," he told his father-in-law.

"Are you telling the truth?"

"Go look for yourself!"

"Fine!" said his father-in-law. "The planting is tomorrow. The next day you harvest!"

The sonofabitch wasn't worried because he had seen his wife work.

She planted. Lord, it was ready.

Then she harvested. It was done immediately.

"Now you can marry!" said his father-in-law.

They took each other. They were married. The man became the chief, the king of the world.

—Rey Komis

The Bear's Son

A woman was taking some tortillas to her husband.

But a fucking bear appeared. The woman was carried off to his cave. She hadn't any clothes. She was naked. Berries were what the poor woman ate.

His child was born. The boy had legs like a bear, his face was human.

The bear's son grew. "Mother, why don't we leave?"

"Can you open the door?" she asked. The door was a rock.

"I'll try," he said. He moved the door a tiny bit. "I guess I'll grow for three more days. Then we'll see if I'm strong enough."

When the three days for him to grow were up, he could move the rock a little more.

Another three days passed. The door was nearly opened.

Another three days passed. The rock came out. "Let's go, mother!"

Ooh, they fled. But the fucking bear chased them. He was about to drag off that woman again, but she had already entered the town. The bear stopped at the bridge .

The woman was completely naked. The awful boy was naked too.

Soon a man took her bear husband's place. The woman was treated kindly. She was given a skirt. She told how she had been abducted long ago.

"It doesn't matter," said her new husband.

That boy of hers grew. She sent him to school.

The bear child learned right away. He was well-liked by the teachers.

Now his friends didn't learn, and they were beaten by the teachers. The bear child was called "Pig's Foot" by the boys. He lost his temper. He slugged them. Because he was so strong, they died. Their souls departed for good.

The teachers got tired of the way he hit the other students. "Get out once and for all!" he was told.

"All right, I'll go," he said. "But please get a walking stick for me."

They got a walking stick for him. "Lord, what good is this to me? I want a bigger one," he said.

He was given a bigger one. It was some walking stick! It took two men to carry it.

He journeyed a great distance.

He met up with one of our countrymen on the way. "Where are you going, friend?" they asked each other.

"As for me, I'm going to wherever I fall dead. It makes no difference," said the bear child.

"Sonofabitch, it's just the same with me!" said the Zinacantec. The two went on together. They met another of our countrymen on the road. Now there were three.

Soon they got terribly thirsty. His companions longed to drink some water.

They came to a pit. "There's probably some water down there," said the bear child. "Let me down."

They tied vines together and lowered them into the pit. The bear child climbed down to the bottom.

There he met two girls. He helped one out. "Pull me up now!" he called.

Then he helped the other girl out.

"Now I'm coming out myself. Pull me up!"

But it was a big rock that weighed just the same. Lord, they lifted it halfway up the pit. Then they dropped it. They thought it was the bear child.

Oh, the black gentleman arrived. He was the lord of that cave. There was no longer a way to escape. Quickly the bear child grabbed his knife. He cut off one of the Earth Lord's ears. He held it in his hand.

"If you don't carry me out, I'll bite your ear," he said. He bit the Earth Lord's ear.

"Ow, don't bite my ear! I'll take you out," said the Earth Lord.

Halfway up the pit, he was about to be tossed down. He bit the Earth Lord's ear again.

"Ow, don't bite my ear!" said the Earth Lord. The bear child was carried to the surface.

He reached another town. He had taken along the ear of the Earth Lord.

He saw two beautiful rocks in the meadow. And next to them he met a girl.

"I guess I'll bite the black gentleman's ear. We'll see if he brings me some money so I can marry this girl."

He bit the Earth Lord's ear. Who knows where the owner of the ear was.

"Ow, don't bite my ear!" said the Earth Lord from far away.

"Give me some money," said the bear child.

"Take it!" said the Earth Lord. "Just don't bite my ear!"

The bear child was given the money. He placed one rock over the money and one rock under his head to sleep on.

The girl spoke to him. "What's that?" she asked.

"This is a charm, of course!" said the awful bear child.

"Do you want to give it to me?" she said.

"Ah, I'll give it to you, but only if you marry me."

She thought it over.

"Shall I come sleep with you now?" he asked.

"Come on, sleep with me, then!" said the woman. She had made her decision.

"Can I put my arm around you?"

"Yes, you can!" she said. He embraced her.

"Can I touch you a little bit lower?"

"You can!" she said. He touched her a little bit lower.

"Can I climb on slowly?"

"You can!"

"Can I poke it in slowly?"

"Poke it in!" he was told.

Lord, he poked it in! Sonofabitch, the blood certainly flowed! She was screaming. Who knows what horrible length his tool was! He was an evil animal, you see.

Lord, he was going to be arrested and jailed.

But he wasn't arrested or jailed. He fled. He went to another town. And he did just the same.

—Rey Komis

How to Take Care of Jaguars

Once there were lots of jaguars. They lived in a large cave. They didn't let people pass by. Everyone met his end there.

There was a man. He said too many people had been lost.

He took his machete. When he reached the cave he looked for plenty of rocks. He looked for seats for all the jaguars.

When all the seats were ready, he called to the jaguars. "Hoo ha!" They all came out of the cave, the young and old.

"I'm going to eat you right up," said the jaguars.

"Wait a minute! If there are still little ones inside your house, tell them to come too. All of you will eat me," said the man.

The little jaguars came out.

"There are your seats, sit down!" said the man.

All the jaguars sat down on the rocks.

"Wait a minute. I'll take my clothes off. It will be easier for you to eat me if I'm naked."

"Hurry up. I'm getting hungry," said the big jaguars. They were huge, with long whiskers. They were delighted now. They were laughing.

The man was naked now. He lay down in the middle. All the jaguars were seated around him.

"Well, come eat me! You'll be satisfied with the morsel you'll be eating," said the man.

"Fine!" said the jaguars. They all tried to lift their asses, but they couldn't get up. They were squirming about. They were glued to their seats.

"When are you coming to eat me? Hurry up!" said the man.

"We can't," said the jaguars.

"Hurry up, hurry up! Come eat me! How much longer do I have to wait?"

The man lost his temper.

"What are you good for? You are jaguars. You eat people. All our countrymen are dead. Just so, eat me too! You get away with eating so many people. Now today you are going to enjoy my machete."

Quickly he swished his machete until he killed all the old jaguars. He left three cubs to breed. If it weren't for him, we wouldn't outlive the jaguars.

—Romin Teratol

When the Soldiers Were Coming

The soldiers came up from Chiapa. They came to wage war. They were stopped by the sight of many bowls dancing. They danced until they broke. That's why the place is called "Bowl Spring."

They paid no attention. They came on up. Above Tzoj Lum [Red Earth] a pine tree was dancing. That's why the place is called "Pine Tree."

They paid no attention. They reached Ik'al Vo [Hurricane]. Our countrymen fought with wind and rain. Black rain and wind were hurled at them. They weren't afraid. They didn't die.

They continued on. They came to Tz'akav Uk'um [River Fork]. The flow of water in the river stopped. They paid no attention at all.

They came on up. They arrived at Yav Ch'ivit [Market Site]. They entered the market to buy a little fruit. They enjoyed themselves. Some disappeared there.

The others came on up. They arrived at Jolob Na [Weaving House]. They saw many women weaving, but they paid no attention.

They came on up. At Tz'ajom Pik' there was a lake. Many naked women were bathing there. That's why the place is called "Submerged Clitoris."

The soldiers went as if they were herded, as far as the cave of Lachchi-kin [Pricked Up Ears]. There they stuck in the earth. There they became gods.

—Romin Teratol

The Revolution

At the beginning of the war, one group of Obregonists was gathered at the graveyard. Another group was gathered at Window Pass.

Now while they were eating, they were discovered by Pineda's soldiers. Pineda's soldiers killed them all.

There were heaps of meat, beef, mutton, chicken left uneaten. Is there anyone who would eat chicken like that—cooked in lard in a frying pan!

It looked fine, if you don't know fear, of course!

I was eleven years old. My neighbor's son had some sheep. We stuck the sheep in the pen. We came right home, since the bullets were sputtering at the top of Horned Owl House hill.

Pineda's soldiers were coming to kill us. We hadn't a chance of going anywhere. "Forget it, let's each of us lie down at home. We can't say we don't know about the shooting," we said.

They took all the animals. There were twelve sheep, three cows. The cows that had already been killed were tossed up on the horses. The sheep were hung up and skinned. All the meat was left at the courthouse. The soldiers divided it up amongst themselves. But the food that was already cooked—it made no difference who took it.

By the cross above Blessed Spring we went to stick the sheep in the pen. There were two chickens cooking, each one in a frying pan. The owner was gone.

"Come on, let's take them!" my neighbor's son told me.

"If he comes back, what if he kills us?" I said.

"That's the way awful girls always are! They're so scared. Ach, keep on gabbing!" He was walking off with one frying pan.

Now I really didn't want to take the other frying pan. "Shall I just take the piece of liver to eat?" I said to myself. I took it, but I was looking around behind me. I was scared.

But the owner was an Obregonist in one of those advance groups that was destroyed at Window Pass. There were only three men left to bury the dead. Their arms were wounded. Their legs were wounded. One was wounded in the lung.

The next day we opened the pen for the sheep. It was probably ten o'clock when the fighting broke out.

The fields were ripe with corn.

"Why did we take our chickens home for our mothers to eat? We should have eaten them here by ourselves!" said my companion. "Let's go look at the fire over there to see if there is any food left."

Ooh, a pot was bubbling away on the fire. A pot of chicken. "Come here! See how good the food is! Let's eat!" he told me.

"Where will we get the tortillas for it?"

"Look! There are tortillas stacked at the foot of the fence!" he said.

We each ate two pieces of chicken. We drank its broth. Whatever we couldn't finish eating we took home. Four pieces for me, four pieces for my companion. We stuck the sheep in their pen. I carried the meat in the little old pot. My companion wrapped his up in a tortilla. We were lucky!

The next day the countryside was deserted. The governor's soldiers were gone. "That's probably how it will be. Old Pineda was able to take the town," we said.

Four days later the government came in force. Who knows how many soldiers. But they had no mercy.

We had a few tortillas among us. We had some watermelon squash flavored with chili. We had cut it in chunks to eat. The Obregonists scooped out the watermelon squash. They took our tortillas and ate them. It didn't matter if you died of hunger, yourself!

They found the sheep hanging up. They roasted them and ate them. They surely were satisfied with that! If they hadn't found them hanging there, if there weren't someone guarding them at the courthouse, who knows!

More sheep-stealing and chicken-thieving began. The governor's soldiers only ate stolen food. They'd scarcely buy it!

I had a hen turkey crouching in the tall weeds. They made a path through the weeds and grabbed the turkey. They took away two chickens too. My turkey and my chickens, they did go!

On the fourth day, my pots went, my bowls went. They stole a ball of wool. They sold them at a store. I saw my bowls there. They were huge. What good were they now?

I had a chest. I had some books. They stole them all.

"God, how will we be freed from our hardship, mother, suffering as we do?"

"Never mind, daughter! We'll see what we'll live on," said my mother.

In the end, they returned more than they stole. One day

Obregon's soldiers came to our house to ask a favor. They had stolen a mule-load of flour at the pass. "Do you want a third of the flour in exchange for making tortillas for us to eat?" asked the soldiers.

"We do!" we said. A sack of flour!

We made a huge stack of wheat tortillas every day. Every day they ate them.

A half straw mat of flour was used up. They ate it and we ate it.

"If you will still be so kind as to make tortillas, we'll get some more flour," they said.

"Bring it!" we said. One of them brought another bag. "We'll store up the rest," said my mother. "We'll be happy to eat it when we haven't any corn." We put it away. The straw mat was empty.

"What can I do with the straw mat? Take it!" the soldier told us.

"It's probably payment for our firewood, mother."

One day he brought two turkeys. Probably Chamulans' turkeys!

"Fix the turkeys for us to eat," he said. "You eat half, we'll eat half."

My mother fixed a whole turkey. He had said that he would just eat half. But he was carrying the whole turkey off, together with my pot.

"I told you, ma'am, 'One today, one tomorrow.' But never mind. Since there are three of us eating, you'll just have to figure it out." So he took six pieces of turkey and our little pot. He left the big pot with our own portion.

Other times he would bring a chicken or a rooster. We would fix the food and his tortillas. Our pay was half a bag of flour. We lived on it.

"The trouble is, my firewood has run out," my mother told him.

"There's a lot of firewood," he said. "Take it from the paths! Take it from the fences!" They warmed themselves with the fences!

"But my neighbor will scold me! Don't you see, it's my neighbor's fence," I said.

"What does it matter to you?" he said. "Don't be scared to steal!"

He had brought a bag of green broad beans for us to cook.

"But I don't know how," said my mother.

"Do you know how we should eat them, mother? We'll shuck the pods and then we'll boil them."

"What if they don't eat them that way? What if they only eat them fried," she said.

I shucked the pods. I boiled them until they were good and soft, like corn. "Do you eat them like this?" we asked.

"Ah, these are better!" he said.

He had an enormous bowl. We filled it up for him. "There's enough here for supper and breakfast," he said. He took the beans. He took his wheat tortillas. We ate wheat tortillas for more than a month.

Then the soldiers were sent off to fight. One rooster, two legs of mutton, roasted in the oven, were left at our home. There was still a quart of corn. That became our pay, of course!

Pineda's soldiers came. They marched along the tip of Raven House Mountain. They blew their bugles. Their bugles sounded good.

But the advance force met them at the cemetery. Pineda's soldiers were chased across the top of the mountains. They ended up at the Church of Guadalupe in San Cristóbal. They fled. They fled to this day. Obregon was established. There haven't been any more battles. That was the last battle, indeed!

—Tonik Nibak

It's Cold in the Crocodile's Belly!

There was a man who went to draw water from the Grijalva River. He discovered a crocodile, warming itself in the sun.

Quickly it caught the man. He was swallowed whole.

When the man woke up, he felt terribly cold. The crocodile was lying under water.

He regained his senses when its belly warmed up, because the crocodile came out to lie in the sun.

"But what can I do about this?" the man said to himself. Inside the animal's stomach he prayed to Our Lord. "My Lord, how can I get out of here?"

He remembered. He took out his knife. He ripped open the crocodile's belly. When its belly was ripped open, the man rolled out.

He arrived to tell his friends. "Where did you go? Why did you disappear?"

"Man, I had an accident. An animal swallowed me. Thank God I had my little knife. I ripped open its belly. I climbed out."

"Are you hungry?" they asked.

"I'm famished! I was stuck inside the crocodile's stomach. I haven't eaten in three days!"

"Eat, then!" he was told.

He had killed the crocodile that ate him and escaped in one piece.

—Manvel K'obyox

The Man Who Lived a Dog's Life

Once a boy and a girl got married. They acquired many maids.

Every night the woman went out, but the man thought she just went out to pee.

It was the same every night. Finally he noticed it. When he went to bed he had his gun and machete ready.

He didn't fall asleep. At midnight the woman got up. She felt her husband's chest to see whether he was asleep or awake. Her husband didn't move.

The man took his gun and his machete. He followed his wife wherever she went. "Could she have a lover?" said the man. "I'll kill both of them now!"

His wife arrived at the graveyard. She began to dig. She took a bite out of a corpse. She left it. She went to another grave and dug it up. Then she found good meat. She ate it all.

The man was watching from a distance. "Well, never mind. I've seen now what she's doing."

He went back home and went to bed. He pretended to sleep. His wife opened the door. She came to bed.

"Where did you go?" he asked his wife.

"I went outside to pee," said the woman.

"Hell, that's a fine thing you're doing! Are you a dog? Are you a buzzard? Why do you eat corpses?" Quickly he hit his wife with the flat of his machete. "There's no need for me to have a corpse-eater to sleep with," said her husband.

The woman cried and cried.

The next morning the man turned into a black dog. The poor dog wasn't given its tortillas. It just ate shit.

As a man he had been familiar with another town. He used to go there on trips. He had a good friend there. "I'm going. I can't stand it. I'm starving," said the dog.

He arrived at the store. He sat down on a chair. There were newspapers scattered about. The dog looked at them.

"But this isn't a dog. It knows how to read," said the store-keeper. "Have you always been a dog?" he asked.

"No!" it said.

"Are you a human being?"

"Yes!" it said. The dog made signs with its head.

At lunchtime the dog was given meat and tortillas by the storekeeper.

An old woman arrived to buy bread. She saw the dog eating at the table. "I'll take you home," she said.

"Let's go!" said the dog. It went off with the old woman.

"Have you always been a dog or are you a human being?" she asked.

"Yes, I'm a man," it answered with its head.

They arrived at the old woman's house. "Do you want to turn into a human being again?" asked the woman.

"I do!" said the dog. Suddenly it became a man.

"Is it you?" said the woman.

"It's me," said the man.

"What happened to you?" she asked.

"My wife was doing all sorts of things, so I hit her. It was like thus and so."

As for the maids, they missed him. "Mistress," they said, "where is our master?"

"Who knows, maybe he went to look for his girlfriend," said the wife.

"Ah!" said the maids.

The man finished his story. "What do you think you'll do to her?" asked the old woman.

"I don't know. I'd like to do something, but I don't know how."

"If you give me plenty of money, I know what to do. She and I learned together. But she knows less. I'm stronger."

"Please, I'll give you as much you want," said the man.

"All right. Go back to your house," said the old woman. "She can't do anything to you now."

The man went home.

"Master, you've come back!" said the maids. "We thought you had died."

"No, God doesn't want that," said the man.

He was given his meal. He ate well. The maids embraced him and kissed him.

His wife appeared. "Have you come back?" she asked.

"I've come back," he said.

Suddenly the woman turned into a mare.

"Daughters," the man said to his maids. "Take the mare away! Tie it in the stall. Let it starve to death. Don't give it its meals, because it has done wrong."

Tied up, the mare starved. It grew thin. It died.

"Where did our mistress go?" the maids asked their master.

"Who knows. Maybe she went to look for another husband."

"Ah!" said the maids.

Just so ends the story for now.

—Romin Teratol

How Toenails Won a Bride

He had a mother. "Mother!" he said, "I really long to marry the princess."

But that princess already had a husband. The princess was the king's wife.

"Oh God, son, poor child, *you* marry *her*? It's the king seated there, you know. She would be hard to ask for. What makes you think a princess would want you?" the old woman told her child.

"But I'm mad about her. I'm simply going to try to speak to her. I've fallen completely in love."

"Well, go on, then!" said the old woman. The man left his house.

On the road he came upon a dead cow. Buzzards, coyotes, flies were circling round.

"Man, won't you do us the favor of dividing up our food for us?" said the animals. "We are simply quarreling with one another over our food and we're not getting anything to eat."

The man pulled out his knife.

"We want the bigger animals to have bigger meals," said the buzzards and coyotes. "Give the tiny animals a smaller amount."

The man cut up the cow into little pieces. He portioned them out equally.

"Take care of yourselves! Don't quarrel with each other," he told the animals.

"Thank you," they said. "It's not much, but we are going to give you our toenails as a present. They will be a real help to you when you travel."

The animals and flies cut off little slivers of their nails. The man clutched them in his hand. "But how can they help me?" he said to himself.

"Adios, Fly!" said the man.

Lord, he was flying.

"They really work!" he said. He put the animals' nails away carefully. "Now I must get to speak to the princess.

"Adios, Eagle!" He soared as an eagle.

"Adios, Fly!" He saw the princess sitting alone, high in the palace.

"Adios, Ant!" He turned into an ant and crawled up the princess' face. The princess flicked him off.

"Princess, it's me!" he said. He turned into a human being. "I'm mad about you. I'll marry you, even if it seems impossible."

"But you can't kill my husband," she said. "The king has seven souls."

"But where?" he asked.

"Here behind the wall. As soon as you leave, a deer will come out. Inside the deer are three doves. And inside the doves are sparrows. Inside their stomachs is an egg. That's the last soul, of course. But who knows if you can win out!"

The man approached the wall. "Adios, Lion!" he said. The wall only moved a little. "Adios, Tiger!" he said. It moved quite a bit. "Adios, Lion!" he said again. The wall toppled over. A deer came bounding out.

"Adios, Eagle!" he said. Now he was an eagle following close behind. "Adios, Tiger!" The tiger went to work. He jumped on the deer's back and killed it.

Three doves flew out and soared away. "Adios, Eagle!" The eagle killed them. He cut open the doves' breasts.

Three sparrows came out. They flew into the ocean. Now the man couldn't do anything at all. He cried and cried.

Some fish appeared. "What are you crying about?" asked the fishes.

"Three sparrows dove into the ocean. The trouble is, I can't swim."

"Don't worry, we'll find them," said the fishes.

The fishes brought the little sparrows to the surface.

The man cut open their breasts. There was the egg.

"Adios, Eagle!" said the man. He flew to the window where the princess was sitting. "Here is the egg," he said. It was as big as a chicken egg.

Now the king was thrashing about, since his powers were exhausted. When the king came staggering in, she knocked him on the head with the egg. He died right away.

The king had soldiers who were guarding the princess.

"See here, princess, when you have asked for permission to come down, I will pass by quickly and scoop you up. I will turn myself into an eagle," said the man.

The princess begged permission and came down to the ground. Lord, that eagle appeared. He scooped her up the way they catch little chicks. The soldiers tried to shoot him, but he wasn't hit by the bullets. The man who killed her husband carried the princess away.

He had a wife now—the one he was mad about, you see.

—Rey Komis

The Adventures of Johnny Fourteen

Once there was a man named Johnny Fourteen. He was called Johnny Fourteen because he ate fourteen meals a day. At each meal there were enough helpings for fourteen men.

Since he never could get enough food, he left home. He would travel wherever he traveled. Wherever there were big animals he caught them. Because he had no use for them, he killed them.

It was learned that there was a Johnny Fourteen. "Come and do some work!" said the boss who summoned him. "But I won't pay you any money. You'll just be paid your meals."

"All right!" said Johnny Fourteen.

"You are to roll these rocks. Sixty rocks. If you can move them, then you can eat."

"Fine!" said Johnny. The rocks were the size of a house. He pushed them aside.

"How is your work going?" asked the boss.

"It's finished," said Johnny.

"Do you mean it?" the boss said.

"I mean it," said Johnny.

"Good!" said the boss. "Now tonight you will guard my banana trees." But he was being tricked. It was known that wild animals would come to eat him.

"All right!" said Johnny. He took his machete with him. He spent the night at the foot of the cliff, guarding the banana trees. He couldn't get to sleep.

Jaguars and snakes came out of the cave. He killed them all with his machete.

At daybreak he returned.

"Didn't anything happen to you?" asked the boss.

"No, nothing," said Johnny.

"Do you mean it?"

"I mean it."

"Now you are going to deliver a message," he was told.

He arrived at the house and spoke to the Ladino at the door. "I've come to deliver a message," Johnny told him.

"Go inside and speak to the owner," said the Ladino.

Johnny went through sixty doors. The gentleman inside read the message.

"Ah, good, the message says you are to stay here. We will be together now," said the lord of the house.

"But who says so?" asked Johnny.

"I say so!" said the gentleman.

"Are you the one who gives all the orders?"

"It's me, as I told you. Get out if you can! But how are you going to get out?"

"If I want to, I'll get out," said Johnny. "I'll think it over and see whether I get used to it here or not."

Now when Johnny Fourteen lost his temper, he kicked one door after another until he broke down all sixty doors.

"I'm back," he told the boss.

"But how did you get out?"

"I opened the door," said Johnny.

"Fine," said the boss. "Now you are to go to the graveyard. You don't have to work. Just spend the night there."

"Okay!" said Johnny Fourteen.

He went to spend the night at the graveyard, but he couldn't fall asleep. He kept pacing around.

At midnight all the ghosts came out. "What are you looking for?" they asked.

"I'm not looking for anything. I'm just having a good time," said Johnny.

"Let's go to our house, then," they said.

"Who's giving the orders?" asked Johnny.

"It's whatever we say," said the ghosts.

Johnny was taken through sixty levels of the earth. He was at the very bottom of the world.

"God, but how can I get out?" said Johnny. He thought carefully. "I guess I'll try."

In a minute he kicked his way out of the underworld. Johnny Fourteen escaped.

"I've come back," he told his boss the next morning.

"Eat, then!" the boss said.

Johnny ate and ate. He ate fourteen helpings.

"Now," said the boss, "you are to go to the graveyard again."

"Okay," said Johnny.

A troop of soldiers was waiting to attack him, since it had been heard that he couldn't be killed, that one man had the strength of fourteen men.

They fired their rifles. Johnny Fourteen was standing unconcerned. He just dodged the bullets as they passed. Finally the soldiers ran out of bullets.

Johnny rushed at them, swinging his machete. He wrestled all the soldiers. He finished them off.

He returned to tell his boss.

"Have you come back again? What kind of a man are you?"

"Really, I'm no special kind of man," said Johnny.

"Didn't anything happen to you?"

"Nothing," said Johnny.

"So, you bastard, stop eating here, then! You just eat and eat. Go on, go far, far away! Go jump into a war or something! Today there is no food for you."

Johnny went on. He disappeared. That's how the story ends.

—Romin Teratol

When One Stupid Indian Won

Once the Mexicans had a dispute with another land. Who knows where the country was. Ooh, even the Mexicans couldn't win. They did their best in battle. Many of them had died. But the enemy soldiers were terribly fierce. The Mexicans couldn't overcome them.

Now the Mexicans had heard that the Zinacantecs were stronger. The leaders sent a message. "All of you are wanted," said the message.

The Zinacantecs came to a decision. Only one man would go.

He arrived in Mexico City dressed in his ceremonial robe, his red turban, his fine ceremonial sandals, carrying his net properly.

"Sir, what are the orders?" asked the Zinacantec.

"Where are the others?" asked the general.

"I have come alone," said the Zinacantec.

"But what help are you? Ugh, stupid Indian, forget it! Go back home!"

Happily the poor Zinacantec left, carrying his net, dressed in his ceremonial sandals. "Since I'm not of any use, I'll return," he said.

At lunchtime the leaders of the troops were talking together. "A Zinacantec came here," said the general.

"What did he say?" asked the others.

"He asked what the orders were. 'Are we to help each other perhaps?' he said."

"But could one help?"

"That's why I told him to go home."

"You should have delayed him. If you had told him to stay, who knows what he could have done."

"I didn't stall him. 'Go on, poor Indian. You don't know how to do anything!' I told him."

"Oh no! Have the soldiers catch up with him on the trail and bring him back," said the other war chief.

The soldiers caught up with him. "Zinacantec! You are supposed to return."

"Eh, I won't go back now. I've come too far already. I'm tired," said the Zinacantec.

"You must return, because the leaders want to talk to you."

He returned.

"Will you be so kind as to help us? Please stay!" said the leaders.

"Who knows if I can do anything. I'm no help, since I'm a stupid Indian," he answered.

"Forgive me for having told you that. On the contrary, please help us! We aren't able to win by ourselves," said the general.

"If I am to help you, I'll help you. It's no trouble, if you really are too worn out to do it by yourselves. Send out a message. Have the enemy wait three days!"

They sent out the message. The enemy was to wait three days so that the Zinacantec could work as he pleased. The Mexicans stretched out a rope in the path of the enemy. When the rope was absolutely taut, the enemy would be blocked off.

The Mexicans were ready. They sent out another message. "Come on!" said the message.

The enemy advanced. Well-satisfied they came, since they knew they were winning. Wherever they tried to cut through the rope, they got entangled. All the soldiers were burned up as if it had been an electric wire. Heaps of ashes were left.

That's how the dispute was settled long ago.

—Romin Teratol

The Three Suns

Long ago there were three suns.
There was no darkness. The suns took turns.
There was always day because of the three suns.

They traveled together. They went for a walk.
They went to look for fruits.
The two older brothers climbed a tree.
The younger brother stayed below.
   "Give me some fruit," said the little brother.
      "Throw one down to me."
   "Come on, climb up!" said the older brothers.
   "I can't climb up. Throw some down!"

The fruits were thrown down, but just the chewings.
He picked up the chewings and made them hind legs and forelegs.
He buried them at the foot of the tree.
They turned into a gopher. It gnawed the roots to pieces.
The older brothers felt the tree moving.
   "What are you doing, Xut?" asked the older brothers.
   "I'm not doing anything. Eat the fruit."
The tree fell. Down came his mean older brothers.
Xut went home.
   "Mother, I'm hungry. Give me six tortillas."

He went back and grabbed his older brothers.
Quickly he stuck noses and ears on them.
He made their noses and ears out of the six tortillas.
He turned one into a peccary, the other into a pig.
The peccary ran away.
He caught it by the tail, but its tail came off.
It fled into the woods.

He drove the pig to his house.
   "Mother, I've brought a pig. The pig is hungry.
      Let's fatten it up."

"All right," said his mother. "But where are your older
  brothers?"
"I don't know. They must be having a good time
  someplace," said Xut.

The first day she believed it.
Then his mother cried and cried. Her tears flowed.
Now the moon's light is faint at night.

                                 —Romin Teratol

When the Ashes Fell

Long ago ashes fell. I was a teenager. It certainly was long ago. First
there was an explosion to the south. It was after midnight. Then I felt
the earth shiver. It was like a mortar.

    The next morning everybody was afraid. "But what fiesta could
it be?" they came to ask in San Cristóbal.

    "A mountain is exploding. But you watch, ashes will fall! Who
knows if it will be midnight, who knows when," they said. "The
ashes will fall today."

    At sunset we fled to the woods. We went to my grandfather's
house. It was packed tight with people. "The mountain will explode.
The mountain will explode here!" everyone said. But it was far away
where the mountain erupted.

    Ooh, when it grew light, Holy Mary! The ash was a handspan
deep on the holy ground. The horses, the sheep, Holy Mary! They
couldn't eat, they couldn't drink the water.

    Dawn came over the holy earth. We reached home. The ash
stopped falling. Nothing stirred. The sun appeared. The dry season
began. It was just before the Day of the Dead. Just like today. The
rocks exploded at this time of year.

    After it erupted, the horses and sheep got diarrhea. They drank
the water. They ate their food. The ashes were hot. Long ago the
punishment was a little too stiff. A mountain exploded. Ashes fell.

Then candles were offered in the mountains. The shamans said that candles should be offered.

The earthquakes had started in October. Everybody was scared. Everybody cried. We were afraid we would die. There was quake after quake after quake. For a month it rained, rained and rained like it's raining now. The earthquakes continued, Holy Mary! Then the earthquakes stopped. The mountain exploded. The ashes fell.

—Xun Vaskis

When the Church Rose and Saint Sebastian Was Saved

The Church of the Martyr wasn't built by masons. It was built by the Vaxakmen, the Gods of Creation. It was made in five nights and five days. Darkness took hold. There was no day and no night. It was the Creator Gods who carried the stones. It was the Creator Gods who stirred the lime. It was the Creator Gods who lifted the timbers. That's why the land was in darkness.

Day and night the land was in darkness. Dawn never came. "Why is the land so dark? It's unbearable," said the people.

"Who knows why. Maybe god is punishing us for something. If the things we live on run out, we'll die of starvation. We won't live through it," said the people.

But when five days and five nights were over, the church was standing. Its walls were up. Its tiles were on.

Our Holy Fathers, the Creator Gods, gave the order. "You go in here!" When the stones heard, they knew where to go. They knew how to build the church by themselves. When the trees were told, "Let's go!" they dragged themselves along. They had legs long ago. That's why it didn't take long to build the church.

The bell tower isn't tall. It's low, because it was built by the Creator Gods. The bells aren't big either. You see, there were no big bells long ago. That church wasn't built this morning or yesterday. Who knows what year it was or how many centuries ago. There isn't anyone living who saw it built. Our ancestors saw the church being built.

There used to be a cemetery where the church is. There were white stones standing on the graves of the dead.

Our Holy Fathers, the Creator Gods, built the church for the Holy Martyr.

The Holy Martyr, Saint Sebastian, was a captain. He came from deep in the woods with his little slit drum. I don't know what Our Holy Father's crime was. They left him in the heavy forest to be killed by mountain lions, coyotes, jaguars. They did their best where they threw him. They tried their hardest where they tossed him, but he didn't die. He returned.

"How can it be that he doesn't die? We thought he would be killed by coyotes. We thought he would be eaten by jaguars, by some wild animal in the woods, but he returned just the same, alive."

The Lacandóns were sent to shoot him with arrows. He was wounded in his breast. He was wounded in his legs. He was wounded in the belly, in his thighs, in his ribs. They tried to kill him because he was an army captain. How would we know he was Our Holy Father the Martyr? He looked like the image of Our Holy Father the Martyr in the church.

Raven came. The Spooks came with their squirrels.

And then the Spaniards came.

It was the Spaniards who defended him long ago. "Don't kill him. He is our captain," said the Spaniards. "He will come to live here in the church."

The Church of the Holy Martyr has never collapsed. It's never come apart. Saint Sebastian is happy there. It has a roof. It has everything.

If you ask Him for grace, for blessing, if you go to Him and weep, Our Lord always gives you your food. Our Lord has miracles. Our Lord is good-hearted.

That's why the church was built by Our Holy Fathers, Vaxakmen. It was built to last to this day. The Church of the Holy Martyr is ancient work.

—Tonik Nibak

The Priest and the Bell—
The Epidemic and Me

Three Zinacantec shamans dreamt. They dreamt about Our Holy Mother, Muxul Mountain.

"Children, I'm giving you a bell. Go see for yourselves, children! I left it for you."

The next holy morning the three shamans went by daylight to the top of the mountain of Our Holy Mother. There was the holy bell! Its rim was peeking out above the holy ground.

The news spread to all the children of Our Holy Father Saint Lawrence. They came to pray to Our Holy Mother to learn if she would kindly let them remove it. Candles were offered.

"Take it!" she said. Our Holy Mother, Muxul Mountain, gave them permission.

Our Ancient Mother is so good-hearted. Holy Mary, place of recovery, place of revival. Even if you are sick, when you leave her shrine you will come back well. The sickness is left beneath the feet of Our Mother.

They dug. After three holy days the bell came free. The holy bell was secured with chains. It wouldn't go anywhere now.

The trouble was, the elders were stupid. "Let's go eat!" they said.

While the elders were in the midst of eating, the priest came. The trouble was, the priest happened to bring his maid along. The priest walked around the bell. His maid was standing beside it.

God, the bell leaped out of its chains. The great chains for the holy bell were left lying in a knot. The candles were left standing in rows. To this day there is a huge pit there. Let the young look! Let the old look! It was a very broad, big bell. The bell was bright green. It was gold.

Me, I saw the bell. I am its child. I am its offspring. I was a little boy then, but it won't be long before I'm a hundred years old. So it was a hundred years ago, Holy Mary!

It lifted itself out from the place where it was lying. It soared into the sky. It sailed to Raven House hill. It went "Bong" there. It disappeared in the mountains.

The people of Zinacantán Center wept. The shamans wept. Their efforts were all in vain.

The elders were denounced. "It's wrong for a woman to watch. Men were taking it out." Don't you see, it was the elders' fault. They lost their heads. They didn't take authority.

The priest was condemned too. "Your crime is too great, father. Why did you have to bring that woman along? Women aren't supposed to watch everything." Women musn't come close, because women are "cold." Men are men! Don't you see, Our Holy Father has a beard. Men have beards. Women never have beards.

The three shamans were just stupid. They should have offered candles to the gods at all the shrines. They should have offered candles at the Church of Saint Lawrence, place of recovery, place of revival, where stands the sustainer, the protector.

No, they simply prayed to Our Holy Ancient Mother, Mary Muxul. She gave permission for the bell to be taken out as a gift to Our Holy Father Saint Lawrence.

The elders were dumbstruck.

All the elders met at the Church of the Holy Martyr. They were dressed up in their ceremonial shirts and pants. They were well-prepared, Holy Mary! Loads of gunpowder, rockets, mortars blasting off.

But Our Holy Ancient Mother was heartbroken. The priest, then, died. His maid, then, died. Too bad! Don't you see, they were doing evil. Then the elders died. The shamans lived. They weren't at fault. They just gave their counsel. They dreamt. They saw the bell. Our Ancient Mother showed it to them.

The bell was hurt. "Since I won't be installed, you will be punished. I should have been seated next to Our Holy Father Saint Lawrence. We would have watched over our children, our offspring, but now you can wait!" said the bell.

See how it is now—some have lice and some are well-off. The land became poor. The famine came. Zinacantán lost its luck when it lost the bell.

Look at the bell in the Church of Saint Lawrence! It is cracked now because a disgusting woman went up into the tower. When the schoolboys went to ring it, the bell cracked.

The other bell, the None bell, has never cracked. It isn't struck by lightning, because it is virility itself. What a bell!

My Lord, when the epidemic came, the None bell rang three times at midnight. But there was no one there. The holy church was locked tight. The bell rang by itself.

In November, God, the dead! In sevens and eights they went into the grave. I was a full-grown man. I carried the bodies. I did the burying.

If there was a chicken standing there, grab it! Eat it! If there was a bottle standing there, grab it! Drink it! Pick up your hoe, go on.

If there was a tortilla or if there was still someone to give you a tortilla, eat it! If not—have you ever seen a jaguar?—the chickens were gulped down without tortillas. That's how I got the strength for the constant carrying of corpses.

I buried one body. I came back to pick up another. I buried it. I came back to pick up another. I was worn out. My strength was gone. I was bedridden for seven days, but it wasn't so bad. I'm still walking around.

My wife died. I was left penniless. One son was left, one daughter was left. My little boy was still crawling. I cried. I went home to my mother.

Afterwards, I decided to get a wife. She has been with me ever since.

—Xun Vaskis

The King and the Ring

Long ago there was a terribly wretched man. He had nothing to live on, nothing at all.

He kept rolling about by the courthouse door. He would beg from the elders. He would be given a tortilla or two by the civil officials. He was terribly poor. He couldn't earn a thing in the world.

He would come to the foot of Muxul Mountain time and again. He would spend the day there, rolling about, playing. He was a grown man, but he didn't know how to earn a living.

He was rolling around. He kept tossing sand up into the sky.

Suddenly a golden ring came flashing down. He caught it. He put it on his finger.

He went home.

Lord, money appeared! All his little pots and baskets were filled to the brim.

"Sir, do you want to visit my house? Our Lord has given me a little something," he started saying to people.

"Where would you get anything, you loafer?"

"Really, it isn't a story. It was given to me by Our Lord. Come see for yourselves!"

The civil official went to see if the pauper was telling the truth. Quickly the pauper scooped up a gourdful of money and gave it to the civil official. The coins weren't counted out. They were poured from a gourd, like corn.

"Lord, you were telling the truth after all!" the official said.

Little by little word spread that there was a king in Zinacantán. It was heard as far as Mexico City that now there was money in our town.

A strong order came from the government that he was to go to the capital. Soldiers came to escort him. They brought three beautiful girls along. He was to choose whichever one he wanted for a wife.

"Well, I'll go," said the king. "What else can I do, since they have heard about me."

All the money was carried away on mules. Zinacantán was left penniless.

And when the king arrived in Chiapa, his wife stole the ring.

Then a Ladino appeared. "Let's see your ring!" he said to her. The woman showed it to him. Lord, the thief dashed off with it.

Ooh, the money simply stopped coming. The king was about to be killed, since the Mexicans had no use for him now.

But a dog and a cat spoke. "Don't worry, we'll find your ring."

The thief had already crossed the Grijalva River. But when he was swimming, he swallowed the ring. Now it was sitting in his stomach.

Sonofabitch, the dog and the cat seemed to know it. The dog carried the cat across the Grijalva, since the cat didn't know how to paddle in the water.

They found that thief sound asleep in the deep forest.

The cat looked for a mouse. It gnawed the seat of the thief's pants, to make a path for the ring to come out.

The dog looked for a little lizard. The lizard kept wiggling his tail in the thief's nose. The thief was rolling around sneezing. "Hatchoo! Phht! Hachoo! Phht!"

The ring came out. The cat grabbed it in his teeth.

"Let me take it," said the dog.

"I won't give it to you," said the cat. "I'll take it myself."

"But don't lose it!" said the dog.

The dog carried the cat back across the Grijalva.

But that dumb cat dropped it in the middle of the river.

The dog dove under the water. He spoke to the fishes. They searched for the ring. They found it for him.

The dog brought it back. "Here it is!" he told the king.

The king was overjoyed. They wouldn't kill him now. He had the ring. He was rich again. He went on to Mexico City with all his money.

It was there that he grew old. When he was close to dying, he asked to be shut up in a water jug. He said he was going to be restored.

"Don't open it for three days!" he ordered.

But they opened the jug before the three days were up and they looked inside. So he died once and for all.

Ever since there has been no more talk of Indian kings.

—Rey Komis

The Donkey and the Spring

They were looking for mushrooms at the foot of a cliff.
They saw a donkey standing there.
Three days later, and the donkey was still there.
They were going to catch the donkey that didn't move.

They saw the corral at the mouth of the cave too late.
They were shut up in the corral. They joined the donkey.

Their friends who had stayed on the hillside came with candles.
They prayed to the Earth Lord.

"What are you looking for?" asked the Earth Lord.
"We're just taking a walk," said one of the men.
"Come watch my donkey for me!" said the Earth Lord.
"No!" said the man.
"I won't let you go!" said the Earth Lord.

They offered candles. They were released.

For three days the man was free, free to die.
He was going to look after the donkey.
He told his friends the Earth Lord's name.
He said that Lupe was the Earth Lord's name.

He said, "There is water." He said, "There is a spring.
In exchange for my soul, in exchange for my body,
the Earth Lord will let you live by the water in the cave."

The dead man talked as he was lowered in the grave.
"Now I will watch the well and the donkey.
I'm going to see everything there is under the world."

—Xun Akov

John, Head of Gold

There was a man who met up with the Earth Lord. The man had
three sons.

"Compadre," said the Earth Lord.

"Compadre," said the man.

"Won't you give me one of my godchildren? Let him come and
guard my house for me."

"Why not, compadre?" said the man. Quickly the little boy
mounted on horseback. He was taken to the Earth Lord's house.

The boy was given seven keys. "Don't touch anything! Guard
my things!" he told his godson.

As soon as the Earth Lord left, the boy opened all the rooms. Silver was dropping everywhere. The boy dipped his fingers in the silver. He couldn't get them out.

His godfather returned. The boy was killed. His corpse was stuck in a bin of silver.

The Earth Lord went to speak to his compadre again.

"Compadre," said the Earth Lord.

"Compadre," said the man.

"Give me another of my godchildren! The first boy feels at home. They would be happy talking to each other. Lord, he's really content now!"

"Take him!" the father said.

The boy rode off with the Earth Lord. He was given the same seven keys. The fool opened up all the rooms.

Then he saw the skeleton of his older brother sticking out of the silver. But he dipped his fingers in. They wouldn't come out. He just reached his brother where he lay dead, and he died.

The Earth Lord went to bring the third boy back to his cave. "Compadre," he said when he arrived.

"Compadre," said the man.

"Won't you give me another one of my godchildren? Hell, they really feel at home. Let all three be together and guard my house!"

"Sonofabitch, why not let him go!" said the father.

The boy was given the same seven keys. He opened all the rooms.

When he reached the room where all the treasure was stored, he washed his hair in the gold.

But there he stuck fast. "What the devil can I do?" he said.

Now he saw the skeletons of his older brothers. And next to their bones was a magic wand. It belonged to the Earth Lord. He pulled it out.

"Magic wand, is it long before my godfather will return?"

"He's coming near now," it said. "You ought to leave right away!" The boy took off with the magic wand.

There was a very skinny horse. The horse bucked and bucked, but the boy held on. He rode away with that little devil of his that talked.

Ooh, the Earth Lord came galloping after him. You see, the boy had stolen his power.

The boy tossed down a comb. It turned into a thicket of hawthorns. The Earth Lord stumbled, but he kept on riding.

The boy tossed down a mirror. It turned into cliff after cliff. But the Earth Lord kept dashing after him on horseback until he caught up to the boy.

The boy tossed down the ribbons from his hat, I've heard them say. The ribbons turned into a swamp. The Earth Lord was stuck. Finally the boy came out on the earth's surface.

He arrived in Zinacantán Center. He had wrapped his head in a neckerchief, but people saw that his hair was gold. John, Head of Gold, he was called.

He still had his devil with him. He wouldn't give away that magic wand. It talked to him, you see. It was his companion.

One day he met a beautiful girl. "Sonofabitch, wouldn't you like us to get married?" he said. It was the magic wand that coaxed her. It deceived her, that devil.

She let him sleep with her, but he never married her.

He went to another town. Wherever he traveled he tried the women out. That's what I've heard, indeed!

—Rey Komis

The Little Bird

Little Bird was a general. He led the Chamulans into war. They went to Acala, Chiapilla, San Lucas, to Kakav Te', Rincon. They stole a Christ Child. They stole icons. They grabbed women. They grabbed little girls. They cut them with a pocketknife.

They would startle people. They would break into houses and grab the men, tie them up, truss their legs, make them kneel. Then they would assault the women. They would search for the women until they had finished with the whole household.

Then they would steal money, or an icon, or a Christ Child. Whatever you had they would steal. That's what they did in Acala, Chiapilla, Rosario.

They had guns, machetes, knives, spears. They had something

like a dagger, a metal-tipped walking stick as thick as your finger. They would kill people with them. They hunted down their own people and murdered them in caves where they had hidden. You used to get a fright long ago when the Chamulans went about.

There was one Zinacantec who became a follower of Little Bird. His name was Palas Rodriguez. He went with them to Totolapa. He stole a Saint Anthony, two Christ Childs, three icons. Who knows how much money, because we didn't see. But what I saw I'll tell about. The old man lived next to our house, so we saw what that Little Bird brought home.

In Chiapilla he stole a telephone and sold it to a Chamulan. He stole two thermoses too. He thought they were bottles, the fool. He was glad to get a peso for them.

Then they went to Acala. There he stole the Holy Mother, Our Holy Father Saint Anthony, and a little Christ Child. They went to Rincon Chamula just to steal money, to steal pigs. They went to Ixtapa to sell them. The pigs sold for a hundred and fifty, the chickens for fifteen pesos. For twenty-five pesos they sold the turkeys—the ones they didn't eat up. They split the money among themselves. That Old Palas himself brought home two heifers and a sheep. Four turkeys. Three watches. One jug of peach cane liquor. They celebrated with it. They mixed the liquor with chicha and drank it all.

When they went to Simojovel, they stole yarn and cloth. They had a mule load of stolen goods. On their way home they tethered their mule in the woods. At night they would take the stolen goods into the house. Who would know that all their things were stolen goods? That's how Palas became a rich man, Tall Old Little Bird, as he was called.

Once my mother nearly killed him, because he stole our land. All the land that reaches to the edge of the ranch used to be my own. Stolen for nothing. He didn't pay a single cent. That was the tricky Little Bird, Palas.

He was a friend of Juan Perez Jolote, the second Little Bird.

The first Little Bird, the Chamulan general, was the one who was always armed with spears, with metal-tipped walking sticks, with shotguns, with knives wherever he went from house to house to steal.

Little Bird didn't die easily. He couldn't be killed. In Chiapilla his army was attacked. Those who were captured had their ears cut off.

The dead were piled in a heap. The dogs ate them. The buzzards flocked. The government soldiers poured gasoline on the corpses. They burned like firewood. Their flesh turned to charcoal. Their bones glowed.

Old Little Bird, Palas, died in the epidemic. He had no children of his own. He was impotent. His offspring were the children of his younger sister's husband. The daughter was Marta. The boy's name was Maryan. They baptized him Maryan Rodriguez, but he wasn't Maryan Rodriguez. We called him Maryan Seto.

When Little Bird and his wife were still alive, a man arrived to borrow money. He set down two bottles of cane liquor.

They drank the cane liquor. They got drunk. Little Bird sent for the boy.

The poor old woman did an ugly thing. She raised her skirt. "Would you be happy with this, compadre?" she said to the man who had come to ask for a loan. She pulled up her skirt. She slapped her legs.

That son of hers lost his temper.

Quickly he cut off her head with an axe. God, curled up tight the poor old woman died. Her neck was thoroughly cut. Holy Mary! Her hair was simply stiff with blood.

The house was closed, so how would we know she was dead? The day after her death I passed by on my way to gather firewood. The house was shut up. The next day and the day after that, the house was still shut up.

She had a comadre, wife of Rejino who lives in Sek'emtik. She was the one who found her. She opened the door. "Comadre, comadrita!" she called, since the old woman was Spanish. Her name was Loxa Seto. Rosa Buluch was her name.

But her comadre was completely dead. Her legs were simply curled up. Dead, murdered.

That's what happened to Little Bird's wife, indeed! That was the third Little Bird.

The first Little Bird was the one with real Chamulan flesh. The second was Juan Perez Jolote. The third was Old Palas, the thief. The fourth was Maryan Seto, the murderer. Until they all died. Died. Shot. Cut to pieces!

—Tonik Nibak

Still Another Spook

Long ago there were a great many Spooks. The Spooks would steal chickens. They would steal money. They would go from house to house to steal women away.

We couldn't go anywhere. We couldn't go out to gather firewood or fetch water. From three o'clock in the afternoon until eight o'clock the next morning we were closed up inside the house. At nine o'clock we could go out, but only nearby, and never alone. We couldn't go far because it was dark under the trees. They would be squatting there, waiting to grab us as we were gathering wood or drawing water.

Once a Spook came to the house of one of my neighbors. "Nanita, won't you please do the favor of preparing my meal?" asked the Spook, carrying a stolen turkey with him.

"Give it to me! Come in! Sit down!" said the woman. She put her pot of water on top of the fire. When the boiling water was bubbling, she dipped the turkey in it. She put another pot on the fire. "Wouldn't you like to drink some posol while you wait for your meal?"

"I would!" said the Spook.

While he was drinking his posol, she threw boiling water on him. He was scalded like a chicken.

But it didn't kill him. He just rolled out the door. He was rolling around the whole day at the door, since he was burnt. But in three days he was well again and walking around. He tried to grab a baby girl.

You see how tricky they were. They would grab whatever they could get. There weren't any good Spooks. They were wicked.

"Forget it," said the woman when she saw that the awful Spook couldn't be killed.

"But we shouldn't be scared. We should be brave now that there are several families nearby," said the women of Zinacantán. "Now that he has seen our houses there's no time left."

The women gathered together. The Spook arrived again.

"Nanita, Nanita. You gonna make dee meal!" said the Spook in his awful Spanish.

"But he's a countryman of ours. Don't believe he's a Spook. He's fooling us," said the women, trying to humor him.

"Give it to me! Where is it? Come on! We'll fix it! If you want to eat a meal, I will grind the corn. I will make the tortillas," said the woman of the house.

"Grind it. I'll wait, Nanita!" said the Spook.

She patted the tortillas. She cooked the chicken. He ate.

"If you want a little coffee, I'll make it," she said.

He was in the midst of drinking his coffee. Then he was shot at. God, he didn't die from the bullets.

The women attacked him with a machete. He was cut up properly. They didn't cut his body into just two pieces. He didn't get just a single blow!

But he was sewn up. He revived, since he just wouldn't die.

A week or two later he returned again. He brought two hens and a crate of bread along with him. "Nanita, fix dee meal. I eat!" said the Spook.

"Ah, give it to me! If you are hungry, I'll fix it. I'll rinse my corn and make the tortillas."

"Oh, his horrible eyes, his horrible teeth. They'd give you a fright!" said the woman who told me about it.

"His horrible wide eyes were red. You'd be scared of him. You certainly wouldn't eat with him."

"Did you eat with him?" I asked.

"I ate with him," she said, "because we had already decided what to do."

The tip was sharpened. She served his meal, her meal, and her children's meal. They finished eating.

The gentleman burped. "Ahh!" he said. "Burr! Well, Nanita, thank you for the meal. Do your children have enough to eat?"

"They do!" she told him.

"Fine! Spend a good night, Nanita!" said the Spook. He stretched his legs and went out the door.

He landed on a sharpened stake. It went up his ass, came out his mouth. He was spitted.

"Now we'll roast him on the fire."

They roasted him on the fire the way we roast a rabbit. Wouldn't he die of that?

They turned him over from side to side. They used up eight logs.

They cooked him until he was well-done. Then they set him afire. They poured kerosene on him so that he would die. Die for good.

The Spooks have disappeared to this day. There are very few left. Only where a road is being made or a bridge is being built do we hear of Spooks. But we don't see them much anymore. Long ago we couldn't even go outside. It was scary because we were killed by Spooks.

—Tonik Nibak

Long Hairs

Once there were peanut sellers from Tenejapa who tried to get to Simojovel, but they couldn't continue past that bend in the deep woods where the Long Hairs held up people long ago. They confiscated beans, wheat, any little thing they could find. Sometimes they let people go. Sometimes they killed them and ate them.

The Tenejapans were tired of it.

A merchant from Zinacantán Center arrived in Tenejapa to sell salt. "How can you buy your clothes, how can you buy your muslin, how can you buy your thread now that you can't trade anything from San Cristóbal?" the man asked.

"There's nothing we can do. We have no way of earning a living, and besides, no one in San Cristóbal will accept the money we have. Who knows why the money situation has broken down," said the people of Tenejapa. The Ladinos in San Cristóbal would only accept Cabreras from Guatemala.

The man from Zinacantán Center spoke. "Long ago I had an uncle who was terribly strong. You have to say that the gentleman was the very last word in strength. There were a good number of people he was able to beat up regardless of how tall or well-built they were. He was strong, but he was killed by the Long Hairs. Do you think if it were us we wouldn't die?

"But I have a remedy for the highwaymen. If you will pay twenty-five pesos for a gourdful, I'll get the remedy and bring it. You'll see, you will be able to go trading. You will be able to buy cloth. You will be able to travel to Guatemala or wherever your hearts desire. You will look for your pesos the way I do when I come to your land. Just so long as you pay the price of the remedy. The medicine that I will bring is fine powder."

"What kind of medicine could it be? What is it called?" he was asked.

"I'll let you know what its name is when I have prepared it and brought it. We'll talk together then."

"Twenty-five is its price," said a Tenejapan, "but give it to me on credit, because I haven't that much money."

"No, if it's bought it is twenty-five, but if it's on credit it's fifty," said the medicine-seller. "I'll be back in a week. Get your load ready! You'll see if you don't win. I'll teach you what to do. I'll prepare twenty-five staves for you too!"

In a week the salt merchant arrived with twenty-five staves and a gourdful of the medicine. "You hold it in your fist like this! You wrap it up like this! You slip it in your waist like this! When you see the highwaymen approaching, you say to the remedy, 'Let them come to kill me, let them do whatever their hearts desire!'"

The Tenejapan wrapped it up and slipped it in his waist. When the Long Hair came out swinging his machete, the man tossed the remedy at him. "I'll give it to you too!" the Tenejapan shouted.

The awful murderer was thrashing about. He couldn't stand up. He got a terrific beating with the staves.

The Tenejapan traveled on for a half a league. Another Long Hair came rushing out in a fury, menacing him with his awful bow and arrow. He was about to shoot when the Tenejapan grabbed away the bow. Then he tossed the medicine at him. The Long Hair landed way off, on his knees. He had no strength left. He was helpless. The man attacked him with a stave. The second Long Hair died.

The Tenejapan arrived in Simojovel. "How did you get past all the highwaymen?" asked a storekeeper. "One of my customers, a gentleman like you, came back with an arrow in his back. Blood was pouring out of the poor guy."

"I have some medicine," the Tenejapan told him. "I paid a hundred and fifty pesos for this little handful. But see how many staves I was given! I win with my staves." It was probably because the sticks had soul.

"But what does the plant look like? How does it grow? Does it have a trunk? Do you add anything to it?" a Ladina asked the Tenejapan.

"I don't know. It was prepared for me by a salt merchant in the town of Zinacantán."

"Ooh, but I'll buy some too. I'll pay whatever you say. I'll take any amount," said the Ladina.

The Tenejapan sold the little wad of medicine for a hundred and fifty pesos.

He asked the owner of the remedy for another twenty-five staves. The Zinacantec sold them for ten pesos. The Tenejapan sold them for twenty. He had no more worries.

Before we couldn't travel. Even if we went a short distance, we were sure to be wounded or killed by arrows. The highwaymen had never been afraid, because if someone came along, they covered their faces with their hair. No one recognized who they were or where they came from.

But we had clever eyes. We were the first to scatter "chief" at them.

When the remedy was found, the road was opened up. Now people come and go everywhere. If you know what to do, anyone, even Spooks, are afraid of that medicine.

It was twenty-five years ago when I heard my mother say that that remedy was very useful. When she had a toothache she stuck it in her mouth. It was my late mother who told me that tobacco is medicine. "Chief" is what we call it.

—Tonik Nibak

A Medley of Remedies

To incapacitate a devil or a snake, tobacco or garlic is thrown at it.

When corn is stolen from a field, the owner may make a cross of the corn stalks that have been stripped of ears and stand it in the center or in a corner of the field so Our Lord will punish the robber with poverty or death. That same effect may be produced by drawing a cross on the footprints of the robber.

To prevent a weasel that has crossed one's path from shortening one's life, and to ensure that it will die in its den, three crosses are made on the path with one's foot.

Should a Ladino foreman on the coffee plantations not let his workers rest, they may sprinkle tobacco on his back when he is asleep. This is reputed to cause him nausea and diarrhea, laying him up for at least a day.

To cause hail to stop falling, three pans of embers, three loom bars, and three bodkins are flung at the hail.

To calm a violent storm, tobacco is sprinkled on the ground.

To make an enemy's field of corn die, a person sprinkles tobacco on it.

To make an enemy's peach tree die, a stick of pine is buried at its foot.

If the wife of the owner of an avocado tree is pregnant, she must take three bites out of three avocados lest the fruit be spoiled.

When a religious official or bridegroom has a bull slaughtered, their assistants bite the raw meat three times lest it be contaminated by the pregnancy of the wife or mistress of one of the party.

To tame a mule, its neck is rubbed three times with a broom.

To rid a corn field of raccoons, a naked boy and a naked girl walk around the edge of the field three times.

To rid a corn field of june bug grubs, a man may take a greasy old skirt of an old woman and, holding it aloft like a flag, walk around the field three times. Alternatively, he may take two grubs and place them head to head or one across the other and bury them in one of their tunnels in that position.

To prevent wind damage, a strip of the palm fronds distributed on Saint Peter Martyr Day is tied to the corn plants at the four corners of the field. To protect a corn field in high wind, the owner will call out, "Be strong, my little corn fields, please do not fall down."

If a pregnant woman is sleeping alone, she will keep her husband's shirt or pants in the bed lest a monkey come to steal her baby.

A person with gas on his stomach puts three crosses of ashes on it and says, "Take the Tuxtla road, take the Chiapa road," so that the "wind" will leave.

To cure a mule of "wind," its belly is struck three times with a woman's sash, its tail is cropped in a cruciform design, and a copper coin is passed over the tail.

To cure a person of a yellow spot on his eye, thirteen black beans, three or thirteen silver five centavo pieces, together with white salt are placed outside overnight to let the dew fall upon them. Then they are applied to the eye to reduce the "heat."

Swelling may be treated by smoking the patient with the smoke of a black vulture's bones, wax myrtle, butterfly bush, and sage.

To ensure that a rifle fires well, thirteen chilis are put in the barrel which is then held over the fire until the chilis are roasted.

To ensure that a jaguar will not toss back one's bullets, a person sleeping in the woods will wrap the wad with three pubic hairs and three hairs from the arm pit and insert it in the rifle barrel, or he will simply break wind on the rifle.

from *The Great Tzotzil Dictionary of San Lorenzo Zinacantán*

The Flood

Long ago the world was flooded. My late grandmother told my mother about it. My mother heard it and she told me.

The land was flooded. The world was deserted. Only two people were left. They fled to the top of a mountain. They hid there for months until the water dried up.

When the water receded, they sent off a buzzard. It never returned.

The "red beak," the turkey vulture, came down. It didn't return. The king vulture came down. It didn't return. It got used to the food. There were plenty of dead things to eat. The grackle came down. It filled up on corn. The rusty-crowned sparrow came down. It grew fond of eating worms, whatever little tidbits there were. The towhee came down. It didn't return. The bobwhite came down. "There is corn, I'll eat it," it said. It didn't return. The sharp-shinned hawk came down. It got used to it too, since there were dead horses, dead sheep, dead dogs. The cowbird, the caracara, the yellow bird came down. They never returned.

"Why is it that not a single bird returns? Why don't they come back to tell us how the world is?" said the woman and the man who survived.

"Who knows, but you'd better wait or you'll just go and kill yourself down there," said the wife.

The man waited three days. Nothing returned. He sent one of his little dogs. It grew fond of eating horse meat. He sent a white-winged dove. It never returned.

"Maybe the water hasn't dried up yet," said his wife. "If there is still water down there, forget it, I'm not going, I'll just die."

He waited a week for the earth to dry out properly. Then he came down to the valley. But you see, the mud was up to his knees. He hurt his calf. Who knows if it was slashed with a machete. Who knows if it was cut with a knife. His leg had a long gash.

He went back up. "Skip it. It's impossible to walk on the ground. Look, my leg got hurt right at the start."

"Didn't I tell you, 'Don't go yet!' Didn't I say that?" said his wife.

"I'll wait one or two days more. Otherwise I'd just be going off to kill myself."

"That's better. What's there to lose?"

He came down when the stated time was up. He opened the first house. It was flooded with water. He was soaked.

But the smell! It stunk terribly where people had died. He broke into the houses with a club. Don't you see, the doors had swollen from the water.

"I shouldn't have come down. It wasn't worth it. The earth stinks horribly!" he said. "Never mind, I'll wait for the rainy season to end. The trees still have their leaves."

He lit a fire. He warmed up his tortillas. He ate, and after he finished eating, he slept. He didn't return that night because the trail was so slippery.

The next day he climbed back up the mountain.

"You shouldn't have gone, you should have waited until the earth had finished drying out properly, you hear! I was right. What good did you do by going?" his wife said.

"Yes, you're certainly right. It's absolutely impossible to rest, because of the smell inside the houses. It stinks horribly."

"Never mind, wait until the earth is good and dry. It's useless for our livestock to leave now. The raven will come to take us."

The raven flew down to the valley when the earth seemed dry enough to walk on easily. It looked to see if it left footprints.

The bird returned. "It's fine now. It's dry now. I've come to take you. See for yourselves. The mud is well-cracked in the houses that were closed up. As for the others, just the tips of their roofs show. They're just buried in mud," said the raven.

"How many of the houses are still good?" asked the man.

"There are six or seven good houses. Those that had strong walls."

The man came down. He looked in all the houses. In one house he found seventy solid pesos, the money of long ago. In another house he found twenty-two. In another house he found fifteen, ten in another.

"My Lord, I can't live on this. The amount I've found isn't enough for me alone. It's true I still have corn. But when it runs out, what will we eat?"

He had two girls, two boys, and a baby. Soon they were starving, and their mother took sick. She got sick from eating famine food— banana roots, fern roots, wild yam roots. Her face grew big. Her belly grew big. The poor thing was horribly bloated. She died.

"God, what can I feed my children?" said the man.

He spoke to the raven. "My corn has run out. I haven't any seed corn. What do you think I can plant, holy raven?"

"Shush up!" it said. "There are two bins of corn in a cave on Upper Raven House Mountain. There's yellow corn there. There's white corn there. There's black corn there. There's red corn there. I'll go steal one ear apiece for your seed corn. That's where I go myself when I haven't anything at all to eat."

One by one the raven carried off four ears of corn in its beak and gave them to the man. "Here is your seed corn," he said. "See if you can support yourself, because they won't let me take any more. 'What do you keep doing with the corn? How could you have finished eating up all that?' the owner of the cave asked me."

"I understand," said the man. "Thank you. Now that I have hoed my little plot of land, I'll plant it. I have nothing to worry about now. Until the corn is ripe, I'll be satisfied living on the tassels."

It was at that time that the Spaniards arrived. The man joined them. He sought out a wife. When his time came, the man died. He left five children behind.

Others survived when it flooded long ago. Those who were saved could see Our Lord.

When Our Lord himself came down to look, all those who were saved were angry.

"How did you escape?" Our Lord asked.

"We climbed to the mountaintop," some said. "We fled to the woods," said others.

"Where, what woods!"

"Wherever there were any," they answered.

"And your houses?" he asked.

"Oh, who cares?" they said.

"What did you live on?"

"We didn't live on anything much. We lived on vine berries. We lived on nuts." They talked back angrily now.

"Do you want to go on living?" asked Our Lord. "Look behind you, then!"

When they looked behind them, their tails appeared. Their fur appeared. They were turned into monkeys.

Monkeys are the people of long ago. Their faces look human except that they have fur. They have fur and long tails and live in the forest because they didn't obey Our Lord's command. If you don't obey the command, your fur will appear! Go eat the berries of trees and the berries of vines for the rest of your life!

Those who didn't say a single word were left to repopulate the world.

The man's children married. The people multiplied.

Those who didn't talk back to Our Lord, who didn't speak improperly and didn't make a sound, bowing low, weren't guilty. They are humans now. Just like us.

—Tonik Nibak

Our Lady of the Salt

Long ago when Salinas was formed, the Virgin appeared to a young boy.

"What are you doing, son?" asked the Virgin.

"I'm taking a walk around my little corn field, ma'am. I'd like to clear the brush, since the planting season has arrived."

"So that's what you're doing! I am very pleased by this holy place. I'd like to be seated here. I'd like you to build a little house for me.

"Think it over, son. Talk about it with your friends, those who are the wisest, the manliest. I'll come back in two weeks to learn what they have said."

"Oh, it's no trouble, ma'am. I'll tell at least one family. Whether I'm answered favorably or not, I'll come back and wait for you."

"I will be sitting under the avocado tree," said the Virgin. "If they want to build a house for me, then I will bring a gift. You will have salt. You will make a sluice. You will make griddles to crystallize my salt. You will earn your pesos with it. There will be no problems at all. I will help you if you build a house for me.

"I am the youngest sister. My eldest sister lives in Zinacantán Center. My second oldest sister lives in Ixtapa. My sisters are content. They are settled in their houses. The men did as my sisters said immediately. Now I'd like to have my house too, if you'd be so kind."

"If you come, ma'am, if you won't deceive me, if you aren't just tricking me . . . "

"Why wouldn't I come? I want to settle here, if you will build a house for me, however small. We'll produce salt here. You will crystallize it, then you will sell it. With the money you earn you will eat and drink."

"I guess I'll chat about it," said the boy. "You will hear what I'm told in two weeks."

"Wait for me here, son. Take care," said the lady.

She vanished.

"Was it a real person who told me she wanted a house? Could it have been some kind of dirty work? Could it have been something

Romin Teratol and Anselmo Peres in Santa Fe, New Mexico (1963).
Photograph by Helga Gilbert

Petul Vaskis. Photograph by John Swope

Manvel K'obyox. Photograph by Frank Cancian

Xun Akov. Photograph by John Swope

Tonik Nibak. Photograph by John Swope

Anselmo Peres's daughter learning to weave. Photograph by John Swope

Xun Teratol, Romin Teratol's son, typing tales. Photograph by John Swope

announcing my death? Will I die from it?" the boy said to himself. "I'll ask my grandfather if it's a messenger of death. If he tells me it's something bad, that will be terrible."

"Don't worry, son," said the grandfather. "She might be the Virgin, since you've learned that she has two older sisters. It is known that there are three of them, and each one lives wherever she chooses to have her seat. Could it be that I am not conversing properly, for that is what I heard? All the men should meet. 'We'll build her house, collect the money,' they should say. If they don't agree, then we aren't good for anything at all. 'I will ask my grandfather,' you should have told her."

"The lady set apart a two-week period," said the boy.

"Two weeks is still plenty of time. Decide what you want to do. Tell whomever you want to tell. I'll tell my compadre, Maryan, and see if he will help."

The old man talked about it with his compadre. "My grandson says there is a woman who wants to settle here."

"Could she be the Virgin?" asked his compadre.

"And if she's not the Virgin? If she's a woman who simply wants to fluff wool, to spin, to weave in our homes would we turn her down? We'd be satisfied that she makes our shirts and our neckerchiefs. Lord, how can we refuse to let the poor lady live here? It's worth it to build her a little gabled house, however small."

The men gathered together. "What else can we do?" they said. They built a gabled house for her in the place she had chosen.

Who knows how many years afterwards, the ground split open. A little stream descended from the cliff and ran by the door of the Virgin's house. Her house was completely flooded with water.

The Virgin leaped out.She landed at the foot of the avocado tree.

It became apparent that she was the Virgin. When she talked, you wouldn't think she was a saint. She seemed to be a person. But she came and went like a spirit.

After the ground split open and the stream appeared, her house was rebuilt. They collected the money in Zinacantán Center. Her little gabled house is a big church now. The Virgin came and sat down on the altar.

A river passes by the entrance to the Virgin's house now. The sluice was moved to this side of the river. The trunk is a good meter wide. The well where the salt comes out is fifteen meters deep.

They celebrate a fiesta there, the Fiesta of Our Lady of the Rosary.

The civil officials, the scribes, the aldermen, the justices of the peace, the magistrate attend. Whoever is actually in charge of the fiesta, the stewards-royal, the tithing man, are the servants of the Virgin.

Musicians enter. The Stewards of Our Lady of the Rosary carry censers from house to house. A band plays. They offer meals. They celebrate, just as it has come down from long ago. They hold a fine fiesta, because that's what the Virgin wants. The town of Five Pieces is prosperous now.

—Tonik Nibak

When the Bell Was Lifted

When the world was made, the Creator Gods left a bell for Our Holy Father Saint Lawrence. It was quite a bell! When the bell rang, it could be heard as far as Chiapa, as far as Tuxtla.

The Chiapanecs said to the Zinacantecs, the children of Saint Lawrence, "Bring us the bell! Come hang it here!"

The foolish elders talked together. Who knows if it was given or bought. Who knows how much the ancestors sold the bell for, long ago.

The blotchy Chiapanecs were just Hairy Hands. Their chests, their shoulders, their arms, their legs were covered with hair. You don't think their legs could be seen like our legs? Hairy legs. Hairy Hands. They were rain creatures.

Among the Zinacantecs there were Thunderbolt, Wind, and Rainbow. The bell was lifted in the Wind. It was struck by Thunderbolt. Rainbow arched over. It was hung in Chiapa.

But the next morning the bell was back in Zinacantán. The holy bell was bonging in the Center.

The elders carried it to Chiapa again. And the next morning it was back here in its country. The holy bell had a hard time getting used to that place! It didn't feel at home there.

The elders took it to Chiapa a third time. "Watch out! See how it turns out for you!" said Our Holy Father, the bell. "You think I'll hang?"

The bell was never hung. The blotchy Chiapanecs, the Hairy Hands, were strong, but even they couldn't hang it.

A house was built for it in the churchyard. If you look at the bell, it sprays you. Watch out for the water!

The holy bell has been face down ever since.

It won't stir itself to come back. Wind lost. Rainbow lost. Thunderbolt lost. It was their fault that the holy bell left.

But it didn't turn out well for the Chiapanecs either. Some are poor, some are assassins. Some long, in vain, to eat. The holy bell was angered, so Zinacantán grew poor and so did Chiapa, since they came to steal the bell.

There has been punishment ever since for the young and the old. Now some snatch women, now others lie in wait, now some play loudspeakers, now others are barkeepers. How brutish! They're not worth a whoring damn! Some Zinacantecs can't ever accomplish anything, since things got out of order. So it is the punishment of the holy bell to this day.

—Xun Vaskis

Saved from the Horned Serpent

There is a rock with horns. It goes out on Wednesdays and Thursdays.

A man went to see why the rock had horns. The rock moved. The rock spoke.

It said its name was Xul Vo' Ton. There was a horned serpent living under the rock. It plowed the ground with its horns.

There was a spring that flowed from the rock in the forest. The spring was the path of the snake.

The man ran home to tell what he had seen. The people came to live by the spring. They called the rock "Horned Serpent."

But the Earth Lord didn't want us to drink the water.

The serpent crawled across the land. Our corn fields turned to gullies. The earth quaked.

The people prayed. They celebrated Cross Day where the rock stood.

The Earth Lord was appeased. He was contented.

"Thank you for praying to me," said the rock. "I will hide the horned serpent. It won't dig up the ground again."

Thunderbolt came. The rock was struck. The rock's horns were knocked off.

The people living there still drink the water. The May celebration is never abandoned.

—Xun Akov

The War of Saint Rose

Will you hear about a war?

Once in Chaklajon they had something that wasn't worship at all. Chaklajon, what brutes! They prayed to the caves. They danced. Oh, the girls, the women! Hah! It was quite a dance, Holy Mary!

Saint Rose was the mother of dissension. Little by little she lost her senses completely. She was a devil.

Wherever there were pretty women, the followers of Saint Rose embraced them, deceived them. They escorted them to the dance. It didn't matter if they were from San Andrés or Magdalenas. They went everywhere to mislead them.

The women sang and danced, dressed up in fine ceremonial huipils, fine skirts, the men in fine ceremonial robes and high-backed sandals.

Then they came to kill the people of their town.

The Chamulan magistrate protested to the authorities. One hundred soldiers were dispatched. They left from San Cristóbal on foot.

The Chamulans, the followers of Saint Rose, assembled in Chaklajon. Who knows how many thousands of the brutes.

The women lifted their skirts and turned their asses to the enemy. Their asses were bared to put the bullets out of action.

But it was steel at play, foreign gunpowder.

Who knows if a hundred women died or more. It's true there were some men, but they fled. It was the women who were trying to cool the bullets so the bullets wouldn't fire.

But how would the bullets cool off? Why wouldn't gunpowder explode?

All the followers of Saint Rose were pursued until they died. All the houses in Chaklajon were set on fire. The mother devil was burned.

When Saint Rose burnt up, the war cooled down.

—Xun Vaskis

He Saved a Snake and Won a Wife, Slapped His Wife and Lost His Life

Once there was a Chamulan who was hunting on the trail to the lowlands.

A snake appeared and stretched out in the middle of the path. "You've come to block my way, you bastard!" the Chamulan shouted at the snake. Quickly he slashed at it with his machete. He cut the snake into three pieces.

But in a flash its head spun round. It received another blow of the machete. The snake was left in four pieces.

"Please, my Chamulan," said the snake. "Won't you be so kind as to carry me home."

"Where is your house?"

"I'll show you where it is if you'll carry me away. It won't be for nothing. My father will give you whatever payment you want," said the snake, the Thunderbolt.

"But I haven't anything to carry you in," said the Chamulan.

"Spread out your neckerchief, then put me in your net."

"But your juice will stain my net and my neckerchief."

"I'll give you money for the soap. Carry me away. Please, my father will pay you."

"All right, I'll carry you home," said the Chamulan. "It's because I pity you, sliced up the way you are."

It was no ordinary snake. The pieces piled themselves up on the trail. The Chamulan carried them off.

"If I feel heavy to you, rest please," said the snake. "I have a terribly sharp pain where my back was wounded."

"I'll set you down, then. You certainly are heavy!" The man rested on top of a rock. The snake's yellow juice stained the rock where he rested.

"Shall we go now? Come on, I'll carry you," the snake was told.

"Let's go!" said the snake.

They walked on and on until they reached a cave. The fog was thick. "I can't see at all," the Chamulan said.

"It's just a cloud," said the snake. "The cloud will rise. We go down this path. My house is a little bit further."

They followed the path. "Knock on the rock. This is my house."

The man knocked. The snake's father opened the door.

"Sir," said the Chamulan. "Is this your son you see wounded to death? I've come to bring him back to you."

"Yes, that's my boy. Thank you for bringing him to me. How much do I owe you?" the father asked.

"You don't owe me anything, sir," the Chamulan said. He laid the snake down on his bed.

The father treated his son's wounds. Slowly the bones began to mend.

"Was it you who carried me back?" asked the snake.

"It was me," said the Chamulan.

"Take your choice, then. Do you want money? Do you want beans? Do you want corn?" asked the snake. "Or do you want mules or cows?"

"I don't want anything at all," the Chamulan said.

"Do you want one of my younger sisters?" asked the snake.

"Oh, if you'll give me one of your sisters, I'll gladly take her home!"

"I'm sure my father will give her to you, since you did me the favor of bringing me home."

"Do you feel strong now?" asked the man.

"My back hurts horribly," said the snake. "But I won't be sick for long. The medicine my father gave me is so good. But if I am to recover completely, my father must treat me again. It will grow dark. A terrible black cloud will appear. But don't be afraid," said the snake. "Bury your head in the sand!"

First the father came out. Right behind came the patient. The door rattled and banged. Fire flared up. Lightning cracked! The ground shook this way and that. The Chamulan fellow had his head buried in the sand.

But the fool peeked. He was knocked over. He was too weak to stand.

"Why didn't you bury your head? You watched to see what we were doing. You think I didn't see you?" the man was told by the burden he had carried.

The man was left with the smell of gunpowder all over his body. He had been burned.

That Old Thunderbolt had medicine. The Chamulan's face and body were rubbed carefully with cotton.

"Stupid, what good did it do you to watch? You've seen how and where and why we work. Today you lived through it, but the next time you may die.

"Now choose one of my daughters." Four girls were standing there.

"I want the one in the middle," the man said.

"Take her! But only on condition that you treat her well. If you hit her or scold her, I'll send fire and lightning as before. You'll die, you hear!"

"I won't scold her, provided that she does what I say, prepares my meals, takes care of my sheep and horses. She'll gather corn stubble for my horses. She will watch my sheep in the meadow."

"Don't worry. If it's a question of her watching the sheep, they know how to look after themselves. They know to get in the corral when the rain comes," said Old Thunderbolt.

"Take your wife. Be kind to her! May God repay you for carrying my son back to me. If my son were to die, I wouldn't have anyone to keep me company. My son is my constant traveling companion."

"Your daughter and I will visit you," said the man.

"Yes, if you haven't any money, if you haven't any corn, come back and ask for it. You've seen that I have money. You've seen that I don't go hungry. Come and ask. My house is far away. If you can't come, send my daughter."

"I'll come," said the Chamulan, "even if I have to spend the night here."

The man left on good terms.

His wife prepared the meals. She tended the sheep.

She went to the fields to pick a tiny basketful of beans. She poured the beans in heaps next to the wall. She went to pick a net of corn. The corn filled a corner of the house.

With an awful angry face her husband watched her. "Why the devil did you pick such a terrific amount of corn? We won't have anything left to pick when the time comes for the harvest. You shouldn't have picked so much," said her husband.

"When did I pick so much? Go see for yourself! I just picked a net full of corn. It's because your corn has done well," said the woman.

The husband went to look. She hadn't even picked a whole row.

"Oh, you told the truth. I thought you weren't following my wishes," said the man. "Now I've seen that the corn increases in your hands. I won't scold you, nor will I complain again."

The poor woman had children. They were baptized. They grew.

Her husband had never hit her. Then one night he went and got drunk with his compadre, and when he came home he slapped his wife. The woman wept. She went and complained about it to her father.

"Where did you go?" her husband asked when she returned.

"I went to our father's house. I spent the night there, so you wouldn't hit me again."

"I hit you, but it was because I was drunk. You don't think I would hit you for nothing! But I hardly hit you at all. My hand didn't hurt."

"Your hand didn't hurt! But now my eye is wonderfully blue!"

"Oh, you shouldn't have gone to tell our father. Would it please him? He said he would kill me if I hit you. See here, I'd better settle the matter tomorrow."

The next day he went to talk to his father-in-law.

"Come in, come in! Won't you eat some fish?" said his father-in-law. The man sat down to a big piece of fresh fish.

"What's to be done to me, father?"

"Please don't hit her. Please don't scold her," said the father.

"I don't hit her, father. It's just because I was drunk."

"Oh well, then," said the father.

The man returned home. "I've brought you a little piece of fish folded up in a tortilla," he said to his wife.

"I know when my father wants to eat. I'll go eat with him. You should have eaten it yourself," his wife said.

The man went hunting in the lowlands. He came back sick. He died.

She bought a coffin for her husband. They buried him. The people gathered. They killed chickens.

After she buried her husband, she went home to her father. "Father, things aren't right. My husband died. You gave me away long ago, just because of my older brother. He suffered so. Now I'm left alone with two children. It would be better if I came back to join you. My little girl and my little boy can stay at home, since that leaves an owner for the land and an owner for the house. They can grow up there.

"Do you know what I did, father? I gave them a little pot. They turn it upside down and rap on it several times. 'I'm hungry, mother, I'm hungry,' they tell their pot. 'Eat!' it says, and beans and tortillas fill the pot. That's what the children live on. That's what I taught them."

"Ah! That pot of yours, where did you get it?"

"I took it from home," said his daughter.

"Did you ask your mother for it?"

"Of course I asked my mother for it. 'Take it! It will feed the children,' my mother told me."

"Well, leave the children. You can visit them when you aren't busy. Come!" said her father.

She began her work again. She became a Thunderbolt again.

The dead Chamulan's children were left by themselves. They looked after each other. They had enough food to eat.

But one day they broke their pot. They hadn't anything to feed them anymore. The boy learned how to work in his corn field. The girl learned how to grind their corn.

Finally they went to see their mother. "Mother, we don't know what to do. We dropped our pot. I tried to catch it, but I dropped it. It's split in two."

"Never mind, I'll give you another one," their mother told them.

The children grew up. They supported each other. They ate. They drank. They had nothing to worry about. Their mother came to see them when she wanted to.

"What did you bring, mother?" asked the girl.

"I brought a little fish, if you want to eat it."

"You can stick it in my pot," said her daughter. When her mother stuck it in the pot, the fish grew and grew. The children ate well.

"This is the last time that I've come to see you," their mother said. "See this! I'm leaving you a little chest full of money. I'll put the key underneath it. Open it! Your money is there."

The boy opened it. The money jingled and jangled.

Gradually they used up all the money in the chest. "Now we won't have anything to live on," said the boy.

"It won't run out. More will come," said the girl.

When they looked again, money filled the chest. It just came and came and came.

The girl acquired a husband. The boy got a wife. With the help of the money they had everything they needed. The money kept appearing and appearing.

It was a Thunderbolt that did that, a Thunderbolt girl.

—Tonik Nibak

How the Weak Ones Won, Rabbit Wins and Rabbit Loses

Once upon a time there was a man who went hunting with his wife. They went to a spring to wait for deer. There they found many toads.

A deer came along. "Look, Toad," said Deer, "Let's make a bet to see who can run faster."

"Okay!" said Toad. One toad made the deal.

All the toads lined up along the path.

"Let's race!" said Toad.

Deer ran, but he was worn out trying to outdistance Toad. "Don't you ever get tired, Toad?"

"Why would I get tired? We're invincible," said Toad.

Ooh, Deer ran as fast as he could, but he didn't succeed.

Deer went on. He stopped at a hollow to drink. Swarms of mosquitoes were buzzing around.

"Why don't you let me drink?" he asked the mosquitoes.

"First let's see if you can race," said Mosquito.

"Fine, let's race!" said Deer.

Mosquito perched on Deer's ear. Ooh, Deer dashed off.

"Hey, did you fall behind?" asked Deer.

"Eeee," said Mosquito in his ear.

Deer raced on. Every few seconds he would speak to Mosquito. "Eeee," Mosquito kept saying in his ear.

"Well, I can't do any better," said Deer. "You fly too fast."

"I race because I'm the best," said Mosquito.

"Forget it! I can't win!" said Deer.

Now the hunter had left his wife behind when he went to follow the deer. But when he came back to the spring, his wife was gone. The woman had been taken off by the devil.

The man sat down and sobbed.

A jaguar came along. "What are you crying about?" asked Jaguar.

"Oh, Mr. Jaguar, I lost my wife. The King of the Devils stole her."

"Don't worry. I'll get her back in a minute," said Jaguar.

"Please, then, because I'm heartbroken."

Jaguar knocked on the devil's door.

"Who is it?" asked the King of the Devils.

"I'm Mr. Jaguar."

"What do you want?"

"I've come to take the poor woman back because her husband is crying," roared Jaguar.

"What's that to you?" said the King of the Devils. He beat Jaguar's ass with a stick. Jaguar fled.

"I didn't win out. My ass is broken," said Jaguar. Ooh, the man cried even more.

A bull came along. "Why are you crying, friend?" asked Bull.

"Look here, Bull, my wife disappeared. She was taken off by the devil."

"I'll go right away and bring her back," said Bull.

"You can't succeed. You're even less of a match. A jaguar's already gone. He failed and he's stronger," said the man.

"But I'll break down the door. I'll bring back your wife," said Bull.

"Fine! Please do!" said the man.

Bull banged on the door.

"Who is it?" said the Devil.

"I'm Mr. Bull."

"What do you want?"

"I'm going to take the woman back," said Bull.

The Devil grabbed a stick and broke Bull's horns. Ooh, Bull ran.

"I couldn't do it," he told the man. Oh, the man cried even more.

A donkey came along. "What are you crying about?" asked Donkey.

"My wife disappeared," said the man.

"Indeed! Well, I'll bring her back," said Donkey. "You'll see!"

"God, now it's *you* who thinks he can win. You're just a poor donkey! Jaguar tried. Bull tried. But they didn't succeed."

"But I'll kick the door down!"

Donkey knocked on the door.

"Who are you?" asked the Devil.

"I'm Donkey."

"What do you want?"

"I want to take the woman back." Donkey quickly kicked the door. Oh, his hoof fell off. He hobbled away.

"I couldn't do it. My hoof came off," he told the man. Oh, the man cried even more.

An army of ants came by. "What happened to you?" they asked.

"My wife disappeared," said the man.

"We'll bring her back," said the ants.

"Poor ants, you can't win. You're even smaller!"

"Oh, but we can!"

Off they went and knocked on the door.

"Who is it?" asked the King of the Devils.

"We're ants," they said. They swarmed under the door.

The Devil threw hot ashes on them. Some of the ants were killed by the hot ashes, the others fled.

"We couldn't do it, man." Again the man cried.

A rabbit came along. "What are you crying about?" he asked.

"Man, my wife disappeared."

"If you want me to, I'll bring her back."

"God, but do *you* think you can do it?"

"Of course I can do it, why not?" said Rabbit.

"Please do, then!" said the man.

"First get a gourdful of wasps, a gourdful of hornets, and a gourdful of honey bees. With three gourds I'll go."

Rabbit arrived at the Devil's house. "Knock, knock, knock!"

"Who is it?" asked the Devil.

"I'm Uncle Rabbit."

"What do you want?"

"I've come to visit you," said Rabbit.

"Come on in!" said the Devil.

Rabbit walked right in. He saw the woman sitting by the fire.

He went up to the hearth. He shattered all three gourds. All the devils were stung to death by the wasps and hornets and bees. Quickly Rabbit picked up the woman and carried her out.

"Don't cry anymore," said Rabbit. "Your wife has come back. But you'll pay me a little at least."

"What's your price?" asked the man.

"Oh, I don't want money," said Rabbit. "I want to sleep with your wife for just one night."

"Fine, let's go to bed!" said the man. "My wife can sleep in the middle. You can sleep behind her."

In the middle of the night the woman let a great fart. Rabbit thought it was a bullet. He thought it was a gun. He fled.

That's why rabbits are timid now.

—Romin Teratol

The Spook and the Saints

Once there was a Spook who went asking for permission. He went to the Church of the Holy Martyr. "Marty, give me one or two of your children as presents, for I long to have some company," said the Spook.

"I don't know what my younger brother would think. Go talk to him! If Larry tells you 'Take them!' then what else could I say?" said Our Holy Martyr.

The Spook went to talk to Saint Lawrence. "Larry, won't you please give me one or two of your children. You have so many. It isn't as if you hadn't any to spare."

"I'll never give away my children," said Saint Lawrence. "They remember to bring me flowers. They remember to bring me candles, at dusk and at dawn. Sometimes some of them forget to come, but whenever it occurs to them, then I'm content. You, what have you brought me? Step aside, nuisance! Please don't get me angry or I'll hit you."

The Spook waited. Then he went back to talk to the Holy Martyr. "Marty, favor me with one or two of your offspring, because I need a little company," he said.

"But you are certainly telling a lie! You won't befriend them. You'll just stick them somewhere in the mountains, in the caves. But me, I'm satisfied that they sweep my house. They always come to give me my flowers. They always come to give me my candles. They always come to give me my incense. I'm happy with my children. It's true not all of them come every day. They take turns. One day, one. Another day, another. Or another day, none. Still, I'm satisfied with my children. You, what do you bring me? You, what do you offer me? You just pester me at dusk and at dawn. 'Oh, Marty, give me one of your children! Oh, Marty, give me one of your sons, one of your daughters! Even if it's a girl, that's good enough for me!' you say. But I won't give away my children. Go to Johnny's house. Maybe it won't take long if you talk to him."

But the Spook couldn't remember where Saint John's house was. So he went back to the Church of Saint Lawrence and chattered away.

"Larry, give me one of your children. I need one. I'd be happy if I just had someone at home to talk to."

"Oh, if you want one I'll give you one, because I'm tired of you pestering me so," said Saint Lawrence. "Look! There's one coming down the path now. Go meet him on the trail!"

But it was a great big horse he went to hug. It was a good kicking that he got.

He was struck in the back of the head. The horrible Spook went home in pain. But two weeks later he was up again.

"You did this to me, Larry! See this lump! Was it a human being that you gave me. No, it was a great big horse!"

"It's not my fault that you're half-blind," said Saint Lawrence. "A man was walking down the trail, and he had a good laugh when you landed on your back."

"If only you weren't so mean-hearted," said the Spook.

He went back to Marty's. "Marty, favor me with one of your children. I'd be content to have someone fix my meal while I'm gone."

"Where in the world do you go?" asked Our Holy Martyr.

"Oh, I go to churches, I go visiting at houses. I go wherever I can find bread to eat. I only eat bread. I don't eat tortillas," the Spook said.

"Where in the world do you get money to pay for the bread? You just steal it, stupid loafer!"

"Yes, but now I'm *asking* you."

"Oh, take one! I've been sick and tired of this from the start. There's one coming on the Chamula road."

The Spook rushed out. He went and hugged a hawthorn tree.

"Marty, I'm pierced! Thorns are stuck in my mouth, thorns are stuck in my face. You tricked me. It was a hawthorn I hugged."

"It's because you can't see! There he is, walking across the bridge. Look!"

The Spook landed in the water, pushed off the bridge by the kick of a mule that was crossing over. He was carried off by the current as far as Roaring River. There he was tossed out by the flood.

He came back to the church, sopping wet. "You know, Marty, I fell in the river. I almost drowned."

"Don't fall in the river! Why were you walking on the edge of the bridge? The mule pushed you off because mules walk on one side, people on the other. You can't succeed the way you are. Don't keep coming back and making me lose my temper! My children are sick and tired of being frightened. Only yesterday one came to complain. She says you nearly dragged her out of her house. You caught her chickens. You killed her chicks. You drank a gourdful of eggs.

"Now those eggs are used by my children to pay for my candles and my flowers. What happened to the poor woman's eggs? You sucked them all. Are you a weasel?

"Look for someone else to give you others. Go to Johnny's country! He has lots of children. Mine can be counted. He has so many more. See if Johnny will give his to you," said Our Holy Martyr.

That night the Spook arrived in Johnny's land, Chamula. "What can I think up? Would it be a good idea if I bought a candle? Or should I buy him some cane liquor? If I say, 'Let's drink!' would he drink?" said the Spook. "No, it's better if I buy a candle."

He planted his candle at the church door. Maybe he thought Saint John would come outside to talk. He rang the church bell. "Bong!" went the bell at midnight. The saint didn't stir, but oh, the poor Chamulans were terrified.

"A robber has entered the church," they cried. "There's no time left. Our saints will die!"

The Chamulans blew their horns. They swarmed out of their houses. They fired their rifles. The horrible Spook fled.

"Why can't I find one saint who will be kind to me?" said the Spook to his Spook friend at his cave. "Johnny's children almost killed me. Their guns were cracking!"

"Try again! It's you who have always gone out. Do your best now that your face has been seen already. Go talk to Johnny alone!"

The Spook flew to Chamula.

"Johnny, give me one of your children. You have too many. You can't be happy letting them eat fish, letting them eat June bug grubs, letting them eat maggots. Give me one! I won't eat him, not me! I want one for company."

"Take her!" said Saint John.

The woman who was given to him was a little old lady. She wasn't good for anything. She couldn't even see.

Quickly at vespers he caught her and carried her off. "Where are you taking me, son?" she cried.

"Wait, Nanita! Wait, Nanita, I'm going to take you home!" answered the horrible Spook.

"But I know that my house has been left far behind," the little old lady was screaming.

The old lady's heart was worn out. She fainted with fear. The Spook arrived and threw her down in the cave. The little old lady passed out.

"Darling, let's sleep together! Darling, let's eat!" the Spook was trying to tell her. God, the old lady didn't move. She was speechless. At dawn the next day the little old lady was dead.

That horrible Spook went to offer candles to Saint John. "You tricked me! The little old lady you gave me was already dead."

The next time he went to ask, he was given a boy. The boy was riding a horse. The Spook endured the horse's kicking. But when the horse bucked, the boy fell out of the saddle. The Spook grabbed him and carried him off to his cave. That was surely the first time he won.

Another time, an old Chamulan woman and her granddaughter were digging up clay by a stream. "Take your clay home, daughter! Knead it awhile after you arrive," she told the girl.

The girl went home. She was kneading her clay by the door when the Spook came whooshing down. She thought it was a buzzard. When the grandmother returned, the poor girl was gone.

The Spook carried her off. "Stay here, girl! We're home now. See which chicken you'd like to eat. Do you want the black hen or the barred one? Kill it! Then put aside my share for me. I'm going to bring more food for us," said the Spook.

"All right," said the girl. She had pots, gourds, whatever she needed to prepare her meal. She fixed the chicken. She ate. But the poor girl was upset being stuck in a deep cave.

The Spook arrived with a crate of white bread from Chiapa. "Here is the bread for your meal. You have nothing to worry about. Please don't be sad!" he said.

On the third night after her arrival, the girl had a child. A little baby Spook was born. "Nanita, Nanita!" said the baby Spook. It grew up over night.

The girl was frightened by it. "Why does my child talk like this? Why does it say 'Nanita'? My Lord, can it be some kind of dirty business? Could his father be a devil?" The poor girl didn't know what it was that had carried her off.

Some hunters passed by on the trail. "Hoo heigh, come take me out!" she called. "I'm helpless. I'm sick. I'm suffering terribly from the cold down here."

"It's me, niece. I've come looking for you. What more do you have to tell me?"

"I'm sick. I have a child now. It's the child of the man who brought me here. Take me out, uncle!"

"Wait, I'll get my lasso. I'll get you out on condition, niece, that your husband isn't there."

"He'd kill us," said the other Chamulans.

"He's gone to bring bread for us to eat. Don't be afraid! Please take me away, uncle, because I'm beginning to swell in the frightful cold. Please, may the Holy Virgin enter thy beautiful heart, uncle. Take me away!"

"Grab the lasso, tie it around your waist!" he told her.

He threw three lengths of rope down into the cave. Ooh, it was hard pulling the woman out.

"Nanita! Nanita!" cried the little Spook hanging on to her skirt.

"Pull it off with your hand, niece! It's clinging to the hem of your skirt. Don't you bring up the spawn of your companion in deviltry!"

With one hand she held on to the rope, with the other she grabbed the little Spook and threw it down. "Nanita!" could still be heard echoing inside the cave.

When the girl reached home she was already swollen. Her dirt had washed off. Her face was white, a sign of her having been submerged in water for so many days. She was swelling because the horrible Spook's prick was six feet long.

It was only three months and three weeks that she was alive. The girl peed lime water. She died.

You see how it was long ago, and how it's been ever since. The Spooks were given a few Chamulans to appease them. Saint Lawrence didn't give any of us away at all.

—Tonik Nibak

The Charcoal Cruncher

There was a man sleeping with his wife.

She was a Charcoal Cruncher.

The man touched his wife in the dark. Just the stump of her was there. She had no head.

He lit a match. "Where did my wife go?" he said. "How could it be? Could someone have cut off her head?

"Who knows. There must be a reason. Maybe she took a walk. Maybe she's bad. I guess I'll see if she's a devil."

He put salt on the stump of her neck.

When the woman's head rolled home from crunching coals, it wouldn't stick to the rest of her. Her head was flopping about like a chicken. It bounced and bounced.

"Why are you doing this to me?" the woman asked her husband.

"Why do you go out wandering?"

The woman cried. "But where can I go now that my flesh doesn't fasten on?"

"See for yourself! I don't want to be with you any longer. You're a devil!"

Her head bounced. It landed on her husband's shoulder. Now the man had two heads.

"But this is no good at all," he said. "If her head sticks on, I'll have two faces! One a woman's, the other a man's."

He prayed to Our Lord. "My Lord, what can I do about this? If Our Lord would only do me a favor. If only there were some way to get rid of it."

The husband decided to trick it. They went for a walk in the woods. "All right, come down a minute, stay on the ground! I'm going to climb that pine tree. I'm going to get pine seeds for you to chew."

He climbed the tree. The woman's head bounced and bounced at the foot of the pine.

"God, My Lord, if only there were something that would come and take it away."

A deer came along.

Her head landed and stuck on the deer's back. The deer ran in a panic. Ever since deer have been wild. And that's how the woman's head was lost.

—Manvel K'obyox

A Bellyful

Dogs used to talk. Dogs used to say whatever they said. Today they don't talk anymore. It's because the dog told its master about his wife's sin.

Its master was going to the lowlands to prepare his corn field. The poor man didn't know about his wife.

"Let's go, my dog, let's go to the lowlands to look for deer!"

He never got any deer no matter how many days he hunted. If he saw the deer, they fled. If he fired his gun, he missed them. One even tricked him. The awful deer was lying on its back, thrashing and moaning. But when the poor man aimed his rifle, the deer jumped up and bounded off.

"Why is this happening to me?" he said each time a deer escaped him.

At first the man blamed his dog. "Why are you so utterly useless? You don't track them. You don't round them up. It's your fault, you bastard. I'll cut off your head!"

"Don't scold me! I'm not the one who's at fault. It's my mistress. There's something I'll tell you about," said the dog.

"As soon as you leave home she fixes a chicken. She eats with your substitute. While you are in the lowlands, another man stays to eat with her. Then they dig a hole and bury the bones in the ground. If she had let me take the bones, I certainly wouldn't have told you!"

"Are you telling the truth? Is there really another man who eats and drinks with her, who goes to sleep with my wife? If you aren't telling the truth, I'll cut off your head!"

"Of course I'm telling the truth," snapped the dog.

"Then I'll sharpen up my knife. I'll see what I'll plan for her," said the man.

They returned home. A few days later the man was ready. "We are going to the lowlands, my little dog."

But you see, they went to the edge of the woods to wait for night to fall. The man hung his bag of tortillas on a high branch. They sat under the tree and waited.

"Don't you bark, for if you bark, we'll surely get into trouble. Please don't bark, even if you see something suddenly land with a thud. It's none of your business. Keep your mouth shut!" the dog was told.

They could hear the woman talking away with her other "husband." "Aren't you hungry now? Shall I put chili in our meal?" she asked.

"Have you finished fixing the tortillas?"

"Of course I'm finished!"

"Then put the chili in your pot and we'll eat together," the woman's other husband told her.

She lifted the griddle off the fire, put their tortillas in a gourd, and dished out the chicken. She gave the drumsticks to her two little children. She and the man ate the breast and the heart. Her baby had already nursed and was sound asleep.

"Do you want more broth?" asked the woman.

"I do," the man said. They drank the broth together.

"Ooh, we ate so much our tortillas are finished. You won't have any for the morning."

"I'm leaving early tomorrow, or else somebody might see us," said the man.

"But there's no way for us to be found out. When the dog is here, it wants to chew the bones. Now we can throw the chicken's bones in the gully!"

"But the principal might just come by."

"Oh, maybe you're right," said the woman. "If you won't eat before you leave tomorrow, then I won't save any of our broth. We'll drink all of it before we go to bed. I'll turn the pot face down."

They finished eating. She spread out a cloth and put her little children to sleep next to the wall. Then the woman's lover joined her in bed.

"Did you see them? Didn't I tell you they were eating chicken?" said the dog.

"But what can I do? The man won't come out now," the husband said.

"Oh, he may just get up in the night. 'I'm going to take a piss,' the man may tell my mistress. 'No, don't go outside. There is a little opening in the wall where my husband pisses,' she will say."

"If that's what you have seen, then we'll win out later on," said the husband. "We'll crouch down and not move."

It was no story. Two, three hours passed.

"Woman, I'm going to piss."

"Don't go outside. Here is an opening in the wall where my husband always pisses," she said.

When the man poked his prick out, the husband grabbed it and cut it off with a knife.

The lover fell on the bed. "What happened to you?" she asked.

God, the poor man was too far gone to answer. Her blanket and her straw mat were covered with blood.

"What can I do about this? My children will wake up. They'll see."

She took the old straw mats and wrapped them around him. The man was just groaning when his spirit departed.

She dragged him out like a dead dog. She threw him in the gully. She started a rock slide. He was buried under the rocks. She knocked down the earth with a hoe. The earth covered the rocks and her lover. She finished burying him in the night.

The next morning, by daylight, she went to the stream to scrub her blanket. She scrubbed her straw mat. She scrubbed her pillows. She scrubbed the pillow cases. She spread them out in the sun to dry.

"If for some reason he returns early from his corn field, if for some reason he didn't do any hunting, or he got a deer right off, then there's no time left at all. There will be no way of knowing how I was involved with what happened to the man," she said.

She turned the bedclothes over. Her blanket dried out, since it was a good hot sun.

As soon as she came home she made the bed. She swept her house carefully. She scraped the floor wherever the ground was stained with blood.

"Let's go!" the dog said to the man after he had finished cutting off what he had cut off. "Did you wrap it up carefully?"

"Of course I wrapped it up. I've put it in my shoulder bag."

"Let's go, then! You'll see, when I find the deer you won't say that it dodges the shots from your gun. I'll be surprised if we hit just one, if we don't hit two," said the dog.

The dog rushed off. It played and played. They arrived at the corn field.

The man hung up his tortillas. "Shall we look in our corn field or shall we go looking for deer?" asked the man.

"Let's go hunting first. We'll eat a piece of the meat at dawn."

The master slung his gun over his shoulder. He went into the tall grass beyond his corn field. A deer started up. The man didn't lose any time. Quickly he aimed his gun and fired. The stag stretched out. It was stone dead.

"See! Was I lying to you? We got one!" said the dog.

The deer was hung by the legs from the crosspoles over the fire.

The man cut off the deer's penis. He skinned it, skewered it, and roasted it. The penis of the woman's lover was skewered too, and roasted until it was well-browned. He cut off the foreskin so that the woman wouldn't recognize it.

The deer's penis and the penis of the woman's boyfriend were packed away. The deer's liver, the lungs, the spleen were put on the fire. The man and his dog ate them freshly cooked.

After he looked over his corn field, the man went hunting again. "We'll see if we can get an iguana or an armadillo," he told his dog.

They hadn't gone three steps when they caught an armadillo.

They walked a half a block and they found a little fawn. Then a doe appeared in the clearing. It had doubled back to where the little fawn was bleating.

Quickly the man shot the doe. He caught the little fawn in his hands.

He tied up the baby deer while he skinned its mother. After he skinned her, he roasted one haunch and one foreleg. He carried the rest of it back in a burlap bag.

He met a fellow corn farmer. "Let me rent your mule," he said, "because I have a lot of deer meat to carry."

"If you give me a haunch, I'll give you the mule," said the farmer. "My compadre is coming down tomorrow, so return my mule with him. I'll enjoy eating the venison with my tortillas."

"Take it! I also brought a lot of toasted tortillas because I thought my corn field had been knocked down by the wind. I thought I would have to lift up the plants, but no, my corn field is fine. And then I got two deer. I'm taking the little fawn home with me. That's why I don't want to have a burden."

"We would never have gotten the deer," said the dog, "if my mistress still had a lover. If you had spied on her long ago, we would have begun eating venison much sooner."

"Where do you think she put him?" asked the man.

"Oh, she must have thrown him somewhere."

"Or will we arrive to find him lying face up? We'll see. Don't you admit anything!" he told his dog.

"What's it to me? It's you who had better watch what lies you tell about it! The only thing that offended me was that when you came to the lowlands and left me behind, they ate chicken and didn't let me eat the bones. They didn't let me eat the gizzard. They didn't even let me eat the chicken's beak. They thought I was a terrible nuisance. They dug a deep hole for the bones and covered them up with stones. I couldn't possibly dig them up. That's why I opened my mouth, of course. That's why I'm guilty, but who cares?"

"Never mind, now you can gorge on the deer's guts. Eat up!" said the man to his dog.

"Of course I'll eat today. It isn't as if I won't eat! But what good is it, because who knows what you're going to do to that mistress of mine? Who knows if you aren't going to kill her?"

"Why would I kill her? We'll arrive to sustain her. We'll give her the deer penis to eat. I can't kill her. I can't beat her. We'll just look her in the eye. Our Lord will punish her when he wishes to. I'm grateful for what he has done for me. He has treated me well. He gives me what I eat. He gives me what I need. There is venison when we return from corn farming. I couldn't get any deer before because of what the poor woman was doing to me. Never mind now. Only Our Lord knows. As for us, we only know that we eat."

The man returned. He brought his burden on muleback. He carried the little fawn in his arms.

When he reached home, the house was tidied up and carefully swept. Her pots were sitting face down in order. The floor was well-scraped.

"Why is the house so clean?" asked her husband.

"Maybe it's because I've suddenly become industrious," said his wife. "Ooh, where did you get your mule? Did you pay for it?" she asked.

"Of course I paid for it. I gave our compadre a meal in return for it. Thanks to Our Lord, I got some food. Now I want a few tortillas. I'm hungry," he said.

"Eat!" said the woman.

"Won't you eat?" he asked. "I've brought some roasted deer penis. I've brought some roasted liver. Try eating the penis. It's wonderfully tender," said the man.

He gave a piece of the deer penis to each of the children. But he gave the woman her lover's prick to eat. She ate a lot. She ate well.

"Oh, why do I feel so full? I feel like a drink of water," said the woman.

She drank a gourdful of water. She had a craving for more. Every few minutes another gourdful, another gourdful. The woman's belly became so bloated. One water jug. A second water jug. God, the woman's belly was bulging.

"What did you give me to eat, husband? Why am I so thirsty? My belly is bursting. I can't sit down. It feels as if the skin of my belly will rip apart. I just don't know why I drank so much water."

"Then don't drink so much, for heaven's sakes! You obstinately keep on drinking. It seems as if it's your madness. You should endure your thirst a little. As for me, I'm hungry. I'd eat if our food is cooked, if the chili is ground."

"Our meal is almost done. The trouble is that this full stomach of mine can't be lifted on top of the metate."

"I'll grind the chilis, then. I guess I'll see what it's like to grind on the metate. Why do you drink so much? You're awful. Hand them over! How many chilis shall I put in our meal?"

"Put in four," she told her husband. The man ground the chilis. He poured the chilis in the pot. He put coriander in. The meal was ready.

"Won't you eat?" he asked.

"God, I'd certainly like to eat. I long so for it. The food is good," she said.

"Eat the meat. You don't have to drink the broth now, if your belly has no more room."

My Lord, no sooner had she drunk a bowl of broth when "Boom!" went her belly.

"Oh, My Lord, Jesus Christ, why did your belly burst, wife?"

"Ah!" she said. "Ah!"

A minute later her soul departed. She died from her lover's prick.

Today the dog is dumb, since the poor dog told clearly why his master didn't hit the deer. How would the man have known what the trouble was? His wife seemed to be a good woman. As it turned out she was deceitful. There isn't anyone who would speak well of her to you.

Long ago the dog was your companion. You conversed with it, since it was guiltless. Now the mouth of God's animal is closed, because the dog told about its mistress's sin. The man was delighted but the woman was dead.

One day a neighbor passed by the gully where the woman had buried her lover. The husband was thrown into jail. "You just rob and kill people. Why would the bones be stuck inside the pants and the sash? You buried him. Who knows who you killed," they said.

"I never killed anyone. I wasn't at home. I'm not an assassin. What were people looking for there? They searched. They dug. Who do you know is missing? Who is lost if it was me who killed him? I never killed anyone," said the man at the courthouse. "If anyone was killed by me, there must be someone who watched me. Maybe someone who is resentful of me buried him near my house to incriminate me. As for me, I never killed anyone. Is there a witness who saw me?"

"There is no one whom we know about who died," said the magistrate. "We haven't heard any talk about it, except what is being said now. There wasn't anyone who said, 'My son has disappeared, my son was killed by an assassin.' There was no one who reported it. Maybe the poor dead thing was swept down the river. We can't make this man bear the blame.

"Forget it, son, go home, you aren't guilty of anything. There isn't anyone who saw you kill him. Only his clothes, his sash, his hat were seen where he was buried.

"Who knows, maybe someone disappeared from his house, fell in the flooded gully, and was washed down by the water. Maybe it isn't our concern where we die. It makes no difference now how people died long ago. The man disappeared. Maybe the corpse had no wife or mother, or anyone at all to complain. So he died. No fuss. None."

—Tonik Nibak

The Dwarfs

The rabbit is the dwarf's mule.
When they load the rabbit's back, the pack slips to the side.
The world will turn upside down if the rabbit's pack stays on top.

At night when the sun passes over, the dwarfs put mud on their
    heads.
It is a hot place. The mud is used for their hats.

They want to come up, because they suffer from the heat down
    below.
They want us to see their underground country.
They want to come up now to our world.

—Xun Akov

He Followed the Sun and Swallowed the Gold

There was a man, long ago, who asked the buzzard for its wings. He stuck them on and flew toward the sun.

"My Lord, I am going to follow you. I want to go as far as you go. I want to know where the world ends," he told Our Lord.

"Poor creature!" said Our Lord. "You will be a real man if you can keep up with me!"

The man followed close behind. By three o'clock he was exhausted.

He perched in a tree. Our Lord went on.

The man flapped his wings. He caught up with Our Lord on the path.

"Please wait for me, My Lord. I'm doing my best, but I'm worn out," he said. "Please don't leave me behind."

"You surely are a rugged traveler! Me, I'm used to it. That's how I watch over the young and the old," said Our Lord.

At the end of the day they reached the ocean where the sun sets.

"If you really want to cross over," said Our Holy Father, "dunk your head three times."

The man dunked his head. After the first dunking, Our Lord had not crossed over the ocean. Nor after the second dunking. But after the third dunking, Our Lord was on the other side of the sea.

"Cross on over! The ocean is dry now."

The bottom of the ocean was covered with gold. There was money on our side. There was money on the other side. There was money from one side to the other.

"Why should I cross over now, since I long for the money?" the man said to himself. He picked up a handful of coins and tucked them inside his sash. They felt so heavy he could barely stand.

But he wasn't satisfied. He filled his neckerchief with money and wrapped it tightly around his waist. Then he flew home.

He arrived late that night. He didn't return with Our Lord at dawn.

"Never mind, wife, I carried out my wish. I have seen where the end of the world is.

" 'Dunk your head three times and cross over!' Our Lord told me. I dunked my head three times. I never saw how Our Lord crossed over.

"But the money, wife! I didn't want to come back. You wouldn't be sad scooping up the money! I just scooped it up in my hands. Look how much there is! See how the money is to the touch! We just pick it up at the place where Our Lord disappears.

"The trouble is, I had a hard time returning all the way with it. At Calvary I grew weary. I dug a hole and buried some. Take this much! I'll be right back with the rest."

He flew back holding the money in his teeth. But he swallowed it. Maybe it was the price his body had to pay for his efforts.

He flew off again. This time he gathered up the money in his neckerchief. He carried the bundle home. "Look! See how much money there is!

"The trouble is, I took pains to get it. I cupped the money in my hand. I put it in my mouth. I didn't think I would get thirsty on the way.

"But my heart was bursting with air at Calvary. I drank some water. It was then that I swallowed the money. I don't know if I'm not dying from it. My stomach feels dreadful."

His wife gave him refined sugar and water to drink. Then she went to report it at the courthouse.

"See here, magistrate, I don't know what to do. It's the fourth day since my husband's return from the end of the world. He found some money there. He gathered it up and flew home.

"The trouble is, he grew thirsty on the way. He drank some water. But you see, he swallowed the money at the same time. Now I don't know what to do. Should he be operated on? Do you think he would come back to life?"

"Oh, we can cut him open, but I certainly won't give you the money. If it's true that your husband swallowed some, I'll keep the money myself. It costs money for the efforts of the justice of the peace who examines him. But who knows if you are telling the truth. When will I ever go so far off in the world, loafers!"

"Well, if you don't want to operate on my husband so that he won't die . . . " said the woman.

He wasn't cut open. The poor man, having swallowed the money, died. His children lived on the money he had brought back from the end of the world. Gold and silver from the place where Our Lord disappears.

—Tonik Nibak

The Famine

Our Sustenance suffereth: it lieth weeping. If we
should not gather it up, it would accuse us before

Our Lord. It would say 'O Our Lord, this vassal
picked me not up when I lay scattered upon the
ground. Punish him!' Or perhaps we should starve.

—Aztec Prayer

Long ago the famine came. The famine was a punishment from Our
Holy Father.

The first year it rained and rained. It was raining then like it's
raining now. The holy rain didn't let up at all.

The corn grew well. There was a good harvest.

The second year there was no rain at all. The lowlands were laid
waste by the sun.

Those who had sold much of their corn nearly died. We had no
tortillas. People ate tortillas made of banana roots, fern roots. As soon
as the corn fields flowered, the poor people pulled all the tassels off to
eat.

In San Cristóbal there wasn't a tortilla for sale. You could buy a
wheat bun for a peso. But that's if there were any, and there weren't.

The Ixtapanecs went mad. They sold corn for five pesos an almud. Solid money, not paper like it is now. Five peso pieces, round
silver pieces if there were any, but there weren't.

People were paid one quart of corn for a week's labor— enough
to eat for one or two days. But that's if there was any work, and there
wasn't.

The Chamulans would fill two ceremonial gourds with a ball of
weed leaves, greens, and amaranth and go out looking for an employer. The Chamulans who weren't given jobs were stretched flat on
their backs, dead on the road. It made no difference if they were old
or young, man or woman, still they perished.

Once a Chamulan girl passed by our house. She was carrying
two ceremonial gourds filled with amaranth greens and spider
flowers. My mother offered her food. But she didn't want to fluff
wool or weed in the field. She was too weak to work. She just lazed
about.

There beneath the redberried hawthorn, in the tiny gully, she
died.

Twice my parents ate banana root. Once my older brother and
my father went scavenging as far as Cherry Trees. They walked all
day, but they found only eight ears of dried corn!

I had a binful plus ten fanegas of flailed corn. If I had sold it, we would have died.

"Never mind, father, I have some stored away. Don't go again! It costs so much effort," I told him. Since it pleased me, I supported my parents, my older brother, and my sister.

In return for three almuds of corn, my father gave me a piece of his land.

I had planted irrigated fields at Vunal. The holy corn was ripening. I guarded my corn with a shotgun and a machete. I stood guard with three friends, long-panted ones from Ixtapa.

When the corn was yellow, the four of us carried it up the mountain. Robbers were killing people. You couldn't travel alone during the famine.

There was no corn. There was no wheat. Everyone ate corn tassels. Some ate fern root. Some ate banana root. If you had any tortillas, you would eat secretly, yes indeed!

Not even in San Cristóbal was it any better. It was a stiff punishment for everybody!

Now the Ladinos haven't taken it to heart. They step on the corn. They throw it out. They eat it on the cob.

We had grown arrogant because we offered them corn for the money we could get. The chastisement is yet to come, you'll see!

The famine will come again, some day, some year! The price of corn will rise, because people spill it and step on it all the time. The holy corn suffers so.

It is offered up for money. The money flows in San Cristóbal. The people keep buying things.

But corn is so hard to raise. There is exhaustion. There are long trips to the fields where the corn is harvested. The holy corn takes so many days!

—Xun Vaskis

When Our Lord Was Chased

When Our Lord was being chased by the Judases, he passed through Zinacantán. One of our countrymen was planting his corn.

"What are you planting?" asked Our Lord.

"I'm planting trees, I'm planting stones!" the man answered.

"Ah!" said Our Lord. "Well, if people come looking for me, tell them that when I passed by, you were just planting trees and stones."

"All right, I'll tell them." That evil man didn't know it was Our Lord he had lied to.

Those devils came along. "Haven't you seen a man pass by?" they asked.

"Yes, he passed by, but it was when I was planting trees and stones." Indeed, his field was full of rocks and trees. No corn appeared where he planted.

Our Lord continued on. He met another planter. "What are you doing?" he asked the man.

"I'm planting a corn plant. Who knows if it will grow."

"Ah!" said Our Lord. "Well, if people come looking for me, tell them, 'He passed by when I was planting my corn field.' Please say that to those following me."

"All right," said our countryman.

Three days later those pursuers arrived. The corn had grown tall and ripened! Some of it was already dry corn. The corn grew immediately because the farmer had answered Our Lord properly.

"Haven't you seen a man pass by?" asked those devils, the Judases.

"He passed by when I was planting my corn field," the man said. "He passed by a long time ago. My corn is already ripe!"

"Oh, hell!" said those Judases. "I guess we'll see if we can find him."

Our Lord went on. When those Judases were about to catch him, an angel appeared on the path. He defended Our Holy Father with a sword. Those Judases turned back.

So the years passed. Our Lord grew up. He became a man. Our Lord was old when he was captured. He turned himself in. He didn't care if he was punished.

He carried his cross. His cross was terribly heavy. The Judases kept poking Our Lord in the ass with a stick.

Our Lord hadn't any strength left. He had reached his limit. He had done all the tricking he could do.

Our Lord was hung on the cross. It was the Judases who hung him.

Our Lord was buried. The Judases buried him under stone slabs.

The Judases were squatting there. For three nights they kept watch. But the sonofabitches grew sleepy and nodded off.

Our Lord came out of the grave. He tossed a stone up. It turned into the sky.

Our Lord rose up when heaven was created.

The sonofabitching Judases couldn't find him anywhere.

Several devils went to look for him. But where would they find him crouching? Our Holy Father was already sitting in heaven.

As for the other devils—a terrific rainstorm came. They tried to hang on to cliffs. They tried to perch in trees. Lord, some of those Judases were killed by Thunderbolt. Some of those Judases died by lightning, others died from drowning.

The devils who were looking for Our Lord escaped. They have been walking ever since. They walk wherever they think they can find him. They travel, but they can't reach him.

Those Judases wander forever and they don't die. They are walking to this day, and they will walk until the time the world ends.

—Rey Komis

The Adventures of Peter

Once upon a time there was a boy named Peter. He was an orphan. He went looking for work. He was given a job as a babysitter.

The baby cried and cried. Peter lost his temper.

He asked his mistress for a needle. "I'm going to sew my clothes," he said.

He went to put the baby to sleep. He stuck the needle in the baby's breathing spot. The baby died.

He went to the kitchen to ask for his meal. "I'm hungry, mistress."

"Wait! The baby is going to cry. I'll go look," she said.

"No, it's asleep," said Peter. The child was stiff.

He swallowed his meal as fast as he could and he left.

He fled to another town and went looking for work.

"What kind of work do you want?" he was asked.

"What kind of work do you have?"

"There is pigherding," he was told.

"Ah, pigherding, yes indeed, I like that!" said Peter. He went to herd the pigs.

A Ladino came along. "Won't you sell one of your pigs?" asked the Ladino.

"Hmm, I won't sell just one," said Peter. "You'll have to buy them all."

"Sell them! I'll pay you a lot of money," the Ladino said.

"All right. But I want silver for them. And I'll only sell the meat. I won't sell the tails and ears."

"Good enough," said the Ladino.

Peter sold all the pigs. He stuck the tails and ears in a mudhole.

He went running to his master. "The pigs are dead! The pigs are dead! They all fell into the quicksand!"

"Sonofabitch! Let's go right away!" said his master.

"Look at their ears," said Peter. He pulled on a pig's ear. It looked as if he were pulling hard. He landed way off on his ass. He tugged at a tail. The tail came off. "Hell, the meat sank further down! Now we can't reach their tails to pull them out."

"Go ask your mistress for a pick and shovel," said his master. "They're leaning behind the door."

Peter ran back to the house. "Mistress," he said, "I was told to ask for a turn behind the door."

"What is it you want?" she asked. "Are you hungry?"

"No, my master says you're to give me a toss behind the door."

"Ooh, could it be this maybe?" Quickly she lifted her skirt.

"Yes, that's what I want," said Peter. The old woman got down on all fours. He gave it to her well.

He stole some flowers from the woman's yard and took off down the road. He stuck some silver coins on the stems.

A Ladino came along. "Do you want to buy these flowers?" Peter asked.

"What are they good for?" asked the Ladino.

"This is my treasure," said Peter. "Money grows on these flowers."

The dumb Ladino gave Peter three thousand pesos for a few little plants.

"I'll just keep these coins," said Peter. "Put the flowers in water and tomorrow when you wake up, the flowers will be blooming with money."

The Ladino was tricked. The flowers were dead the next morning.

Peter saw another Ladino riding along on horseback. "But what can I do?" he said to himself. "Aha! I'll take a shit."

Quickly he squatted down and took a shit. He covered it with his hat.

The Ladino arrived. "Where are you going?" Peter asked.

"I'm going hunting," said the Ladino.

"Oh, I'll sell you a beautiful little bird," said Peter.

"Where is it?" asked the Ladino.

"It's under my hat."

"Let me take a look," the Ladino said.

"You can't look! It scratches and pecks."

"But how can it be taken out, then?" asked the Ladino.

"I'll take it out if you have a cage for it."

"I do, but it's at home."

"If you'll come back right away, go and bring it," said Peter. "Or, if you'd like, give me your horse and I'll go myself."

Peter mounted the horse. He pricked it with a needle. The horse reared.

"Oh, your horse isn't used to me. Give me your clothes, give me your shoes! I'll hurry back," said Peter.

"Take them!" said the Ladino.

"Don't look, because it pecks terribly," said Peter as he rode away.

The Ladino was left by the side of the road in his underwear. He waited and waited. There was no sign of Peter. He was gone for good.

"Well, so what if it does peck me, I'm going to see what the damn bird looks like." The Ladino stuck his hand under the hat. As soon as he grabbed it, he realized it was shit squishing in his fingers. "Oh, the bastard! He's a thief. He fooled me completely."

Peter went off feeling very pleased with himself. Then he met a devil on the road.

"What do you say, Devil?" said Peter. "Do you want to make a bet to see who can make a hole in that tree?"

"Are you a real man?" asked the devil.

"That's what I say."

"Tomorrow, then, we'll see who's stronger," said the devil.

That night Peter cut a hole in the tree. He covered the hole with a piece of bark. The next morning he was ready for the contest with the devil.

"You throw the rock first," said Peter.

The devil threw hard, but he couldn't make a dent in the tree.

"You throw!" said the devil.

Peter aimed well. The rock knocked the bark off and went through the hole. He won two thousand pesos.

"But I won't give up," said the devil. "That money of mine has got to come back. Tomorrow we'll make another bet. We'll see who can roll that boulder."

"Okay!" said Peter.

Peter dug a hole under the rock. On the next day, "Roll it," said Peter. But the rock didn't budge.

"Now rock it toward me!" said the devil.

Peter crouched down in the hole he had dug. "Rock it!" said the devil. When Peter pushed, the boulder rolled away.

"I can't win," said the devil.

Peter went on. He met up with muleteers on the road.

"Ah, here comes Peter!" said the muleteers. "Poor Peter, now he'll die for sure! This one's a real bad robber."

They caught Peter and stuck him in a burlap bag. They tied it up tight with lassos. "Now he'll spend the night here. Tomorrow we'll throw him in the river."

Peter took out his razor and cut the lassos. He stuffed the muleteers' food inside the burlap bag, then tied it up tight. He fled to the other side of the river.

As soon as it grew light, the muleteers arrived. "Poor Peter, he's going to die now. His time has come."

They lifted the bag and went to dump it in the river. Food, dishes, eggs fell out.

"That bastard, Peter, he's scrammed."

"Hurray!" said Peter from far away.

"Well, what can you do?" said the muleteers.

—Romin Teratol

The Spook and the Chamulan

There was a Chamulan who met a Spook on the trail.

"Where are you going, friend?" asked the Spook.

"Sir, I'm going home," said the Chamulan. The sun was about to set.

"Forget your home, you bastard, let's fight!"

"The filth of your mother's cock! I'm man enough if you're man enough."

The fight began. The Chamulan didn't delay. Right away the Spook was slugged. The Spook didn't last half an hour. The Chamulan prayed the vespers, but the sonofabitching Spook probably never prayed the vespers.

The Chamulan gave him a good stab. He pulled off the Spook's wings that were attached to the back of his knees. The wings were long. They were made of yellow metal.

"What would happen if I stuck them on my legs?" the Chamulan said to himself. He stuck them on his knees. He tried to fly.

At first he just crashed. The second time he rose a little way. The third time, ooh, he flew very far, for the wings carried him. Before he knew it, he had arrived in the land of the Spooks. He came down exactly in front of the Spook's house.

"What are you doing here?" he was asked by the Spook's father and mother. "Where is our child? Have you killed him?"

"No, not at all. I am feeding him. I gave him eggs to eat. He is waiting for me at home," the Chamulan said.

"We'll go along with you, then," they said.

They went as far as the border of their country. They gave him a piece of jerked meat. "Eat some of it on the way. When you arrive, give the rest to our son. Take care of him! We want him to come home. We don't want you to kill him."

"He has always been my friend. We travel together," said the Chamulan, so that he would be freed. God, don't believe it. The Spook's flesh had already dried up. Their child was already bones.

"Where is his money?" they asked.

"But you can't think I've come for his money since he really has taken it with him," he said.

You see, the Chamulan had found several thousand pesos in the

Spook's pocket and had buried it in the ground. He didn't carry it with him because the money would tarnish on the way.

If he had tried to change it at the bank in San Cristóbal, they would ask him, "Where did you find it? Where is your invoice?" They don't want you to deposit it. Hold it in your tunic, look at it every few minutes. If you lose it from sight, it will turn into black potsherds.

"We'll keep our child's wings here," they said.

"What filth of your mother's cock! Why are you going to keep your child's wings? How is your son to come back again? I'm taking them to him."

He was allowed to come home. But now the wings wouldn't stick on. He had to carry them under his arm. Who knows how many days it took him to reach Chamula.

He went to dig up the money. The money hadn't tarnished, since it was buried.

Some Chamulans are right smart. The Spook was well-screwed.

—Xun Vaskis

What's Man Like?

Once a pair of oxen were drawing a cart down the middle of the road.

Coyote arrived. "What are you doing, Ox?" he asked.

"I'm not doing anything. I have a load," said Ox.

"Who gave you the load?" asked Coyote.

"Man did," said Ox.

"What's man like? Is he terribly strong? Can't you eat him?" asked Coyote. "Why don't you defend youself? You should gore him."

"But how can I gore him? He'll stick a pole up my ass."

"Exactly what does Man look like?"

"Well, like a man. He walks on two legs. He has two arms. He stands."

"What's the use! There's nothing I can do for you. Take care!" said Coyote.

A jaguar arrived. "What are you doing, Ox?" he asked.

"I'm just plodding along," said Ox.

"Who owns your load?" asked Jaguar.

"It's Man," said Ox.

"What's Man like?"

"Well, he walks on two legs," said Ox.

"Hell, you're so stupid. You should gore him," said Jaguar.

"Oh God, there's nothing you can do. If you act up, he kills you and eats you."

"I'll eat *him*!" said Jaguar.

"Watch out!" said Ox.

Jaguar went on. He met a mule loaded down with packs.

"What are you doing, Mule?" asked Jaguar.

"I'm delivering my load," said Mule.

"Who gave you your load?"

"It was Man."

"Hell, I'd like to see what Man looks like," said Jaguar.

"Well, he looks like a man. He can walk fast," said Mule.

"If I see him anywhere, I'll eat him. He has a habit of tormenting animals. Why don't you kick him?"

"If I kicked him he would whip me more. He'd pull my ears."

Jaguar went on. He reached a forest where he saw a man splitting wood.

"Is that you, Man?" asked Jaguar.

"It's me. How come?"

"Oh, no reason. I'm going to eat you. Why do you torment animals so much?"

"Wait until I finish splitting my wood," said the man. "Sit down a minute."

"I'll wait," said Jaguar. "But not for long. I'm getting hungry. I'm going to eat you."

"If you want to eat me sooner, help me split my firewood," said Man.

"How do I split it?"

"Like this. Stick your paws in the crack in the wood."

Jaguar stuck his paws in. Man pulled the axe out. Jaguar's paws were held tight. He was screaming.

"I can't, it's impossible. It hurts terribly. Help me! Please! I won't eat you any more. Forget it! Free my paws!" howled Jaguar.

"Why aren't you going to eat me? Eat me today, bastard!"

Man picked up his gun and fired at Jaguar. Jaguar pulled his paws out quickly. He ran away. He reached a stream. There he met some women washing clothes.

"What's Man to you?" asked Jaguar.

"Oh! He's my husband," said one of the women.

"Your husband? But he's such a devil. He shot me! A bullet hit me in the ribs," said Jaguar.

"Oh, that's not fatal. He was kind to you. Look at us! He's pierced our flesh wide open. Smell it and see! It stinks," said the women. They lifted their skirts.

"Oh, that's too much. You're already dying. You're wounded too badly. Me, I'm splitting!" said Jaguar.

He ran away. That's why jaguars don't eat us much any more.

—Romin Teratol

A Strange Affair in Totolapa

Once, not terribly long ago, a man went down to Totolapa to work in his corn field.

After he weeded his field, he went to amuse himself in the town. He met a girl on the trail.

How are you, girl?
I long to talk to you.
I see you are beautiful.
The girls in my land aren't like you.
Your back seems different.
Your side seems different.
I long to enjoy your company.
What does your heart feel?
Do you want us to get married?

"You want to talk to me, but are you a real man? Are your pants well-fastened?" answered the girl. "Only with the understanding that you have thought it out well, that you sincerely want to marry me, will I meet you in the meadow. For that is the place where those of us who have fiancés talk together."

"If you are telling the truth, if you respond to my reasoning, I'll certainly wait for you," said the man.

He went, sat down, and waited, looking up and down. At ten o'clock in the morning he was still sitting there.

He was sick and tired of waiting. He didn't know that the girl would come transformed into a cow.

Then he saw it. The black cow glistened beautifully. Its horns were terribly long. The cow was tossing its head from side to side and raising it again and again wonderfully. Before the man knew it, he was lifted into the sky. He landed way off with a thud.

The man was disabled. He wasn't a man any longer. He was a woman.

"How can this be? I thought that the girl was a good person, My Lord!"

He picked himself up and went back to his corn field. He was sick at heart.

"I shouldn't have gone to talk to the awful woman. I wouldn't be feeling so disgusting. But what can I do about it?" he said in his heart. "I think I'd better tie up one or two almuds of corn to take home. I'll make a pretense of carrying my corn. I'll go home and admit it. No, I don't know what to do. If only there was somebody I could ask about it. But I can't ask my friend at work, because he'll just rub it in. I'm ruined. I've turned into a woman forever."

He came home carrying two almuds of corn.

"You're back so soon," said his wife. "You were supposed to return on Thursday."

"I've come back to leave some corn for you," he said.

His wife gave him his meal. He ate quickly and left.

"I'm going to talk to our compadre," he told his wife. But he didn't just talk to his compadre. In the end he looked for anyone who could give him some advice. "Hasn't it ever happened to you? Haven't you ever talked to a woman? Haven't you ever gone crazy from it? I myself went crazy in Totolapa."

"But that wasn't at all smart of you! What business was it of yours to do such a stupid thing? The Totolapa people are very bad. Figure it out! See where the girl's house is. See how it stands. Talk to her. 'Why did you do this to me, child? I feel awful the way you have changed me. If only you had told me you didn't want to be spoken to in good form, I wouldn't have said anything at all. Now I am a poor woman. How can I respond to a greeting since I'm supposed to have my pants on? Don't you see, I'll be tormented. I can't reply to anything that is said to me.' Tell her that!" said his friends.

"Make me a couple of toasted tortillas for the night, wife! They say cattle have gotten into my corn field." He left a lie for his wife.

"Why are you so disgusting? Is there a reason for your never staying at home anymore? You are so strange! Maybe it's because you have an awful mistress there," she said.

"Hell, don't come telling me things like that. I, too, need a master now," said the gentleman.

His old woman, Matal, stayed behind. "Where did your man go?" she was asked by the neighbors.

"He went to the lowlands. He doesn't stay here at all anymore. I don't know why it is. Maybe the disgusting thing has a mistress. Maybe he's turned queer. Have you ever seen him spend the night? Do you think you can join the awful man in bed? Can he do anything now? Nothing!" said the woman, conversing about her husband, since she didn't know what the trouble was.

As soon as he arrived in Totolapa, he went to the market and bought a head of cabbage to take to his fiancée.

"Will my crime cool off?" he asked her. "I thought it was all right if I spoke to you. I thought you would respond to plain speech. I thought you would answer me honestly."

"How does it feel?" said the girl. "Wouldn't you be happier in a skirt? You should have worn your old woman's skirt!"

"But it's known that I'm a man. What would they say if I put on a skirt? I don't have long hair! I am a woman, yet my head is round like a man's. It's not a bit good if my crime isn't forgotten."

He offered a pint of cane liquor to the girl's father. He thrust the head of cabbage at his fiancée.

"I say, sir, please talk to your daughter for me. Forgive me for this little bit!"

"Talk to my daughter yourself! I wasn't watching when you talked to her. Perhaps she did this to you because she was upset, or embarrassed, or mortified when you spoke to her. Maybe she is working off her anger. As for me, thank you, may God repay you for this gift. If my daughter forgives you, we will drink. If my daughter doesn't forgive you, then think about whatever she tells you."

"That was indeed why I did it!" said the girl. "Don't come and play that on me. It isn't as if I said to myself, 'Where could the awful short-rumped men come from?' Our country is different. You have your women in your country and I have my men in my country. It's the first time we've seen someone like you talking to us girls."

"Pardon me!" said the man. "I just can't go on like this. I wear pants but I am a woman. I am ashamed to walk around. They used to address me as 'Sir,' now they ought to say 'Ma'am!'"

"But who knows, sir, if you will take it to heart. It shows in your face that that's what you always do, bothering everyone, talking to all the women. I know that's what you're like at home. Because that's what I was told in my dream last night. 'He goes to get women in their beds. You hear, even if the woman has a husband, he goes to get her in her bed.' That's why, before I will forgive you, I'll roll you over and over with a terrific beating."

"Patience, I can bear it if you beat me. If you reproach me, I'll survive. Just so long as you return my virility. If it's only a punishment, I'll take it to heart. The next time I won't say a word to anyone here, since I've witnessed what the Totolapa people are like."

"See here, sir," said the girl. "If it's true that you have never seen how we behave in our town, then go sit down and wait for me, just as you waited for me before. If you are afraid, pray to God! Ask him for a replacement for your thing or else you will stay unchanged forever. You will have your manhood only if you acquire his strength, paid for and bought."

The girl accepted the cabbage head. The father poured him a drink.

At exactly three o'clock the man arrived in the meadow. The black cow was in a fury. She was snorting at the ground. Ooh, the man was quaking.

"God, My Lord, watch over me, Saint Dennis, watch over me! Don't let me return, a mere woman, to beneath the feet of Saint Lawrence!"

The cow came thundering at him. The lucky guy was able to grab one horn. If it weren't for that, he would have landed rolling, just as he had before. Now he succeeded in grabbing the other horn with his hand.

He turned back into a man. If he hadn't grabbed the cow's horns, he would have been a woman forever.

—Tonik Nibak

The Sweeper of the Path

The great star appeared. The sky grew bright from end to end.

"I am the sweeper of the path, I sweep Our Lord's path so that when Our Lord passes by he finds the path already swept."

Venus is the morning star. She is a girl from Chamula.

The women didn't believe the Chamulan girl who said she was a star.

"She says she is a star! Could she be a star? She's an awful, ugly, black Chamulan. Isn't the star beautiful? It has rays of light. The star is a beautiful bright red," said the women.

"I am the one who fixes the path. When Our Lord disappears, the ocean dries up. The fish come out of the sea. When Our Lord disappears, there is a red sun, the monkey's sun.

"I am the sweeper of the house. I walk when it grows light. When night falls, I sweep beneath the world. When dawn comes, I appear and sweep again, because that is my work. That's why I am a star. Venus appears early in the dawn, say the people, but it's me. I sweep Our Lord's path. It isn't just anyone's path."

She sweeps the path off constantly. When she disappears, she is traveling inside the earth. When the star reappears the next morning, she sweeps the path again, the path of the holy sun.

We didn't believe that it was a Chamulan girl. "It seems to be a star, but a Chamulan, I don't believe it!" we said.

But the poor girl heard us mocking her. If it weren't so, she wouldn't have heard. But she did hear, so it's true.

—Tonik Nibak

Notes, by Robert M. Laughlin

In the Land of the Night Sun: Dreams

Pooh on Him and Pooh on Me

A *compadre* (cofather) is a ritual kinsman whose relationship has been established during any one of a number of ceremonies. The term in Zinacantán has been extended beyond the basic relationships between the father of a child and the child's godfather to include individuals united by a wide variety of bonds. The comparable female relatives are *comadres*.

An Owl Screeches, I Kill a Black Cat

Owls are ill omens throughout Middle America. As the popular Mexican saying goes: "When a screech owl calls, an Indian dies."

Black cats in Zinacantán are not normally ill omens as in the United States.

My Hoe Is Stolen, I Am Chased and Fly Away

Prefects are members of the third level of a four-level religious hierarchy that consumes a great portion of an individual Zinacantec's wealth in exchange for prestige and, hopefully, a long life.

Constables are members of the lowest level of the religious hierarchy. They serve at the courthouse as messengers and officers of the law. To be appointed a constable is a dubious honor, since notorious troublemakers are chosen for this post.

The magistrate acts as the mayor of Zinacantán, in charge of the town's relations with the outside world, but he is also the chief arbiter of local disputes.

I Am Nearly Stoned

Chicha is a thick fermented sugarcane drink. Although it is sold by Chamulan merchants at all major fiestas and is especially important at Carnival, it is associated with informal drinking much like beer in the United States.

I Am Chased by Women

If the earth is "dangerous," this means that the place where the house is standing is next to the Earth Lord's door or perhaps on the middle of his trail. It is further believed that because of our blindness we may unintentionally annoy the Earth Lord by constructing our house or choosing to sleep in his territory.

I Carry Rocks

Four sacristans, who serve for an indeterminate number of years, are responsible for the care of the churches in Zinacantán Center and direct many of the stewards' ritual activities.

Stewards are members of the lowest level of the religious hierarchy.

The syndic serves under the magistrate in a political position similar to vice-president or assistant mayor of the community.

I Am Late for Work and Am Chased by Ladinas

Cane liquor, or *pox*, is a distilled sugarcane drink produced primarily by Chamulan bootleggers in their secret stills. *Pox* is sometimes translated as "rum" though it more closely resembles vodka in taste and potency. It is considered a necessary lubricant for matters of consequence involving communication between men, and between men and gods.

I Am Offered Three Stones

A "contribution at the feet of Our Lord" means a year of service in the religious hierarchy.

Romin addresses his counselors with utmost respect as "My Father," "My Lord," as representatives, if not incarnations, of the saints whom they served.

Two months earlier, on February 24, 1963, Romin had visited the elders and accepted appointment to the Stewardship of the Holy Sacrament six years hence.

I Scold a Shaman

Cross Day, or the Discovery of the True Cross, is celebrated officially on May 3, but in Zinacantán the responsibility for conducting the celebration of this fiesta is assumed by neighborhood groups, which choose any convenient day in the early part of May. Families that share the same source of water gather to clean the waterhole. Offerings are made to the Earth Lord in payment for use of the waterholes and to insure a plentiful supply of water during the growing season.

This dream was directly inspired by a mortifying event that had occurred just three days before. Romin had asked Maryan Teratol, his first cousin, to offer candles to the "Holy Fathers, the Holy Mothers" (the ancestral gods) to inaugurate the completion of his new house. But Maryan proceeded to pray at great length the lines appropriate to Cross Day. Desperate attempts to keep Maryan awake long enough to carry out the necessary rites failed at every step. He was carried from one corner of the house to the next where he instructed Romin's helpers to light the candles as they lay on the ground, as if it were a witching ceremony. He finally passed out and was replaced by one of the assistants who happened to be a shaman, Anselmo Peres. Romin in his dream was able to deliver all the reproaches that must have passed through his mind following the shaman's debacle.

I Work in the Belltower, Give Advice, Distribute Corn

Romin had worked very unhappily for the "gringo priest," who was studying Zina-cantec religion.

George was an American anthropology student who had lived for awhile in Romin's house. He, of course, was not under the priest's authority.

Maryan Sarate had been a school teacher in Paste'. Although he was not the magistrate, he was in fact the political boss of Zinacantán.

The offering of candles to lower the price of corn is an unheard of procedure.

Principals are hamlet representatives who report every Sunday to the courthouse in Zinacantán Center.

This must have been a very gratifying dream episode for Romin, who at the outset of his anthropological employment had aroused the ire and suspicion of the people of Paste' by trying to carry out a census in what was then a very conservative hamlet.

I Have a Drink, See a Plane, Our Clothes Drop in Church

The Cabaña was the headquarters of the National Indian Institute in San Cristóbal.

Courbaril has a pod that is filled with powder. It is eaten by Ladinos.

We Walk through a Deserted Village

A "pinto" is a person suffering from *mal de pinto*, a tropical disease that causes wide areas of skin to lose their pigmentation and become pinkish white. The affected areas eventually turn a dull black. This disfiguring disease frequently is associated with the people of Chiapa de Corzo.

I Gather Snails, I Throw a Black Bull

Mother Pil is Romin's maternal aunt who lived together with his mother in his childhood home.

The thought of driving sheep to the lowlands would strike a Zinacantec as bizarre.

Snails are a Lenten delicacy.

In 1963 no Zinacantecs owned oxen.

A devil ranges in meaning from a hostile person or animal to a witch, a witch's transformation, or any evil force, whether natural or supernatural.

It is curious that Romin would dream of throwing a bull, because his father's father, who was chief shaman for many years, dreamt a similar dream before assuming his shamanic duties.

My Father Is Dressed in Red

The role of the Grand Spanish Lord at the Fiesta of Saint Sebastian is played by the grand *alcalde* (senior elder). Decked out in gold-embroidered red coat, red knickers, and red socks, he participates in a horse race and tilts against a jousting target.

I Am Offered Tassels by a Pretty Girl

Tassels for a man's tunic are usually made by the man himself.

It is said that when a man dreams of sleeping with a beautiful woman and wakes up in the middle of the night, if he gets up and lies down again with his feet where his head was, the woman will have the same dream.

I Am Buying Sandals

Chamulan girls are thought to be bolder in speech, more apt to participate in racy conversations than the girls of Zinacantán. Occasionally Zinacantec men marry Chamulan girls, but in that case the girl would have been commissioned to weave in a Zinacantec home and would have changed into Zinacantec clothing.

What Shamans Are Shown

The elders consist of the grand and petty alcaldes and the four prefects. They are a group of highly respected old men who stand at the summit of the religious hierarchy. They appoint each member of the hierarchy and swear into office all the officials of the top three levels. The elders sit around a large table in the Chapel of Lord Esquipulas where the oaths of office are taken. The elders are human models of the ancestral gods who are conceived as sitting around a table at Calvary. Calvary itself is the mystical courthouse of Zinacantán where the souls of ailing Zinacantecs are defended by the shamans.

Flower water is a necessary element of major curing ceremonies. This water, drawn from sacred wells in Zinacantán Center, is used to bathe the patient and his "substitute," the sacrificial chicken. Before the bath, various herbs, wintergreen, peperomia, Mexican savory, and laurel are steeped in water to provide an aroma pleasing to the gods.

Sweatbaths may be used clandestinely for carrying on daytime affairs but not as sleeping quarters at night.

What Midwives and Bonesetters Are Shown

"Ghost flowers" are Mexican savory. The tea is drunk by women in labor.

I Am Carried from a Cave

For severe illnesses the shaman sometimes prescribes that the patient's bed be decorated with pine boughs, geraniums, and air plants. The bed is the symbolic equivalent of the corral for the companion animal spirits.

I See a Fallen Flesh

Fallen Flesh is a witch's transformation that is believed to leave its flesh in a pile at the foot of the cross to fly about with rattling, squeaking bones, dripping blood. A drop of its blood falling upon an unsuspecting villager is reported to have fatal effects.

I Commit Murder and Am Covered with Pooh

Maryan Seto was a notorious bigamist and murderer. His first murder is described by Tonik Nibak in "The Little Bird."

Lol K'obyox was Maryan Seto's stepson. He is credited with a half dozen or so murders.

More Pooh

The two stewards-royal are the primary stewards entrusted with the worship of the image of Our Lord of Esquipulas. Antun Lopis is the husband of Mal Montixyo.

Every second Sunday the tithing man brings a token amount of salt from the sacred well in the hamlet of Vo' Bitz (Five Pieces) to the Chapel of Esquipulas in Zinacantán Center. When he leaves for home he is escorted as far as Muk'ta Krus, the crosses that stand at the western edge of Zinacantán Center.

The church president is titular head of the sacristans, who, together with the stewards, may form a unitary block when one of their number is under attack.

"Sweatbath" is the jocular name for the jail which then had a barred wooden door open to the elements.

"Wind" is probably arthritis or rheumatic pain.

I Am Offered a Fiddle, I Am Excused from Playing

Posol is a very refreshing drink made of once-ground corn dough mixed with water. Zinacantecs going to work in the lowlands almost always take with them a large lump of the dough from which they break off lumps to mix with water scooped up from a stream.

I Am Offered a Flute

Ensign-bearers are members of the second and third levels of the religious hierarchy. When they march in processions they are preceded by a flutist and two drummers.

My Dead Brother Tells Me How It Is and How It Happened

Tuxtla Chico is a prosperous town close to the Guatemalan border, but in Zinacantán "Little Tuxtla" is the name given to any gully where a murderer's victim has been tossed.

In Tzotzil, as in many other Mayan languages, the verb "to speak" may be extended to mean "to have an affair."

How We See Whether It Will Be a Boy or a Girl

Immediately after a baby's birth these same implements that will characterize the baby's daily activities in adulthood are placed in its hands.

I Am Offered Flowers, Pencils, Gourds

Pinole is a hot drink made of corn that is toasted and then ground and mixed with water, and sugar added.

A shaman begins his practice informally, treating family members and close neighbors. But if he falls ill or if social pressure builds up for him to declare himself and assume the public responsibilities required of shamans, he will seek out the senior shaman of his community, offer him a bottle of cane liquor, relate his pertinent dreams, and ask permission to make his debut. Then he will secure a bamboo staff in the lowlands and return home to ask a veteran shaman to accompany him on the ceremonial circuit of the churches, sacred mountains, crosses, and waterholes in the Center. Together they will journey to the "holy heaven," praying to the ancestral gods that the novitiate's prayers and offerings be accepted.

Two scribes are chosen by the elders to serve for a year. They must maintain a list of all adult males required to pay taxes for fiestas, maintain the list of petitions for future appointments to religious office, and write out the notifications of those appointments. Their term may be renewed as many as three times.

The secretary of the band committee serves for one year. He keeps a record of the expenses incurred when a band is brought to play at a fiesta. He keeps track of the number of songs played so that the three "serenades" of eight songs apiece are played daily. He also sees to it that the musicians' needs are properly attended to and that they do not fall asleep on the job.

I See Dancing Buzzards

Bass viols are played by Ladino mariachi musicians but not by Zinacantecs.

I Watch Dogs Ferry People Across a River

The Zinacantec underworld with its canine ferrymen recalls the Huichol infernal landscape where the sinners are carried across the river on the back of a white-throated black dog. The Aztec sinners were ferried across by a yellow dog because, as Sahagún reported, the white dog refused, protesting, "I've been washed," and the black dog declined too, saying, "I've just been stained with black" (Furst and Nahmad, 1972:59–60).

My Fiancé's Father Brings a Barrel of Cane Liquor

Acceptance of cane liquor under such circumstances customarily implies acceptance of the suit. A gift of a whole barrel of cane liquor is unheard of "on the earth's surface." A proper Zinacantec courtship is initiated by the prospective groom and his family making a surprise visit at night to the house of the girl of his choice. Two or more petitioners must plead his cause before the girl's father. If the visit is successful, a year or two is spent paying the bride price before the girl's family will permit the house-entering ceremony which establishes ritual kinship between the two families. In Zinacantán the house-entering ceremony confirms that a boy and girl will be married, and often this marks the first occasion when the groom can legally sleep with his bride. Several months later the church wedding takes place.

I Am Cooking a Wedding Banquet

The wedding ceremony here is entirely unconventional. Weddings are never celebrated in the woods or the fields. The bride and groom customarily sit at the table with the guests but do not partake of the banquet. The dance follows, but the bride and groom sit inside inconspicuously while the dance continues in the front yard for as long as the participants can remain on their feet.

I Am Given a Chicken, But It Is Taken Away

The man and the woman are probably Saint Lawrence and Our Lady of the Rosary who is the saint in the church of Five Pieces.

Saint Lawrence Asks to Have His Face Uncovered

Apparently the prefects are, in fact, the ancestral gods and therefore address Saint Lawrence as "son," intimating that he is younger.

"The three Maryans" were three sacristans who happened to have Maryan as their first names.

I Find a Pile of Money

"Wind," or arthritic pain, may be caused by seeing copper coins in a dream.

I Gather Firewood and Am Rebuked for Praying at a Shrine

The white-bearded gentleman is one of the ancestral gods.

A cross is conceived as both a doorway and a messenger to the deities.

I Am Falsely Accused in Court and Am Finally Vindicated

That the grand alcalde is acting as the magistrate indicates that he is really an ancestral god and that Tonik has been brought before the celestial court.

A divining basket is made of oak branches and is suspended upside down from a scissor blade inserted in its bottom. Questions are directed at it. When the correct suggestion is made, the basket falls. Divining baskets are rarely resorted to as a means for discovering the location of a lost object.

I Go to Chenalhó

Tonik's annoyance is thoroughly justified as Chenalhó is twenty-three miles from San Cristóbal while Tuxtla is fifty miles distant.

The Day of the Dead is actually a three-day period including Halloween and All Saints' Day. In every home a table serving as an altar is covered with the favorite food and drink of the deceased. Great netfuls of fruit are carried to the graveyard, where the fruit is placed on the graves. Candles are lit, the responsories are chanted by the sacristans, and quantities of cane liquor are consumed. In the Church of Saint Lawrence a large table is studded with flickering candles for the souls that died without surviving kin.

I Am Attacked by a Spook or Was It Saint Michael?

The image of Saint Michael has attracted both Ladino and Indian visitors for many years. Saint Michael reputedly responds to questions directed to him through his Ladino intermediary. He reveals the location of missing objects and the nature of illnesses. His cures combine ritual obligations with pharmaceutical prescriptions. Visitors of confidence are urged to kiss a carved, polished stone which seemed to me, after a furtive glance, to be an Olmec *yugo*.

The Burden of Days: Tales

When the Guatemalans Were Blown Sky High

This legendary conflict between the Zinacantecs and the Guatemalans has no known historical counterpart.

The modesty of archeological remains in the Chiapas highlands suggests that this area was a cultural backwater avoided in preference to the less arduous coastal route between Mexico and Guatemala (Adams, 1961:341). Even so, a sixteenth-century document states that Quetzaltenango, in Guatemala, was subject to Zinacantán and at the outer limits of Zinacantec land (Navarrete, 1966:103).

From Oaxaca to Guatemala come beliefs in the magical powers of the town elders, who could transform themselves into thunderbolts, lightning, wind, hail, and clouds to protect their people. The most interesting reports from Guatemala occur in the historical sources. *The Title of the Lords of Totonicapán*, which traces the wanderings of the Quiché, recalls how their ancestors "being well instructed, used their incantations to make clouds, thunder, lightning, earthquakes" (Recinos and Goetz, 1953:174).

The encounter between Pedro de Alvarado's army and the Quiché forces is also reported. Tecum Umam, the Quiché chief, flew like an eagle at Alvarado, who was protected, the chronicler relates, by a fair maiden and hosts of footless birds that blinded the Quiché soldiers. A second chief, Nehaib, became a thunderbolt, but three times he was blinded by a white dove. Then Tecum reentered the fray. He flew at Alvarado, and beheaded the conquistador's steed, but was impaled on Alvarado's lance. So ended the Quiché resistance (Recinos, 1957:86–88).

Three centuries later and with a keen perception of Indian realities, the great Zapata spurred on the myth of his invincibility by naming his dashing white stallion, "El Relámpago" (Lightning).

After scrupulously searching all the historical and mythic sources of Middle America, I have been able to discover only a Chortí horned serpent that rivals the Zinacantecs' flatulent power (Fought, 1972:83–84).

When Christ Was Crucified

According to Romin, the world as we know it today was made in three stages: first, the rocks and the ground, second, the ocean, the trees, and the animals, and third, the sky.

The person who reveals Christ's hiding place was transformed into a magpie-jay, an extremely noisy bird. Because the rufous-collared sparrow was blessed by Our Lord it must not be killed. Unlike roosters it sings at regular hours. Roosters and hens, however, have been condemned to be the traditional sacrificial offering at curing ceremonies, house dedications, agricultural rites, etc. The chicken is spoken of as the "substitute" of a patient.

It is entirely possible that my translation of *yaxal xixib ton* as a "blue pebble" is incorrect. *Yaxal* can mean gray, green, or blue. Although I know of no local jade, it is likely that the same term would be applied to it, so, in fact, Christ may have created the sky by tossing a piece of jade in the air.

When Christ rises to sit at the right hand of the judge, the "judge" is San Salvador who is seated in the center of the sky. Romin describes him as being the older brother of the sun (of Christ), whom he sends around the world to record and report back to him the sins of man.

A Visit to the Underworld

The use of bones as firewood in Hell must have been borrowed from Christian belief.

The tree infested with masses of lice is a striking analogue to the Classic Maya "tree of life" that rises from the underworld toward heaven, to the Yucatec heavenly tree of abundance, and to the breast tree awaiting the souls of Tzotzil babies in the sky.

The detail of the priest kneeling on the groom's hat as he ravishes the bride is not only a vivid Freudian image but also a neat reversal of Zinacantec custom, for often men use their hats as prayer cushions in church.

How Rabbit Won His Hat and Sandals

Lol's sprightly tale of Rabbit's exploits introduces fresh elements to the standard rabbit-coyote cycle. Rabbit's musical accompaniment has not to my knowledge been heard before. The cheese-as-moon reflection adds another new detail. But Rabbit's bag of tricks is filled here with old ones well-known in Europe, Latin America, and the southwestern United States.

Deer and rabbits are closely related in native lore. In Mexican folk art, rabbits are often portrayed with hoofs and antlers. Rabbits are also identified with the moon. In Zinacantán the deer has underworld associations. During the dry season the Earth Lord is believed to be off mounted on a deer collecting gunpowder for the rainy season.

The Priest and the Constable

The stave used by the constable is of polished palm heartwood so sturdy that an axe can cut it only with the greatest difficulty.

The Spook and the Girl from Magdalenas

Despite the hero's bravery he is derided by the other Zinacantecs with what seems to be a touch of envy for having a Magdalenas girl walking behind him as his wife. But they can write her off as the devil for having obviously had to submit to the devil both body and soul.

The Buzzard Man

The tale of the Buzzard Man appears to be a New World creation. There is some variation in the tell-tale characteristics of the buzzard in man's guise. He hops, has hairy legs, or has feathers on his knees, doesn't wash, refuses chili, or neglects to eat his tortillas, but mostly he stinks. He may protest that his foul odor is caused by hard work or that he was the unlucky target of a bird overhead.

Journey to Irdivolveres

The journey to Irdivolveres is to the Castillo d'Iras y no Volveras, the "Castle of Going and No Returning." At first glance, Mother Wind and Whirlwind seem to be drawn from Tzotzil cosmology. But why does Whirlwind comment on our hero's body odor? The answer is found in a version from Belize, where the cannibal wind giants detect the fragrance of ripe chicozapotes (Thompson, 1930:175–178). This, of course, is an Indian variety of "Fe, fa, fi-fo-fum."

The dialogue in mid-air, equating the size of the world with pesos and centavos, is unique so far as I know.

The Bear's Son

"The Bear's Son," sharing many motifs with Beowulf, is widespread in Europe, especially in Scandinavia. It occurs in India and North Africa and among North American Indian groups (Barakat, 1965:330–331). Rey's Rabelaisian conclusion adds a fresh dimension to this ancient epic.

The very existence of an early Spanish loanword, *tosov*, for "bear" in Chiapas, far from bears' native habitat and where it is not likely that traveling circuses would have ventured, is mysterious. Perhaps this tale holds the key.

How to Take Care of Jaguars

The jaguar is not only a fearsome creature on the earth's surface, he is also the lord of the Mayan underworld.

When the Soldiers Were Coming

When Romin recounted this legend to me, he was of the opinion that it referred to the Mexican Revolution. Both his mother and his aunt were astounded at his ignorance, assuring him that this was dated back many, many years, but, of course, for Romin the Revolution, too, was ancient history that he had only known of by word of mouth.

The Mayan epic *Popol Vuh* presents a scene of bathing girls sent to divert the enemy:

> You are to go, our daughter.
> Go and wash clothes by the river.
> And if you see those three sons
> Then undress yourselves before them,
> And if they desire you
> You are to invite them so that we can come after you.
>
> (Edmonson, 1971:195)

A battle in which black rain is hurled at the enemy also occurs in the *Popol Vuh*, shortly before the scene of the bathing girls (ibid., 192).

Searching elsewhere for clues, three of the place names have proved to be pre-Columbian sites. When I surreptitiously visited "Bowl Spring," I discovered it to be a narrow cave. From the floor protruded a sharp stake surrounded by candle drippings. The potsherds that littered the whole area dated from the Late Classic (600–900 A.D.) and post-Classic periods (900 A.D.-Conquest). "Red Earth" was occupied during the post-Classic. "Market Site" also shows an abundance of obsidian and sherds dating from the post-Classic era. The presence of bones and the shells of fresh water snails suggests that this indeed was a bustling market (McVicker, n.d.:12–13).

Turning now to written records, we find that the enmity between the Zinacantecs and the Chiapanecs at the time of the Spanish Conquest was reported by Ximénez.

> [The Zinacantecs] were men of great valor in war, for it seemed that the whole world was against them. They had constant war with Chiapa over the salt works. Although at times they made peace and exchanged presents, for Zinacantán lacked many things that were in abundance in Chiapa, nevertheless soon they were enemies again, killing and sacrificing each other (cited in Navarrete, 1966:99).

The route that the Chiapanecs allegedly followed was, until construction of the Pan American Highway, the principal access to Zinacantán from the north. By this route Bernal Díaz traveled with two hundred Chiapanec Indians and two hundred Zinacantec porters, spending the night by the salt works and arriving in Zinacantán at noon the next day, Easter Sunday, 1524, where they rested before pressing on to the conquest of Chamula.

Outsiders from the north funnelled continually up this trail. Zinacantán Center was the last stop before San Cristóbal on the trade routes from Mexico City and Veracruz to the Chiapas highlands. Armies marched up and down this trail many times. In 1559 they passed muster in Zinacantán, gathering new forces as they proceeded magnificently toward the Petén. In 1823, when Chiapas was in a turmoil trying to decide whether to be a part of Mexico or Guatemala, the general of the Tuxtla army met in Zinacantán with the representatives of San Cristóbal. Ten years later, when an armed rebellion erupted in San Cristóbal, a hundred government troops poured into Zinacantán surprising and routing the rebel infantry and cavalry—all one hundred and fifty souls! In 1863, 1864, and again in 1866 the liberal forces in Tuxtla representing Benito Juarez were pitted against the imperialists in San Cristóbal. The liberals, forced to spend the night of September 18, 1866, in Zinacantán, complained that no one would sell them a single tortilla. Again in 1869 the governor's armies marched through Zinacantán in the "War of the Castes." In the Mexican Revolution battles were waged in the town in 1920 and 1924. (For historical sources see Castañon Gamboa, 1931; Bravo Izquierdo, 1948; López Sánchez, 1960; Montesinos, 1935; Moscoso Pastrana, 1960; V. Pineda, 1888; and Trens, 1942.)

It is believed that occasionally you can hear the soldiers' trumpets and drums sounding from the cave of "Pricked-Up Ears," though in one tale it is said that these instruments were left there by Saint Sebastian before his martyrdom (Wasserstrom, 1970:212–213). No less mysterious is the transformation of the enemy soldiers into ancestral gods, who guard their descendants from conquest and the forces of evil.

The Revolution

The first scene in Tonik's account of the Mexican Revolution apparently opens on September 19, 1920, when the Pinedists, who represented the conservative clerical interest of San Cristóbal, routed the revolutionary government troops of President Carranza in a battle that raged for nine hours. Tonik mistakenly identifies the Carrancistas as Obregónists, who arrived four years later, not four days, as Tonik recalls.

The battle of Ixtapa pitted less than four hundred Pinedists against three thousand government troops, including infantry, cavalry, and air force, four cannons, and the first airplane ever to be seen in Chiapas. The battle began early in the morning of April 24, 1924, and lasted for thirteen hours.

General Bravo Izquierdo, general of Obregon's army, presents a vivid account of his stunning success, which he felt went exactly as planned. Despite their varying speed of locomotion, the infantry, cavalry, and air force reached Ixtapa sharply at six a.m. The airplane carrying Colonel Pedro Moctezuma dropped the first bomb ever to fall on Chiapas. It was a dud. But undaunted by this mishap, Colonel Moctezuma returned at eleven a.m. Flying low over Ixtapa, he strafed the troops with machine gun fire but, to General Izquierdo's dismay, soon exhausted all his munitions. It seems, too, that the pilot, unable to distinguish the enemy's position from that of the government troops, had misdirected his fire. Fortunately there were no losses.

Later in the day Colonel Moctezuma was to carry out the most extraordinary feat of the whole campaign. He flew over San Cristóbal with orders to bomb the enemy barracks, whose location had been discovered by intelligence. The target was missed, but, as if it had been a "smart bomb," the trajectory landed squarely in General Alberto Pineda's patio, where it decapitated his finest rooster (Bravo Izquierdo, 1948:119–121).

Meanwhile, back in Ixtapa, after a fierce resistance, the brave soldiers of General Pineda, seeing themselves thoroughly outnumbered, attacked from all sides and, sustaining many losses, capitulated. Many officers, including a general, were among the captives. The prisoners had been promised their lives if they surrendered, but no sooner had they laid down their arms than the officers were led off to the cemetery and promptly shot (Moscoso Pastrana, 1960:281).

General Bravo Izquierdo reports that three hundred Pinedist soldiers were routed that same day and pursued up the mountain trail to Zinacantán Center. Eleven hundred Pinedists were camped on the northwest flank of the Center. On the first of May, General Izquierdo launched an attack against Pineda's forces. La Ventana (Window Pass), the pass leading from Zinacantán Center to San Cristóbal and the scene of so many battles through the ages, was finally gained at noon by General Izquierdo after five hours of engagement. The army of Pineda scattered, fleeing to the far side of San Cristóbal. The following month the conservative resistance was completely vanquished. So ended the Revolution in Chiapas.

For Tonik, all the grand ideals, the bullets and battles of the Mexican Revolution, shrink to nothing before the contemplation of a generous stack of tortillas and a simmering pot of well-spiced chicken.

Tonik's mother's quandary about how to prepare food for the Ladino soldiers expresses the distinctive difference between Indian and Ladino cuisine—Indians eat boiled food, Ladinos eat fried food.

None of the accounts of the Revolution reported to me shows the slightest awareness of the political issues involved. The war simply amounted to fear and hardship relived again and again. Evidently many Indians felt admiration for Pineda. Though he represented the San Cristóbal Ladinos, who wished only to keep the Indians under heel, his resourcefulness became legendary. It is said that he escaped detection many times dressed as an Indian charcoal maker. When I first lived in San Cristóbal in 1959, General Pineda, then in his nineties, could often be seen taking walks in the plaza.

When One Stupid Indian Won

The earliest Zinacantec reference to Mexicans occurs in the sixteenth-century *Diccionario en lengua sotzil*, in which they are termed "wrap-around skirt" (*Diccionario*, n.d.:78), a derisive allusion to the mode of dress of the intruders from the north.

It is not clear from historical sources whether the Zinacantecs were allies of the Mexicans. According to Clavijero, the province of Zinacantán was "the last in the southeastern part of the Mexican empire and absolutely the most distant from the capital" (Clavijero, 1964:124). Yet reports that Zinacantán was an Aztec garrison in the fifteenth century are suspect. Sahagún relates that Aztec merchants, eager for amber and precious feathers, penetrated the highlands at the risk of their lives and only after mastering the Tzotzil language and traveling disguised in Zinacantec clothing (Sahagún, book IX, chapter V, cited in Blom, 1959:25–26).

The disguised Aztec merchants, who faced certain death if discovered, evidently made the arduous journey to Zinacantán for reasons other than trade. "They sought land for the portent Uitzilopochtli [god of war]. . . . Secretly they saw (and) entered everywhere in Anauac [Mexico], to travel inspecting as disguised merchants" (Sahagún, cited in Dibble and Anderson, 1959:22–23).

It is reported that in one of the early rebellions in Chiapas, "the Indians used long ropes to impede the progress of the [Spaniards'] horses" (Haefkens, 1969:125).

The Three Suns

Although rodent allies are frequent actors in North American tales, the combination of elements in this story is peculiar to the Mayan area. In the *Popol Vuh* the twin heroes

Hunahpu and Xbalanque (Hunter and Jaguar Deer) are mistreated by their stingy elder half-brothers. But after being persuaded to climb a tree to recover the birds that they have shot, the half-brothers are converted into monkeys; the heroes become sun and moon (Edmonson, 1971:87–89).

The porcine fate of the elder brothers has been recorded many times in the Chiapas highlands. Two variants from Zinacantán identify the hero as Christ (Ritvo, 1972:63–64,T2).

Romin's tale, with its cosmic overtones, also expresses the central tenet of Zina-cantec moral philosophy that food must be shared equally. Because of their stinginess, the older brothers become food for their younger brother. Ritvo argues that the entire sequence represents a developmental model for the Zinacantec child. The tortillas that Xut stuck on his brothers' faces to turn them into pigs are a small oval variety with a hole in the center. In everyday life they are given to little children to induce them to learn to talk, on the theory that the hole in the center inspires them to open their mouths.

Romin did not know why the younger brother's name was Xut. Today that word is otherwise used only as a name for a wild bean.

When the Ashes Fell

When Xun attributes the heat of the ashes as a possible cause of the animals' sickness, he is probably referring not to temporary heat but to a fundamental quality of the volcanic ash. Zinacantecs also ascribe hot, medium, and cold properties to particular foods. Illnesses, too, are categorized along the scale of hot to cold. Herbal remedies are chosen that will restore the patient's balance.

Xun's frequent use of the word "holy" is characteristic of his narrative style. It is an embellishment that perhaps subconsciously emphasizes his close personal relation-ship to the gods that he feels he has earned as a shaman and as one of the most venerable men in Zinacantán.

The fall of ashes from the eruption of Mount Tacaná in Guatemala in 1902 is now probably the earliest historical event of importance that was witnessed and is still remembered by the oldest living Zinacantecs. It is used as a bench mark for dating subsequent events that are fast receding, too, into mythic time.

When the Church Rose and Saint Sebastian Was Saved

This tale of the origin of the Church of Saint Sebastian contains clues to the meaning of the highly complex ritual activity that occurs every year at the Fiesta of Saint Sebastian. Dressed in elaborate masks and costumes, the townspeople impersonate the major figures in this epic drama: the Lacandóns; the jaguars; the "feathered serpent" or Raven, who gave men corn; the Spook (who hurls dead squirrels at spectators); and the Spanish lords and ladies. These and other characters reenact certain aspects of the appearance and martyrdom of Saint Sebastian, as well as the construction of his future home.

The date over the door of the Church of Saint Sebastian is 1872.

The *Vaxakmen* or Creator Gods who built the Church of Saint Sebastian also granted to the ancestral gods of Zinacantán the original bell of the Church of Saint Lawrence ("When the Bell Was Lifted"). They are credited with making the waterholes with their staves. They are also the gods who uphold the corners of the world on their shoulders, and so are surely related to the Yucatec Cuch-caan and the ancient Mayan Bacabs (Villa Rojas, 1969:272). In the neighboring town of San Andrés the original ancestors are said to have come from a place to the east called Vaxakmen, where there was an "elegant palace of stone" (Holland, 1962:14). Perhaps this was Palenque.

Writing in 1794, Ordoñez y Aguiar speaks of a temple in the coastal town of Soconusco that was built by puffs of air and contained jade figures of the calendric gods (Ordoñez y Aguiar, 1907:14). The iconic associations of the *teponaxtle* or slit drum with Saint Sebastian suggests an early assimilation of pre-Columbian Mayan elements. The principal deity of Chiapas was Votan, Lord of the Hollow Trunk, who was also called Tepanaguaste (ibid.). Votan is unknown in Chiapas today, but in Santa Eulalia, Guatemala, Watan is the name for the day that always begins a new year—the "year bearer" (La Farge, 1947:8–10). A slit drum is played every January at the Fiesta of Saint Sebastian. Because the saint played a slit drum, the drum itself has acquired the stature of a saint.

The Priest and the Bell—The Epidemic and Me

The importance of dreams in Zinacantán as the spectacles for true vision is manifest in this legend. The subject of the shamans' dreams is Maria Muxul, the ancestral god of the hill known as Muxul Vitz that stands at the main entrance to Zinacantán Center. At the foot of the hill is one of the major shrines for curing ceremonies, and so Muxul Vitz is addressed by Xun as "place of recovery, place of revival." The hill is personified and referred to as "Our Holy Mother." As such it was offered candles by the shamans.

Xun seems to date the loss of the bell at the time of a famine that must have occurred at the end of the nineteenth century. Apparently the famine began at the Fiesta of Saint Sebastian as punishment for the townspeoples' negligence.

The setting off of rockets and the ear-splitting detonation of a small metal mortar filled with homemade gunpowder are common practice at religious festivals, boldly announcing each stage in the complicated round of ritual activity.

The epidemic, that bore off Xun's wife, was the flu known as "la gripe español" that ravaged Mexico in 1918–1919.

According to Tonik Nibak, the disappearance of the bell occurred in 1923. Tonik described how the priest, Mariano Lievano, later ordered the sacristans either to take the image of Saint Lawrence to the Church of Saint Sebastian or burn it. They carried Saint Lawrence to the other church, and for five days and five nights the rain fell without cease. The townspeople became so frightened that the sacristans returned Saint Lawrence to his rightful home. The priest fell ill. He kept asking those attending him to pull off his shirt, because his back was on fire. He was taken to San Cristóbal, where he died shortly thereafter.

The association of bells with the forces of nature is common in southern Mexico and Guatemala. The Mazatecs of Oaxaca hear bells ringing in the depths of a river (Laughlin, 1957). The Quiché tell of two bells that were stolen in the night and later found suspended by thunderbolt snakes in the mountain (Búcaro Moraga, 1959:30).

Church bells, undoubtedly the single most valuable objects introduced into Indian villages by the Spanish, have become the symbol of community identity and of municipal wealth. They represent not only present riches but also assure good fortune in the future.

The King and the Ring

Although this tale has a decidedly European quality, I know of no tales from outside Zinacantán that follow the same general plot or whose protagonist is a poor boy turned king. The popularity of this legend in Zinacantán may derive from a cultural memory of the prominence of the town at the time of the Spanish Conquest. "The King and the Ring" serves to explain to Zinacantecs why they no longer possess the power and wealth that once was their prerogative.

That Zinacantecs do not see kings in the same light as we do was driven home to me when showing pictures of contemporary European kings and queens to Romin Teratol. He asked if they were immortal. Not satisfied with my negative reply, he persisted, "But they come from caves, don't they?"

The Little Bird

In 1911 the Bishop and the reactionary leaders of San Cristóbal promised the Chamulans land distribution and an end to taxation if they would rebel against the revolutionary government of President Madero. Jacinto Perez Ch'ix Tot, "Robin," known as "Bird" or "Little Bird," who had served in the army, was accorded the rank of general, and his followers were issued arms. A thousand Chamulans carried out guerrilla activity during the summer of 1911, occupying eight lowland towns including Ixtapa, Acala, Chiapilla, and Venustiano Carranza.

The historical and now nearly legendary accounts of the period are unanimous in speaking of the horrifying acts of plunder, rape, and murder that the Chamulans visited upon their opponents, whether they were Ladinos or fellow Chamulans loyal to the government. Romin Tanchak's mother recalls the women advancing with loom swords, chanting, "In red huipils we climb, in red huipils we climb ahead!" Romin's mother remembers that they "killed" the Christ Child in the church of Chiapilla but were destroyed themselves by a "bomb."

Although the Chamulans had been armed by the Ladinos of San Cristóbal, even they became alarmed at what seemed to be developing into a race war. There were many stories of Chamulans hacking pregnant Ladinas and babies to death. The guerrilla army of Little Bird was described with terror as a "wild horde." It was decided by the federal army that these barbarians must be taught to respect civilization by means of a punishment "in harmony with their rudimentary understanding" (Espinosa, 1912:152). And so when the Bird's forces were finally defeated in Chiapilla on October 11, 1911, the bodies of the dead were burned and eight prisoners had their ears cut off. It is only fair to say that the action caused great revulsion among the many Chiapas Ladinos who thought civilization could be better represented.

The survivors of the battle eventually established a new town near Tabasco. The Bird himself, who was hiding out in a small Chamulan hamlet, came in to San Cristóbal before All Souls' Day, 1914, to buy some bulls. He was seized by the soldiers of President Carranza and escorted to the cemetery of San Cristóbal, where he was executed.

Tonik's reminiscences invest several scoundrels with the title Little Bird. Juan Perez Jolote, a Chamulan living in those times, is the subject of an autobiography by Ricardo Pozas Arcienaga. Tonik's neighbor, Palas Rodriguez, perhaps was the only Zinacantec to have joined Little Bird. Consistently, Zinacantecs remained aloof from native rebellions.

Although I have never heard Maryan Seto called "Little Bird," his name is famous in Zinacantán, where his dead soul has provoked nightmares ("I Commit Murder and Am Covered with Pooh").

The gruesome scene described by Tonik was only his introduction to a life of violence. His legendary exploits were chronicled by Romin Teratol, who reported that Maryan Seto, known as "Split-face Man," was the husband of many wives and the perpetrator of sixty-four murders. Three times he was killed and twice he revived. His final demise was assured only after he had been chopped to pieces and his flesh covered with garlic, salt, and tobacco (Bricker, T42). Nor did the violence end with his death, for his two adopted sons were notorious mother-beaters and murderers in 1960; one with five murders to his name, including a poor deaf and dumb Chamulan.

Still Another Spook

Now that the Spook is a thoroughly familiar character, I shall try to present his pedigree.

First is the report of Bishop Nuñez de la Vega:

> In many towns . . . of this bishopric seven Blacks, corresponding to the seven days of the week, are painted on the repertories or calendars for making divinations and predictions . . . and he whom they name Cox-lahuntox (who is the devil, and according to the Indians has thirteen dominions) is painted on a throne, and he has horns on his head like a ram. The Indians are greatly afraid of Negroes because they preserve the memory of one of their original forefathers having the color of Ethi-opia[ns], who was a great warrior and extremely cruel according to a very ancient historical notebook in our possession that is written in their lan-guage. Those of Oxchuc and other towns of the lowlands hold in deep veneration [a god] called Yalajau (which should be corrected to Ical-Ajau) which means Chief Black or, Lord of the Blacks (Ordoñez y Aguiar, 1907:13).

It is possible that Ical-Ajau is kin to Ek Chuah, the principal god of Yucatec merchants, who was always portrayed in black paint. This same god is also a warrior god. The intimate relation between Aztec merchants and conquest, illustrated in the note on "When One Stupid Indian Won," was probably not peculiar to the Aztecs.

Drawing upon a multitude of parallels in Mayan literature from Yucatan and Guatemala, Sarah Blaffer concludes that the Spook is the ancient Mayan bat god associated with sexuality, blood, sacrifice, and death (Blaffer, 1972:57–67). Like the black-skinned, cave-dwelling Earth Lords, the bat demons were believed to be "eaters of souls."

Zinacantán means "bat net." At the time of the Conquest the town had two names, "Place of Bats," and "Black Lord" (*Diccionario en lengua sotzil*, n.d.:5, 78). Two legends from Chiapa de Corzo describe how a nearby town was destroyed by thou-sands of huge black bats (Navarrete, 1964:322–324). Perhaps this refers to a historical incursion of Zinacantecs.

The Spook's negroid features may derive from a memory of African slaves. Al-though Blacks are no longer native to the region, as late as 1778 there were seven hundred living in San Cristóbal. They were treated more as confidants than as slaves, for they were permitted to wear daggers and to dress in European clothing. As such, they served the role of majordomos and foremen who most likely were entrusted with the task of inflicting physical punishment on their masters' Indian serfs (Favre, 1971:81–82). It is not farfetched to assume that the Spaniards increased their authority by spreading stories of the Africans' former cannibalistic appetites. The Spook's cave-dwelling habits may possibly be traced to a memory of African slaves who escaped from the lowlands and sought temporary refuge in the wildest mountain areas. This is supported by the Spanish name for the Spook, "Negro Cimarron," "Black Runaway Slave."

As everyone in Zinacantán knows, Spooks still exist in what we would call "hard hat zones," where they are reputed to be in league with the engineers, providing victims to fuel the machinery and to strengthen the cement foundations of bridges and power plants.

Long Hairs

An unstable monetary situation in the Chiapas highlands persisted into the era of the Revolution when Guatemalan currency was still much in evidence. The Cabrera was a Guatemalan peso minted from 1850 to 1870.

Although the Long Hairs of this tale are highwaymen, they are identified as Lacandón Indians rather than as the devils alternately known as Turnabout Foot. Shielded by his bulletproof hair, this representative of Zinacantec demonology has two remarkable characteristics—his head has a face front and back and his feet have toes front and back.

The Long Hair, known by a variety of names and assuming a variety of disguises, inhabits the spectral landscape from Oaxaca to Guatemala. These creatures may be associated with the Aztec god of war, Huitzilopochtli. Among the Mazatec these demons are also black-skinned and lacking a knee joint. They can be killed by making them collapse in laughter (Laughlin, 1957). According to the Chortí of Guatemala, their feet are especially adapted to enable them to slide speedily down waterfalls (Fought, 1972:73–74).

It is possible that this legend recalls conflicts with the Lacandóns whose raids during the sixteenth and seventeenth centuries terrorized the people living at the edge of the Lacandón jungle of Chiapas. Numerous campaigns were waged to subject the Lacandóns. The first expedition in 1559 was manned in part by six hundred Chiapanecs and two hundred Zinacantec porters. The Zinacantecs, dressed in "scarlet suits and headdresses," paraded with "elegant banners and drums and finely embellished trumpets. . . . Never before had they seemed so elegant or splendid" (Remesal, 1932:1396–397).

The expedition passed muster in Zinacantán and then marched to Comitán. The trappings for two barges were carried into the jungle and one barge was actually launched on the Laguna de Lacandón. After putting several towns to the torch, the expedition continued downstream on rafts. The Spaniards were guided by Indians on reed mats who shot their arrows as they maneuvered the rafts, diving underwater to defend themselves from enemy arrows. In the end, the victorious Zinacantecs returned home with neither riches nor rewards.

The Lacandóns' skill with bow and arrow, their long hair, and their "wild" ways cast them into a demonic role in folk memory. According to the Chamulans, the Lacandón men boast virile members of gargantuan proportions. Mountain lions are their dogs and jaguars their cats. Their name Lakanton [Boil Stone] is derived from their reputed custom of cooking stones as if they were eggs (Gossen, 1974, T168).

I have translated *bankilal*, the euphemistic name for tobacco, as "chief," but it can also mean "older brother." Tobacco is considered to be a guardian, both of the individual and his home. The use of tobacco as a protector on the roads was widespread in Chiapas and Guatemala.

The Flood

For Zinacantecs the flood is an historical benchmark. "Did it happen before the flood?" is a critical question in discussions of early events.

The biblical theme of dispatching birds to report on the firmness of the ground was adapted widely in Middle America.

Although the transformation of men into monkeys is an almost universal element of Middle American creation myths, it seems only in Chiapas that this divine punishment was called down because of the rudeness of men's response to God's questions.

Our Lady of the Salt

The salt wells near Ixtapa have had commercial and ceremonial significance for at least two thousand years. Zinacantán gained control of the salt works around 1300 A.D. (McVicker, 1978:182, 185). The purity of the salt was renowned, even up to the early years of the twentieth century (Zárate, 1971:27). The very name for salt in remote Guaquitepec, Chiapas, is *sotz'leb* or "Zinacantec"! But today there are only a few families from Zinacantán Center that still sell salt from Ixtapa.

The salt from the Zinacantec hamlet of Five Pieces (Salinas, in Spanish) has primarily a ritual use now. On alternate Sundays the tithing man from Five Pieces brings a token amount of salt to the Chapel of Esquipulas in Zinacantán Center where it is distributed among the religious officials. The offering reaffirms the ancient ties between the two towns.

Every year, at the Fiesta of Our Lady of the Rosary, elaborate ceremonies are held first in Zinacantán Center and then in Five Pieces. Ritual activities are centered in the church and at the salt well.

When the Bell Was Lifted

This tale is yet another reminder of the legendary hostility between Zinacantán and Chiapa. Xun describes the Chiapanecs as "blotchy" because so many are afflicted with *mal de pinto*. A similar term of opprobrium, "scabby," is used by the Zoques in referring to their ancient enemies. They relate how they tricked the Chiapanec robbers into donning dance costumes that had been coated on the inside with ashes, beeswax, and ground bones. As the Chiapanecs danced in the tropical heat and sweated profusely, their skin was impregnated forever with blotches and scabs (Navarrete, 1964:321–323).

The magical theft of the church bell is a theme widely distributed in the folk literature of Middle America. So famous was the bell of Chiapa that it is cited in a geographic description of Chiapas in 1845, as being the largest of the department. Containing a considerable amount of gold alloy, it could be heard for a distance of two leagues (E. Pineda, 1845:68). Cast in 1576, it is reputed to be the first bell manufactured in America.

Saved from the Horned Serpent

Horned serpents have inhabited the Middle American cosmos for at least a millenium. Plumed serpent columns at the entrance to the Temple of the Warriors in Chichen Itzá are each endowed with a pair of horns. Their association with water persists to this day in Mexico and Guatemala and among the Pueblos of the Southwest. The Chortí of Guatemala consider the horned serpent to be the alter ego of the god of the earth's center, the lord of water, crowned at both ends with a pair of bejeweled golden horns, with which it plowed the riverbeds (Fought, 1972:83–85, 110–113; Girard, 1962:95–96). As in Xun's story, it may be smitten by the gods for causing landslides. Zinacantecs believe that if the sun or moon dies, animals with four horns will emerge from the underworld to kill the people.

In 1813 a Spanish proclamation to the overseas members of the Empire, pleading for their support while Napoleon's armies rampaged through the homeland, was translated into Tzotzil by an anonymous churchman of Chiapas. Striving to reach Tzotzil hearts and purses, the couplets liken the "murderous" Napoleon to a jaguar, a whirlwind, and a horned serpent (*Proclama del duque infantado presidente*, 1813:2–5).

The War of Saint Rose

The War of Saint Rose, or the "War of the Castes," as it is known in the literature, was fought from 1868 to 1871. A Chamulan shepherdess, Agustina Gomez Chechev, in the hamlet of Tzajal Yemel (not Chaklahon as Xun recalls) discovered on December 22, 1867, three dark blue pebbles which she told her mother had fallen from the sky. She placed them on the house altar and soon the rumor spread that they were "talking stones." They were submitted to the local religious official, Pedro Díaz Cuzcat, for authentication. He put them in a box for safekeeping but was awakened during the night by a terrific racket issuing from the box. From then on he took charge of the cult, installing Agustina as the "mother of god." On Saint Rose Day, 1868, Cuzcat, dressed in a white robe, accompanied by a dozen women in embroidered huipils, consecrated their new chapel, baptized the women, and declared them "saints." A daily market was initiated in Tzajal Yemel. Every Sunday a magnificent procession of saints, chiefs, and the faithful culminated in a service of revelation of the past week's oracles. The major ceremonial centers in the highlands were practically abandoned; their churches deserted, their political officials ignored, and their markets emptied while everyone traveled to Tzajal Yemel.

Responding to the desperate pleas for a restoration of "order" from the Ladino merchants of San Cristóbal, who discovered that their shops and market were also abandoned, a military detachment of fifty men was sent during the night of December 2, 1868, to Tzajal Yemel. The chapel was razed and Agustina and her mother captured and carried off to San Cristóbal. After eluding capture, Cuzcat was identified by a Zinacantec in Ixtapa and taken to jail in San Cristóbal.

Once the movement was quelled and its leaders imprisoned, the governor imposed harsher tax measures. Again the Tzotziles flocked to Tzajal Yemel and stopped attending the churches and markets in San Cristóbal. By May of 1869 the Ladinos were demanding a second, more violent assault on the hamlet.

Shortly thereafter, Cuzcat's wife was awakened in her sleep by the arrival of three Ladinos, Ignacio Galindo, his wife, and a friend, who came to warn the Chamulans of the growing threat. Galindo, a teacher and defender of human rights, was regarded by conservatives as a social revolutionary, sent by Cuzcat to liberate the Indians. It was said that he hypnotised and "brought back to life" several children, claiming that he would revive after three days all who died for their faith. The black-bearded Galindo was identified with Saint Matthew, his wife with the Virgin Mary, and his companion with Saint Bartholomew. Galindo reportedly issued a call to arms.

The news spread terror in San Cristóbal, but the governor ignored the pleas for support. The priest and the teacher of Chamula traveled to Tzajal Yemel to dissuade Galindo, but finding him absent, carried off the saint images. This outrage was quickly answered. An ambush party was dispatched and the priest and the teacher were murdered. Within days a rebel army sacked and put to the torch a dozen ranches. A hundred Ladinos were brutally slain. Several thousand Indian serfs joined the cause.

By June 17, Galindo and his forces poured down the mountain slopes into the valley of San Cristóbal, demanding the release of Cuzcat. Although the army advanced under a white flag, the commandant of the local garrison, with only two hundred ill-trained and ill-equipped men at his disposal, declared San Cristóbal indefensible and ordered the women and children to take refuge in the church.

The commandant then sent word for the governor to advance with three hundred reinforcements from Chiapa. Meanwhile, Galindo agreed to surrender himself, his wife, and companion for three days as hostages in exchange for the release of Cuzcat, Agustina, and her mother.

The rebel army retreated, leaving behind six hundred men to guard the roads from San Cristóbal to Chamula. On the morning of June 21, government soldiers attacked the encampments on the outskirts of the city, killing three hundred rebels. As dusk fell, the Indians withdrew, carrying their dead and wounded into the mountains.

A week later, Galindo and his companion were executed before a firing squad in the plaza of San Cristóbal. In the following months Cuzcat's army was routed by fourteen hundred government troops, and the fugitive rebels were hunted down and executed. Pedro Cuzcat escaped capture but died miserably in a cave in 1871, while Agustina Chechev disappeared without a word. (See Russ, 1983; Favre, 1971; Molina, 1934; and V. Pineda, 1888. Carter Wilson's novel, *A Green Tree and a Dry Tree*, projects with nearly supernatural vision the dramatic events of the War of Saint Rose.)

The failure of the Zinacantecs to join the impelling cause of Agustina Chechev perhaps can be understood only by emphasizing the Zinacantecs' latent and centuries-old suspicion of the Chamulans, who, though considered socially inferior, outnumber them so dramatically. To worship and give one's life for a Chamulan saint would really be beneath a Zinacantec's dignity.

The War of Saint Rose, provoked by the native usurpation of Catholic ritual, is only one of many such events in the history of southern Mexico. The Caste War of Yucatan of 1847 nearly achieved native control of the peninsula.

Although the vain magical tricks of the Chamulan women are not reported in historical sources, they apppear in the folk traditions of both the Chamulans and the Ladinos. Today in Zinacantán, during the Christmas pantomimes, women's supposed magical power is flaunted by the Dames, who attempt to defend their consorts from the Bull's murderous charge by brazenly lifting their skirts. But the Bull, undaunted, makes a mockery of their efforts by goring their husbands in a vital place.

He Saved a Snake and Won a Wife

The trail of Thunderbolt Girl leads north to Oaxaca and finally backtracks to Guatemala.

A cursory investigation of Thunderbolt's activities in Mitla suggests more than a casual resemblance. In one tale two orphans are adopted by Thunderbolts, who give them a magic pot. In another, two mountain spirits quarrel after harvesting their corn. The woman complains that all the corn is white, so her husband promptly punches her in the nose. In disgust she wipes her bloody nose on a corncob, and that is why there is red corn (Parsons, 1936:330–339).

Following the trail south to Guatemala and searching the records of the past four hundred years turns up a fresh lead. The mother of the twin heroes of the *Popol Vuh*, Hunter and Jaguar Deer, bears further investigation. This woman, Blood Girl by name, presented herself, already pregnant, before her mother-in-law, who cursed her and disowned her, telling her that she would never be accepted unless she brought home a big net of corn. Blood Girl went to the corn field, but she found only one stalk of corn. After praying for help, she tore the tassel off an ear of corn. And abundant ears of corn filled her net! The grandmother recognized this as a sign, and she accepted the girl as her daughter-in-law (Edmonson, 1971:83–84).

Only a thread of blood, a net of corn, and two as yet unborn offspring point to Thunderbolt Girl as the bearer of ancient traditions that once flourished leagues apart.

In a version of this tale from San Andrés a man named Usum is offered a daughter by the Earth Lord in exchange for saving the life of a snake. The daughters are fluffing cotton in preparation for spinning. The pile of fluffed cotton grows higher and higher and becomes clouds. Walter Morris believes this tale establishes the religious significance of weaving, its relation to the Earth Lord, and an explanation for many of the symbols that occur in the textiles of highland Chiapas (Morris, 1987).

How the Weak Ones Won, Rabbit Wins and Rabbit Loses

The race between the deer and the toads is run in Africa, Asia, and throughout Latin America.

Rabbit's strategy to defeat the Devil recalls the tactics of the Quiché lords when their citadel was surrounded by thousands of enemy soldiers. With but four jars of wasps and hornets they routed "the Tribes" (Edmonson, 1971:205–208). In *The Title of the Lords of Totonicapán* the Quiché weapons are described as one jar of big wasps, one jar of little wasps, another of serpents, and a fourth of beetles (Recinos and Goetz, 1953:219–220).

Poor Rabbit's final ignominious defeat is couched in terms that seem peculiarly Zinacantec.

The Spook and the Saints

Saint Sebastian's suggestion, that Saint John might contribute some of his children because he has so many, is a true reflection of the much higher population of Chamulans. It is a widely held belief of Zinacantecs that their patron saint guards his children with far greater zeal than does Saint John.

Chamulan subservience is a generally accepted fact of life. According to a Chamulan origin myth, Saint Lawrence and Saint John both raised sheep and so decided to settle together in the highlands, but God wanted the sons of Saint Lawrence to grow corn, while the sons of Saint John were forced to look for jobs in the lowland coffee plantations (Gossen, 1974, T85).

The Charcoal Cruncher

Anyone who has spent a black winter's night in a Zinacantec home, and heard a forest rat munching on the corn stored in burlap bags against the wall, and then minutes later heard the family cat bumping among the pots beside the hearth, can feel in his bones the eerie horror of the Charcoal Cruncher.

Why charcoal is its diet is not clear to me. In Chenalhó charcoal is said to have been the diet of the survivors of the deluge, before they were turned into monkeys (Guiteras-Holmes, 1961:157).

There are a number of tales from Mexico and Puerto Rico that feature witches whose heads sally out at night to eat corpses. Salt is the common means for preventing their heads from rejoining their flesh. But only two tales from Central America show close similarities to the Charcoal Cruncher story. These were recorded among the Pipil or Aztecs of El Salvador.

The two Aztec versions follow the same plot as Manvel's story, but the resolution is far more elaborate. In both, the woman's head falls off the deer's back and dies, and a priest instructs the husband to bury the head. Soon a calabash tree sprouts from the grave, and from the fruit appear many boys (Hartman, 1907:143–147; Schultze-Jena, 1958, 2:22–28).

The boys bring to mind the four hundred sons who emerge in the second creation of the *Popol Vuh*. Their birth from the gourd recalls Blood Girl looking at the gourd tree on which hang fruits that were once the skulls of 1 Hunter and 7 Hunter. As Blood Girl inspects the gourds, a skull spits on her hand.

> And immediately she conceived a child in her
> womb just from the spittle,
> And they were created
> Hunter
> And Jaguar Deer (Edmonson, 1971:77)

Hunter and Jaguar Deer are the two heroes referred to in the commentary on "He Saved a Snake and Won a Wife." The combination of elements from the Aztecs of Salvador and the Quiché of Guatemala is not surprising, since, in the *Popol Vuh*, "Aztec ideas are given in Quiché words and Quiché ideas in Aztec words," reflecting the strong Aztec influence on Guatemala in the fifteenth century (ibid., xv). Despite the extremely low number of Aztec loan words in Zinacantec Tzotzil, Zinacantán was in frequent contact with the Aztecs shortly before the Spanish Conquest. Still, there is no way of telling whether the Charcoal Cruncher is an Aztec concept, a Mayan concept, or both.

A Bellyful

Upon first encounter, this tale seems to be quite simply a story of the consequences of infidelity and the consequences of tattling. Despite the real worries of Zinacantec men, who must labor in their lowland corn fields for weeks at a time, while their wives are left to their own devices in their mountain homes, there is a surrealist quality to this drama—presenting an outspoken dog, a peculiar hole in the wall, an extraordinary abundance of game, a bizarre pièce de résistance, and a wildly thirsty wife. The major plot, revealed in excruciatingly fine detail, offers a series of dramatic contrasts. Lover is like husband. Lover is like dead dog. Wife seems honest and hardworking, but is unfaithful. Lover's penis is like deer's penis. Husband assumes wife's role; he grinds the chilis and serves the meal. Husband gives the wife a delicious repast, but with fatal effect. Lover's penis produces bloated stomach, pregnant with death. Husband appears guilty, but is "proved" innocent.

Lurking behind the cheating wife and tattling dog is the mischievous deer that plays dead only to rush away at the hunter's approach. The man's failure as a hunter is mysteriously linked to his failure as a husband. Following the deer into the folk literature of Middle America, the pursuer soon becomes caught in a thicket of murderous themes. Recall the deer's role in the demise of the Charcoal Cruncher (and the association of the woman's head with the calabash and the birth of the hero twins, Hunter and Jaguar Deer, noted above). The Mixe of Oaxaca tell of two children who murder their grandfather and feed his testicles to their grandmother, saying that they are deer liver. The children later become sun and moon (Miller, 1956, T3, T4). Mixtecs recount the adventures of two boys who, when told by their mother to take their father food, shoot him down. Their father, in fact a deer, is skinned by them and his flesh is fed to their mother. They, too, become sun and moon (Dyk, 1959:10–12). Also suggestive is a Kekchí tale from Belize in which three boys are brought up by their grandmother, who secretly has a tapir for a lover. The boys trap and kill the tapir and feed the tapir's penis to their grandmother. Eventually two of the boys turn their brother into a monkey and kill their grandmother. Later they become the sun and Venus (Thompson, 1930:120–121).

What first seemed to be a story chronicling the infidelity of a humble corn farmer's wife and the tale-telling of his dog was, at least at one time, part of a cosmic epic that must have rivaled, or included, the tale of the three brothers and the fruit tree! Unfortunately we can only guess the religious significance that this tale may have had.

The Dwarfs

The abode of the dwarfs is believed to be located "beneath the world," below even Hell.

Today the Zinacantecs claim that, when the year 2000 arrives, the world will flip over and the dwarfs will be on top.

The Famine

An *almud* is fifteen liters and a *fanega* is one hundred and eighty liters. So ten fanegas of corn would be about fifty-one bushels, and an almud would be a little under half a bushel.

The Aztec prayer, reported by Sahagún, was recited by women as they gleaned scattered corn in the fields (Thompson, 1970:285). The conviction that human carelessness and disrespect toward corn bring divine punishment is a fundamental tenet of Indian communities of Chiapas. In Chenalhó, "white hunger" is caused by men's carelessness, "black hunger" by women's, and "red hunger" by children's (Guiteras-Holmes, 1961:243).

Warnings against mistreating corn stem from the belief that corn possesses a soul. It is said that corn cries if it is not weeded and if it is sold to government warehouses. If beans are "offended," their soul will cry and complain to the Earth Lord and to the gods in heaven, thus calling down a famine upon mankind.

Xun's account of the famine, which occurred around the time of the influenza epidemic of 1918–1919, points explicitly to the dilemma of traditional Indians in a money economy governed by forces beyond their control. Corn that is grown with sacred care must be delivered into grasping white hands so that an Indian can get the money to buy many of the necessities of twentieth-century life.

When Our Lord Was Chased

It is not surprising, in a culture where age and experience are so highly valued, that Christ is imagined as an old man at the time of his crucifixion, even though the images of Christ in the church represent a young man.

The use of Judas as a name and an image to describe the Jews is renewed every year in the Easter celebration, when an effigy of Judas, crowned with a sombrero, clothed in baggy blue pants, carrying an armadillo-shell shoulder bag, and sporting in his mouth a long cigar, hangs above the entrance to the Church of Saint Lawrence until, on Saturday night, it is lowered precipitously to an ignominious end in the waiting bonfire.

If frequency of recording is any indication of a tale's popularity, this story is clearly the favorite throughout southern Mexico and Guatemala. Though many of the scenes are familiar biblical events, Christ's character is startling—only by a slight shift of emphasis Christ has become a hero remembered more for his cunning than for his love of mankind. It would not be difficult to imagine this Christ in the guise of Hunahpu or Xbalanque of the *Popol Vuh*. In the version of this tale from the Popoluca of Veracruz the protagonist is not Christ but Homshuk, the corn god, who is fleeing from his most unChristian mother (Elson, 1947:193–214). Despite its New World flavor, the nineteenth-century folklorist Oskar Dähnhardt determined to his satisfaction that the story of Christ and the farmer originated in the Balkan countries and was brought to Europe by the Crusaders (Dähnhardt, 1912, 2:95–107).

The Adventures of Peter

This account of the merry pranks of Peter conforms quite closely to the Spanish model, usually known as Pedro Ordemales. Many of the episodes can be traced at least to the beginning of the seventeenth century, to the picaresque Spanish novel *El Subtil Cordobés Pedro de Urdelalas* by Alonso Jerónimo de Salas Barbadillo. From New Mexico to Guatemala, Pedro plays these same tricks over and over.

The Spook and the Chamulan

The expletive phrase, "the filth of your mother's cock," is an expression not used by Zinacantecs but is known by them to be typical of Chamulans, whose manner of speech is considered racier and coarser than Zinacantecs'.

The association of potsherds with money may stem from ritual. During Carnival in Chamula a cavern in which a sacred spring bubbles is swept clean of the pebbles and potsherds that litter its floor. Once it is clean, men and women come to pay a visit, tossing an entrance fee or "tribute" of three pebbles or three potsherds to assure their safety during their visit to the dangerous cave (Bricker, 1973:114).

What's Man Like?

I have chosen the colloquial expression "I'm splitting" as it reproduces exactly the Tzotzil.

Jaguar's lesson that man is a two-legged, erect, walking animal who persecutes all others gives a specially Zinacantec slant to this ancient story. Tiger's or Lion's search for the king of the beasts, and his unhappy encounter with the woodsman, form the entertainment for the 146th of the Arabian Nights.

Poor woman's "pestiferous wound" plays no part in the versions recorded in Spain and in Latin America. The most elaborate and thorough treatment of this subject was reported in 1532 by François Rabelais in *The Second Book of Pantagruel* (Rabelais, 1951:301–304).

A Strange Affair in Totolapa

As Tonik finished this remarkable tale, she paused to catch her breath, then turned to me with a wicked gleam in her eye and asked, "Do you know who the man was?"

Then triumphantly, "He is my next-door neighbor!" I shrink from contemplating the implications of a literal acceptance of Tonik's statement and will take refuge in folkloristic and ethnographic footnotes.

Totolapa is a Tzotzil-speaking town in the lowlands, famous for its witchcraft, but known to most Zinacantecs only by tales. According to Tonik, when babies are born in Totolapa they are left in a cave for three days and three nights without nourishment or human contact. If they survive this ordeal, says Tonik, they will grow up to be as strong as the girl in the story.

San Dionisio or Saint Dennis, to whom the poor Zinacantec addresses his fervent entreaties, is the patron saint of Totolapa.

For a Zinacantec to present his girlfriend with so lowly a gift as a head of cabbage, particularly when the stakes are so high, is almost unthinkable. It provokes a retreat into symbolic analysis, but what could a head of cabbage symbolize? At Carnival time in Chamula, cabbage heads are equated with fetuses (Bricker, 1973:118). Perhaps he is requesting the restoration of his fertility in this way. In Zinacantán a man's head may be contrasted with a woman's by its roundness and its braidless sphericity. So with a cabbage head, the unfortunate man may also be reminding his lover of his lost identity.

Witches who assume the form of cows create havoc in other parts of Mexico. Conspicuous figures of Zinacantec dream life, cows are always creatures of unrestrained, unpredictable evil power.

Literature Cited

Adams, Robert M.
1961.   Changing Patterns of Territorial Organization in the Central High-
        lands of Chiapas, Mexico. *American Antiquity,* 26:341–360.

Barakat, Robert A.
1965.   The Bear's Son Tale in Northern Mexico. *Journal of American
        Folklore,* 78:330–336.

Blaffer, Sarah C.
1972.   *The Black-man of Zinacantán: A Central American Legend.* Austin:
        University of Texas Press.

Blom, Frans
1959.   Historical Notes Relating to the Pre-Columbian Amber Trade from
        Chiapas. *Mitteilungen aus dem Museum für Völkerkunde in Hamburg,*
        25:24–27.

Bravo Izquierdo, Donato
1948.   *Lealtad militar (campaña en el estado de Chiapas e istmo de Tehuantepec
        1923–1924).* Mexico City.

Bricker, Victoria Reifler
1973.   *Ritual Humor in Highland Chiapas.* Austin: University of Texas
        Press.
n.d.   Field Notes. [Manuscript.]

Búcaro Moraga, Jaime Ismael
1959.   *Leyendas, cuentos, mitos y fabulas indígenas.* Guatemala City: In-
        stituto Indigenista Nacional.

Castañon Gamboa, Fernando
1951.   *Panorama historico de las communicaciones en Chiapas.* Tuxtla
        Gutiérrez.

Clavijero, Francisco Javier
1964.   *Historia antigua de México.* Mexico City: Editorial Porrua.

Cosio Villegas, Daniel (editor)
1956.   *Historia moderna de México.* 4 volumes. Mexico City.

Dähnhardt, Oskar (editor)
1907–   *Natursagen; eine Sammlung naturdeutender Sagen, Märchen, Fabeln*
1912.   *und Legenden.* 2 volumes. Leipzig: B.G. Teubner.

Dibble, Charles E., and Arthur J. O. Anderson (translators)
1959.   *Florentine Codex; General History of the Things of New Spain.* Trans-
        lated from the Aztec [of Bernardino de Sahagún]. Santa Fe: School
        of American Research.

Diccionario en lengua sotzil
n.d.   Manuscript. Princeton University Library.

Dyk, Anne
1959.   Mixteco Texts, *Summer Institute of Linguistics, Linguistic Series,* 3.
        Norman, Oklahoma.

Edmonson, Munro S.
1971.   The Book of Counsel: The Popol Vuh of the Quiché Maya of
        Guatemala. *Tulane University, Middle American Research Institute,
        Publication 35.* New Orleans: Tulane University.

Elson, Ben
1947.   The Homshuk: A Sierra Popoluca Text. *Tlalocan,* 2(3):193–214.

Espinosa, Luis
1912.   *Rastros de sangre.* Mexico City.

Favre, Henri
1971.   *Changement et continuité chez les Mayas du Mexique: Contribution a
        l'étude de la situation coloniale en Amérique latine.* Paris: Editions
        Anthropos.

Fought, John G.
1972.   *Chortí (Mayan Texts, 1).* Philadelphia: University of Pennsylvania
        Press.

Furst, Peter T., and Salomón Nahmad
1972.   *Mitos y arte huicholes.* Mexico City: Sep-Setentas.

Girard, Rafael
1962.   *Los mayas eternos.* Mexico City: Litro Mex.

Gomez, Ermilo Abreu
1979.   *Canek,* translated and with an introduction by Mario L. Davilá and
        Carter Wilson. New York: Avon Books.

Gossen, Garry H.
1974.   *Chamulas in the World of the Sun: Time and Space in a Maya Oral
        Tradition.* Cambridge: Harvard University Press.

Guiteras-Holmes, Calixta
1961. *Perils of the Soul: The World View of a Tzotzil Indian.* Chicago: University of Chicago Press.

Haefkens, Jacobo
1969. *Viage a Guatemala y Centroamerica.* Sociedad de Geografia e Historia de Guatemala, Serie Viajeros, 1. Guatemala City: Editorial Universitaria.

Hartman, C. V.
1907. Mythology of the Aztecs of Salvador. *Journal of American Folklore,* 20:143–147.

Holland, William R.
1962. *Contemporary Tzotzil Cosmological Concepts as a Basis for Interpreting Prehistoric Maya Civilization.* (35th International Congress of Americanists.) 3 volumes. Mexico City: Instituto Nacional de Antropología e Historia.

Hoopes, Ned E. (editor)
1968. *Ali Baba and the Forty Thieves and Nine Other Tales from the Arabian Nights.* New York: Dell Publishing Co.

La Farge, Oliver
1947. *Santa Eulalia: The Religion of a Cuchimatan Indian Town.* Chicago· University of Chicago Press.

Laughlin, Robert M.
1957. Field Notes: San Martin Soyaltepec, Oaxaca. [Manuscript.]
1975. *The Great Tzotzil Dictionary of San Lorenzo Zinacantán.* Smithsonian Contributions to Anthropology, 19. Washington, D. C.: Smithsonian Institution Press.

Lévi-Strauss, Claude
1963. *Structural Anthropology.* New York: Basic Books.

López Sánchez, Hermilo
1960. *Apuntes históricos de San Cristóbal de las Casas, Chiapas, Mexico.* 2 volumes. Mexico City.

McVicker, Donald E.
1978. Prehispanic Trade in Central Chiapas, Mexico. Pages 177–186 in *Mesoamerican Communication Routes and Cultural Contacts,* Thomas A. Lee, Jr. and Carlos Navarrete, editors. Volume 40 of *New World Archeological Foundation.* Provo: Brigham Young University.
n.d. *A Preliminary Archeological Survey of the Municipio of Zinacantán, Chiapas, Mexico.* [Mimeograph.]

280 The People of the Bat

Miller, Walter S.
   1956.   Cuentos mixes. *Instituto Nacional Indigenista, Biblioteca de Folklore Indígena*, 2. Mexico City.

Molina, Cristóbal
   1934.   War of the Castes: Indian Uprisings in Chiapas. Pages 359–397 in volume 8 of *Tulane University, Middle American Research Institute Publications*. New Orleans: Tulane University.

Montesinos, José María
   1935.   *Memorias del Sargento*. Tuxtla Gutiérrez: [Talleres Linotipograficas del Gobierno del Estado].

Morris, Walter F.
   1987.   *Living Maya*. New York: Harry N. Abrams, Inc.

Moscoso Pastrana, Prudencio
   1960.   *El pinedismo en Chiapas: 1916–1920*. Mexico City: Los talleres de la editorial "Cultura."

Navarrete, Carlos
   1964.   El mal del pinto y la destrucción de Ostuta en algunos relatos chiapanecos. *Tlalocan*, 4(4):321–324.
   1966.   The Chiapanec History and Culture. Volume 21 of *New World Archeological Foundation*. Provo: Brigham Young University.

Ordoñez y Aguiar, Ramon de
   1907.   *Historia de la creación del cielo y de la tierra*. Mexico City.

Parsons, Elsie Clews
   1936.   *Mitla: Town of the Souls*. Chicago: University of Chicago Press.

Pineda, Emeterio
   1845.   *Descripción geográfica del departamento de Chiapas y Soconusco*. Mexico City: Imprenta de Ignacio Cumpledo.

Pineda, Vicente
   1888.   *Historia de las sublevaciones indígenas habidas en el estado de Chiapas*. Chiapas: [Tipografía del gobierno].

Pozas, Arcienega, Ricardo
   1948.   Juan Perez Jolote: Biografía de un tzotzil. *Acta Antropologica*, 3 (3):266–361.

Proclama del duque infantado presidente
   1813.   Manuscript. Princeton University Library.

Rabelais, François
   1951.   *The Heroic Deeds of Gargantua and Pantagruel*. London: Angus and Robertson.

Recinos, Adrián
  1957. *Cronicas indígenas de Guatemala*. Guatemala City: Editorial Universitaria.

Recinos, Adrián, and Delia Goetz
  1953. *The Annals of the Cakchiquels and Title of the Lords of Totonicapán*, translated by Dionisio José Chonay. Norman: University of Oklahoma Press.

Remesal, Antonio de
  1932. *Historia general de las Indias Occidentales, y particular de la gobernación de Chiapa y Guatemala*. 2 volumes. Guatemala City: [Tipografía Nacional].

Ritvo, Phyllis Z.
  1972. *"Christ and his Brothers" as Reflections of the Developing Child in Zinacantán*. A.B. honors thesis. Harvard College.

Rush, Timothy
  1974. The Symbolism and Politics of a Maya Treasure Hunt. [Manuscript.] Files of R. M. Laughlin, Smithsonian Institution, Washington, D.C.

Russ, Jan
  1983. Whose Caste War? Indians, Ladinos, and the Chiapas "Caste War" of 1869, in *Spaniards and Indians in Southeastern Mexico: Essays on the History of Ethnic Relations*, edited by McLeod and Wasserstrom. Lincoln: University of Nebraska Press.

Séjourné, Laurette
  1957. *Burning Water: Thought and Religion in Ancient Mexico*. London: Thames and Hudson.

Schultze-Jena, L. S.
  1958. Nacimiento de los tlaloque. *Archivos Nahuas*, 1(2):190–211.

Thompson, J. Eric S.
  1930. The Ethnology of the Mayas of Southern and Central British Honduras. *Field Museum of Natural History, Anthropology Series*, 17:23–214.
  1970. *Maya History and Religion*. Norman: University of Oklahoma Press.

Trens, Manuel B.
  1942. *Historia de Chiapas: desde los tiempos más remotos hasta la caída del segundo imperio*. Mexico City: La Impresora.

Villa Rojas, Alfonso
  1946. Notas sobre la etnografía de los indios tzeltales de Oxchuc, Chiapas, Mexico. *University of Chicago Manuscripts on Middle American Cultural Anthropology*, number 7. [Microfilm.]

Wasserstrom, Robert
   1970.   *Our Lady of the Salt.* A.B. honors thesis, Harvard College.

Wilson, Carter
   1972.   *A Green Tree and a Dry Tree.* New York: Macmillan.

Ximénez, Francisco
   1929–   *Historia de la provincia de San Vicente de Chiapa y Guatemala de la*
   1931.   *orden de nuestro glorioso padre Santo Domingo.* 3 volumes. Guatemala
           City: [Tipografía Nacional].